Secrets for Successful Sewing

1302

Secrets for Successful Sewing

Techniques for Mastering Your Sewing Machine and Serger

Barbara Weiland

RODALE

Editor: Susan Huxley
Contributing Editor: Marya Kissinger Amig
Cover and Interior Book Designer: Randall Sauchuck
Interior Illustrators: John Kocon and Amy Talcott
Cover and Interior Photographer: John Hamel
Photo Stylists: Paula Jaworski and Randall Sauchuck
Photo Editor: James Gallucci
Technical Artist: Jen Miller
Copy Editor: Erana Bumbardatore
Manufacturing Coordinator: Patrick Smith
Indexer: Nan Badgett
Editorial Assistance: Nancy Fawley, Jodi Rehl,
    and Lori Schaffer

Rodale Home and Garden Books

Vice President and Editorial Director: Margaret J. Lydic
Managing Editor, Sewing and Crafts:
    Cheryl Winters-Tetreau
Art Director: Paula Jaworski
Assistant Art Director: Mary Ellen Fanelli
Studio Manager: Leslie M. Keefe
Copy Director: Dolores Plikaitis
Book Manufacturing Director: Helen Clogston
Office Manager: Karen Earl-Braymer

On the cover: The sewing machines and serger featured on the cover are digitally enhanced images that are based on the Esanté Ese from Tacony Corporation and the White Superlock 2000 Electronic from VWS, Inc. The techniques shown in the foreground and featured on the garments are, from left to right: Invisible appliqué (page 58), lace insertion (page 162), corded pintucks (page 176), sashiko (page 197), piping (page 178), double piping (page 183), charted needlework (page 104), and needle lace fabric (page 167). The garments were sewn by Joyce Edgar, Marcia Ferris, and Vickii Muthard.

Library of Congress Cataloging-in-Publication Data

Weiland, Barbara.
    Secrets for successful sewing : techniques for mastering your sewing machine and serger / by Barbara Weiland.
        p.   cm.
    Includes bibliographical references (p.) and index.
    ISBN 0–87596–776–0 (hardcover)
    ISBN 1–57954–299–9 (paperback)
    1. Machine sewing.   2. Serging.   I. Title.
TT713.W45   1997
646.2—dc21   97–21061

Distributed to the book trade by St. Martin's Press

	4	6	8	10	9	7	5		hardcover
2	4	6	8	10	9	7	5	3	paperback

We're happy to hear from you.
If you have any questions or comments concerning the editorial content of this book, please write to:

Rodale Inc.
Book Readers' Service
33 East Minor Street
Emmaus, PA 18098

For more information about Rodale and the books and magazines we publish, visit our Web site at www.rodale.com

For my mom, Eloise S. Weiland, who, with love and inordinate patience, taught me how to sew. We continue to share a passion for sewing. Most of all, I thank her for her unfailing support through all of my life's challenges and endeavors. She's just the best!

Contents

Sewing and Serging from A to Z

Acknowledgments

A book of this size and scope would never have been possible without the help and support of many. I appreciate and acknowledge the following companies and individuals for their help and generosity throughout the writing and publishing of this book:

Maggie Lydic, for offering me the opportunity to write this book, and Cheryl Winters-Tetreau for guiding the project along.

Susan Huxley, my editor, for her compassionate support and encouragement for the duration of writing and editing this book.

Randall Sauchuck, for a beautifully designed book format.

Erana Bumbardatore, the copy editor who cared so much about the quality and consistency of the instructions and spent many hours managing the numerous aspects of the project.

Brenda Wilkins and Alane Redon, for their unfailing friendship, support, and encouragement throughout the writing of this book. They are strong and special women.

The SPIs—Cheryl Brown, Cindy Knutzen, Janet White, Kathryn Ezell, Kerry Smith, Laura Reinstatler, Marta Estes, Melissa Lowe, Marion Shelton, Sally Schneider, Susan I. Jones, and Ursula Reikes—my sisters and supporters in creative endeavors.

The Husqvarna, Viking, and White Company; Pfaff American Sales Corporation; Elna International; and the Tacony Corporation, for the generous loan of sewing machines and sergers.

Karen Dillon, for a day of lessons on using the new Baby Lock serger.

My friends at Northwest Sewing in Bellevue, Washington, for the use of their Bernette sergers for sample making, and particularly to Bobby Smead and Sarah Pelletier, for their freely given advice and information and the loan of Bernina presser feet for some of the photos in this book.

The Viking White Sewing and Vacuum Center in Bellevue, Washington, and the Allentown Sewing Machine Outlet in Allentown, Pennsylvania, for their valuable advice and guidance as well as for the loan of many of the special presser feet that were used in a number of photographs in this book.

Fred Drexler, of Sulky of America, for the wonderful boxful of sample threads and stabilizers I used while testing techniques and making photography samples for the book.

Jill S. Reed of the DMC Corporation, Meta Hoge of Coats and Clark, Darlene Blanton of Gutermann of America, Incorporated, and Katherine B. Weiland of American and Efird, Incorporated, for their generous donations of threads for testing and sample making.

Lou Kiersky, for the year-long loan of his computer so I could meet my deadlines.

All of the sewing industry professionals who knowingly or unknowingly contributed to my growth in this field and have so helpfully shared their knowledge, ideas, and techniques.

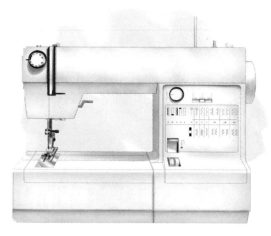

Get Ready to Sew

Over the past year I've been lucky enough to "play" on my sewing machine and serger, plus several others generously loaned by the Husqvarna/Viking, Elna, and Tacony companies, as part of my research for writing this book. I wanted to explore techniques and ideas that would expand the creative options for these machines, as well as find solutions for sewers who aren't ready to part with their faithful older machines. In the process, I've learned many new and exciting ways to use sewing machines and sergers—regardless of brand or age.

Today sewing is so much easier, faster, and more creative than when I first learned to sew, thanks to the vastly improved sewing machines and the widespread availability of the serger, or "wonder machine" as I call it. How did we ever do without the convenience and creativity afforded by this workhorse?

I remember all the handwork that accompanied the machine stitching on my 4-H garments years ago—overcasting seam edges and measuring between each stitch to ensure perfection. (Machine zigzagging was only possible with an attachment, and it was not yet acceptable for competition.) Little did I know that serging would one day replace all that time-consuming handwork.

My first halting and crooked hand stitches were under the close watch of my great-grandmother, whom we affectionately called Big Grandma. With her, I planned wonderful gowns for my doll and watched in awe as she cut simple patterns from my grandfather's well-read newspaper. I still have—and will always treasure—a purple dress and matching bonnet we fashioned for my favorite doll when I was eight years old, using scraps from one of Big Grandma's Sunday dresses.

Big Grandma always had a sewing needle either in her hand or close by. While she sewed, she would entertain me with her stories of the itinerant dressmaker her family had when she was a child. Little did I realize as I stitched that sewing—and writing about it—would become a lifelong passion.

By the time I graduated from college and took my first job in the home sewing industry, my sewing machine had become a constant and faithful companion. It still is—on and off the job. I've been one of those fortunate enough to have enjoyed the luxury of "working" at something I love all of my adult life. Sewing and writing about sewing have provided hours of enjoyment, plus an opportunity to grow creatively. I hope this book will provide you hours of enjoyment as well.

In the pages that follow, you'll learn how to get the very most out of your sewing machine and serger—ways to improve your sewing skills, enhance your creativity, and take advantage of built-in machine features, presser feet, threads, needles, and other helpful notions.

Your sewing time will become more enjoyable, more creative, and more fun.

If you have not yet invested in a serger, or if you have but have not yet removed it from the box or taken the time to experiment with its creative capabilities, this book will give you the confidence and desire to do so. You'll also learn to use it in tandem with your sewing machine to create embellishments that you never dreamed possible.

What's in Store

This book is organized in a handy, easy-to-use format with information for beginning to advanced sewers. The first two sections provide basic information about operating your sewing machine and serger. Guidance on setting up each machine, plus needle selection, thread choices, tension adjustments, and presser feet is also included. (For additional, in-depth information, consult "Recommended Reading" on page 235.)

The last, but most important, section is full of step-by-step directions, organized alphabetically, for a variety of sewing and serging techniques. Since many procedures are known by a number of names and many are variations of other techniques or fall under a broader sewing category, it was often difficult to decide just where they should go. To help you locate techniques that might not appear where you expect to find them, you'll find a comprehensive index at the end of the book.

Stitch settings are given with each technique in this book. They are meant as a starting point and may need fine-tuning, depending on your machine, fabric, presser foot, needle, threads, and the desired results. If a tension adjustment isn't indicated, assume that you use a balanced stitch.

In this book, you'll find both spi and metric equivalents so you can easily adjust the stitch on your machine, whether it's a newer model with metric measurements or an older one with imperial settings. Please note that the metric ranges are written "backwards" because the imperial indicates stitches per inch, whereas the metric is the length of one stitch. When spi increases, mm decreases.

It's a good idea to check your machine's stitch length. To do this, set your machine at 12 spi (2 mm). On a scrap of fabric, stitch a line 3 to 4 inches (8 to 10 cm) long. Mark a 1-inch (2.5-cm) length in the middle of the line of stitching. Count the stitches between your marks. Adjust your stitch length as needed until you get 12 spi (2 mm). Settings on sergers are calibrated for millimeters, so settings are generally given in mm. However, when decorative threads are used or the fabric requires special handling, it's up to you to determine the best setting for the desired result. In these situations, stitch width and length are given in broader terms; for

example, narrow, medium, and wide for stitch width, and short, medium, and long for stitch length.

It can be tough to work with imperial instructions when your machine has metric seam guides on the needle plate. The numbers engraved in the plate represent centimeters. Here are the equivalents:

Metric Equivalents for Your Needle Plate

Metric	Imperial
1 cm	3/8 inch
1.5 cm	5/8 inch
2 cm	3/4 inch
2.5 cm	1 inch

Assume that the thread is to match your fabric, unless otherwise indicated, and keep in mind that you can vary color as desired, to achieve a different effect.

Each technique in this book is presented in a "Get Ready, Get Set, Sew" format. You can tell which machines are required for a specific technique by looking for the icons shown below.

| Sewing Machine Technique | Serger Technique | Sewing Machine and Serger Technique |

"Get Ready" is your shopping list, so to speak. There you'll find listed the needle, thread, special fabrics, presser foot/feet, and notions that you will need to execute the technique.

In "Get Set" you'll find the necessary machine settings and adjustments. When a technique requires both machines or multiple passes on a single machine, you'll find this information in an easy-to-read chart.

In "Sew," "Serge," or "Sew and Serge," I've given you step-by-step directions for the technique.

To save space in the "Get Ready" and "Get Set" sections for each technique and in some illustrations, I've used the following abbreviations:

mm	Millimeter
spi	Stitches per inch
LL	Lower looper
UL	Upper looper
RS	Right side
WS	Wrong side

Below is a sample entry featuring many of the elements I mentioned in the previous paragraphs.

In the pages that follow, you'll learn how to get the very most out of your sewing machine and serger—ways to improve your sewing skills, enhance your creativity, and take advantage of built-in machine features, presser feet, threads, needles, and other helpful notions. Your sewing time will become more enjoyable, more creative, and more fun.

The name of the technique

A TYPICAL ENTRY

A sewing machine technique icon

A brief description of the technique and an accompanying illustration

To strengthen a wide satin stitched edge, add cord along the already-stitched edge and zigzag it in place. If you use a contrasting cord and a contrasting thread, the results are even more decorative. It's a pretty finish for a hem edge where you don't want the added bulk of a hem allowance, making it a great treatment for single-layer collars, pockets, and cuffs.

Diagram 6

Get Ready
Your "shopping list"

Needle	Appropriate for fabric and thread
Thread	All-purpose
Notions	One or more strands of pearl cotton, cord, or gimp; stabilizer

Get Set

	First Pass	Second Pass
Presser foot	Satin, Satinedge, or open-toe embroidery	Braiding
Stitch	Satin	Zigzag
Stitch length	0	15 spi (1.5 mm)
Stitch width	Medium	Narrow

This technique calls for two separate passes on the serger, each with its own settings and adjustments

Sew

1. Satin stitch ⅜ inch (9 mm) from the fabric's raw edge and trim the fabric close to the stitches. Use a water-soluble stabilizer underneath to prevent tunneling, or use the Satinedge foot and stitch over the edge instead. Change your thread and machine settings as indicated for the Second Pass. With the start of the fabric under the presser foot, insert the pearl cotton, or other filler, through the braiding foot, and encase the filler in the stitching.

2. To turn a corner, stop at the corner, disengage the feed dogs, take three stitches in place, and pivot the fabric. Pull out a large loop of the filler, and take three stitches in place. See **Diagram 6.**

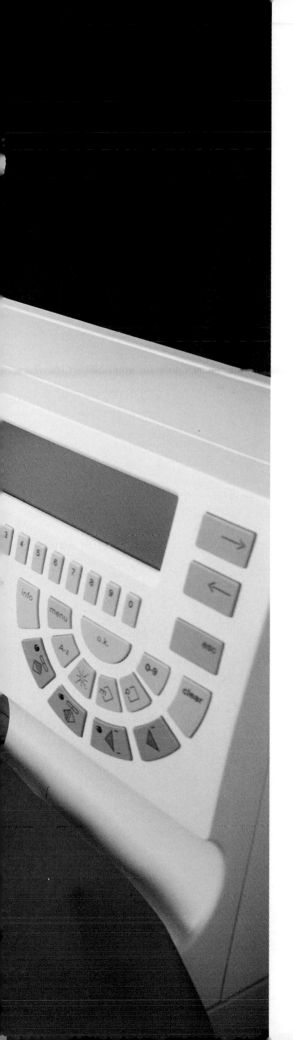

Getting the Most from Your Sewing Machine

Although it has been around for over a century, the sewing machine has changed most in the last two decades. Like everything else in our world, it has been bitten by the computer bug. If you own a computerized machine, you've experienced some of the wonderful conveniences it offers—everything from storing pattern stitches that you designed with a scanner to something as functional as making numerous types of buttonholes.

But even if you don't own one of the newest machines, your simple straight and zigzag stitch sewing machine is probably capable of far more than you've dreamed. In the pages that follow, you're bound to learn something that will change the way you use your machine—no matter how basic or complex your machine might be.

Anatomy of a Sewing Machine

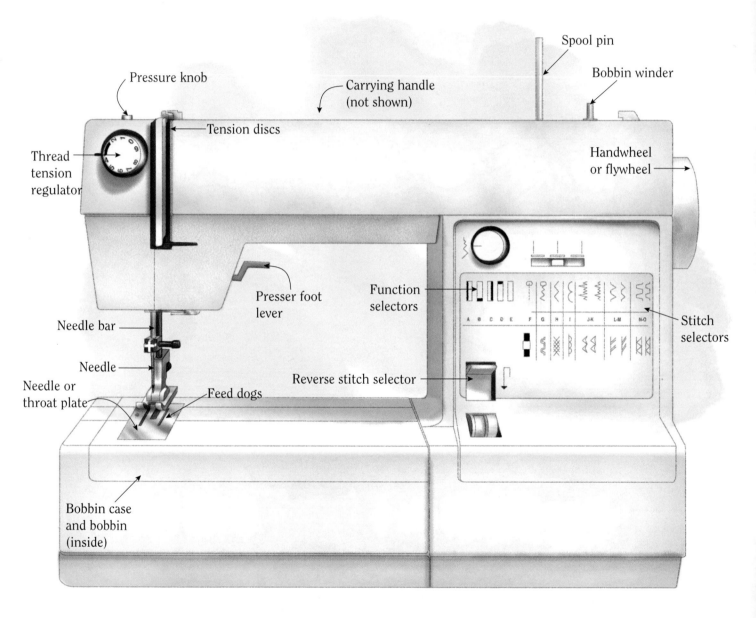

Pressure knob

Carrying handle
(not shown)

Spool pin

Bobbin winder

Tension discs

Thread
tension
regulator

Handwheel
or flywheel

Presser foot
lever

Function
selectors

A B C D E   F G H I   J-K   L-M   N-O

Stitch
selectors

Needle bar

Needle

Reverse stitch selector

Needle or
throat plate

Feed dogs

Bobbin case
and bobbin
(inside)

The sewing machine in the illustration above has some of the most common features that are in use today, whether the machine is mechanical, electronic, or fully computerized. All sewing machines form the basic stitch in the same way, relying on basic parts and a relatively standard threading arrangement. However, there are slight variations from machine to machine. Understanding how your machine operates will help you get more from it. Be sure to read through this section for tips you won't find in your owner's manual.

Bobbin case. To adjust bobbin tension, find the small set screw on the case and tighten or loosen it in very small increments. Work over a light-color surface so that you can locate the screw easily if it falls out. For more information, see "Taming Tension" on page 24.

Insert the bobbin thread through the hole in the bobbin finger, if your case has one, when making buttonholes, applying satin stitching, and doing other decorative work. See **Diagram 1**. This will tighten the bobbin tension, thus keeping the bobbin thread from showing as tiny dots on the right side of the stitching. It also results in a smoother stitch.

Thread bobbin finger

Diagram 1

Feed dogs. On most new machines, you can lower the feed dogs for special stitch functions, such as free-motion stitching and embroidery. On some machines, though, you cover the feed dogs with a plate that prevents them from moving the fabric forward. If your machine requires a cover to deactivate the feed dogs, but this leaves little room for the fabric layers, sew without the cover and dial down to a 0 stitch length. The feed dogs will still operate, but they will not affect fabric movement—you'll do this with your hands.

Needle plate. Zigzag machines have a zigzag or multipurpose plate with a hole wide enough to accommodate the widest stitch possible on your machine. You may also want a straight-stitch plate with a smaller, round hole for sewing on lightweight fabrics and knits. The small, round hole prevents fabric from being dragged down into the plate's hole, called flagging. If you don't have a straight-stitch plate, try covering the zigzag needle hole with a piece of masking tape. Lower

the needle several times to make a hole in the tape. Clean the needle with rubbing alcohol to remove any sticky residue before you start to stitch on your fabric.

Presser foot. For smooth stitching every time, select the correct foot for the stitch. For information on the variety of feet that are available, see "Fancy Footwork" on page 13. If glare from your clear plastic foot makes it difficult to sew, find out if the same foot is available in metal or opaque plastic. If one isn't available for your brand or model, check out the generic presser feet.

Spool pins. Even if your machine has only a single spool pin you can still sew with a double needle if your machine can do a zigzag stitch. See "Threading for Twin-Needle Stitching" on page 16.

Tension discs. If you're experiencing tension problems, especially if the machine was stitching correctly during your previous sewing session, try rethreading your machine because the thread may not be caught between the discs. Check for lint in the discs, too. Try running a dollar bill between them to loosen debris that could be affecting the tension.

Thread guides. These small clips help maintain tension while the thread flows through the stitching mechanism. Don't bypass any of the thread guides, unless you're having difficulty stitching with metallic threads. Then try bypassing the guide just above the needle.

Workroom Secret

I love the convenience offered by the free arm. I often slip a narrow elastic "bracelet" over the free arm of my machine for an adjustable seam gauge. This is particularly helpful for guiding stitching that's farther from the needle than the stitching guide can measure. An added benefit is that it doesn't "gunk" up the machine with a sticky residue, which often happens when you use tape, the most common method for marking a gauge on the machine bed.

Needle and Thread Tips

Choosing the correct thread in combination with the right needle type and size for your project ensures the desired results. Gone are the days when a single needle type would do. If your accessory kit lacks specialty needles, you're limiting your stitching possibilities and quite possibly depriving yourself of superior stitch quality.

Sewing machine needles are available in a variety of sizes and types. Numbers indicate the needle size, while letters designate the shape of the point. American and European manufacturers use different numbering systems.

The needle size that you choose depends on the fabric you're using for your project. Choose a needle that's thick and strong enough to pierce the fabric, but no thicker than necessary so that the needle doesn't leave obvious holes in the fabric.

Both American and European sizes are often included on a needle package or in sewing directions (for example, 70/10). The first number is the European size. The second number is the American size. Both number systems refer to the thickness of the needle shaft. In this example, 70 indicates a diameter of 7 mm. In each case, the smaller the number, the finer the needle. Don't confuse needle size with thread size. For thread, the larger the number, the finer the thread.

Twin and triple needles have two numbers for their size. For example, 2.0/80(12) is a size 12 twin needle with a 2 mm space between the two needles. Select multiple needles carefully, as some are set too far apart to work on older machines that have a narrower maximum stitch width. For more information, see "Twin- and Triple-Needle Stitching" on page 15.

With the increasing interest in embellishment and

Creating a "new" fabric by randomly stitching across material is a fun way to improve your knowledge of needles and threads. Start with a small project, like a vest, because this type of stitching requires many yards of thread.

SUCCESSFUL STRATEGIES FOR NEEDLE SELECTION

Play matchmaker. Choose the appropriate needle size for the thread you plan to use and the look you desire when doing decorative work.

Get to the point. Select a point style that's best for your fabric thickness and type to get the best possible stitch formation.

Heed advice. Buy needles with the system number recommended by your machine's manufacturer.

embroidery, the number of sewing, decorative, and specialty threads has expanded. As you experiment with these threads, you are sure to find favorites that work best for your machine.

Like needles, thread is sized numerically since there are many more types than the all-purpose sewing type that we're used to. The larger the number, the finer the thread. Size 40 quilting thread is thicker and stronger than size 60 embroidery thread, for example. When a number follows a slash (/3), it indicates the number of plies (strands) that are twisted together to make the thread. When there is no ply number, the thread is two-ply.

Fabric and Thread Guide to Needle Points

Type	Abbreviation	Uses
Ball point	S	Delicate and difficult stretch fabrics (including lightweight jersey, swimwear, and elasticized fabrics), and synthetic suedes
Denim/Jeans	J	Denim and other dense fabrics
Embroidery	E	Decorative threads, such as rayon
Fine ball point	SES	Lightweight knits, including lingerie fabrics, and rayon and silk knits
Medium ball point	SUK	Average to heavyweight knits
Metallica	MET	Metallic and rayon threads
Microtex/Sharp	M	Silk and microfiber fabrics
Quilting	Q	Patchwork seaming and machine quilting
Topstitching	N	Decorative or multiple threads
Triple	DRI	Triple-needle stitching
Twin	ZWI	Double-needle stitching
Universal	H	All-purpose sewing on fabrics like cotton
Wedge or leather	NTW or LL	Durable seams on leather and suede
Wing	WING	Hemstitching

It's a joy to have so many threads and fabrics to choose from these days, but it can also be very frustrating if you try to stitch with the wrong needle. Tension problems will abound. The bobbin thread may be pulled to the fabric surface or the needle thread will end up loose. The seamline could pucker the fabric. You can even end up with skipped stitches.

Sewers know that they need to use needles that are appropriate for their particular machines. But it's just as important to make sure that the needle used for a project is suitable for the fabric and thread. For example, a Metalfil or Metallica needle is the best choice for stitching with metallic thread. Certainly this type of thread will fit through the eye of a standard sewing machine size 90/14 needle. A sewer may even have some success stitching, but there is a significant chance that the thread will split. And, again, obtaining a balanced stitch will be challenging.

Some special needles make it easier to stitch on pesky fabrics or use difficult-to-handle decorative threads. Others, such as twin, triple, and wing needles, add a decorative dimension to even a simple straight stitch. So before you change your needle and begin your next project, be sure to check out the "Guide to Specialty Needles" table at right.

While most needles are handled in the standard manner, multiple needles need some special consideration regarding your machine's bobbin, stitch width capacity, and, in particular, the threading sequence. Twin and triple needles attach to a common shank. The width between them varies. Make sure to select a

Guide to Specialty Needles

Type

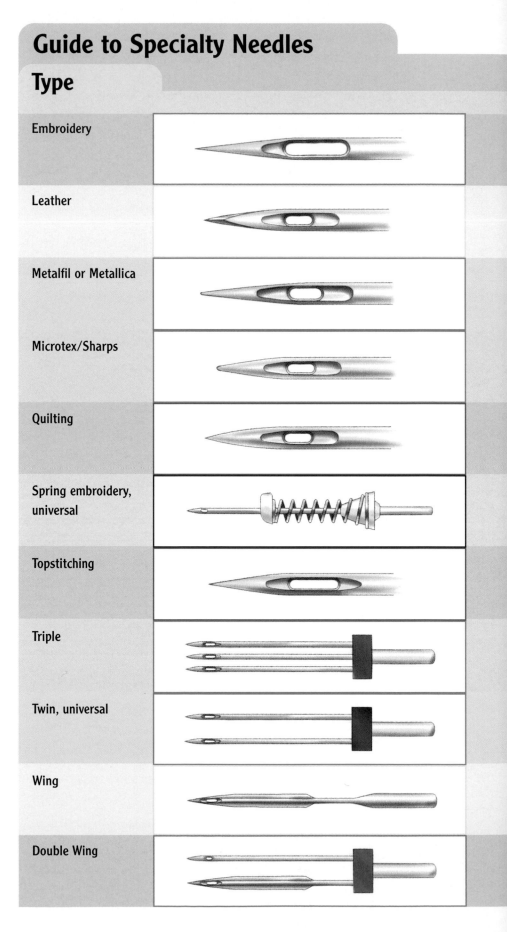

Embroidery	
Leather	
Metalfil or Metallica	
Microtex/Sharps	
Quilting	
Spring embroidery, universal	
Topstitching	
Triple	
Twin, universal	
Wing	
Double Wing	

Common Sizes	Features and Uses
75/11 and 90/14	Scarf prevents thread from shredding, splitting, stripping, and breaking when sewing with finer embroidery and metallic threads
80/12–110/18	Point has three sharp sides for a clean cut through vinyl, leather, and other dense materials; not necessary for synthetic suede and leather
80/12	Larger, elongated eye prevents thread stripping and splitting, and eliminates skipped stitches; use with metallic and rayon embroidery threads
60/8–90/14	Extra-sharp point is great for straight stitching on wovens, especially good on microfiber fabrics and synthetic suedes, ideal for topstitching and edgestitching
75/11 and 90/14	Tapered point stitches through different quilt thicknesses with ease and without skipping stitches
70/10, 80/12, and 90/14	Darning spring is attached so the needle can be used for quilting and monogramming, and embroidery in a hoop without a presser foot; available in other versions, including: stretch 75/11 and 90/14, denim/sharp 100/16, embroidery 75/11 and 90/14, and quilting 75/11 and 90/14
80/12–100/16	Extra-large eye and front groove hold heavier or multiple threads for more obvious stitch definition; used for topstitching; may also work for machine embroidery and quilting
2.5/75–3.0/80	Three needles on a common shaft simultaneously sew three rows of straight stitching; can be used with some decorative stitch patterns
1.6/80–6.0/100	Two needles on a common shaft simultaneously sew two rows of straight or patterned stitching on woven fabrics; used for heirloom sewing; available with special points
1.6/80–6.0/100	Needle shaft has an extension on each side to pierce and spread the fabric weave for decoratively stitched holes; commonly used in heirloom sewing
100/16	A wing and a universal needle are placed side by side to create decorative stitching on woven fabrics

size that will work on your machine. Your machine must have zigzag capability and must thread from front to back in order to use twin or triple needles. It must also have a top- or front-loading bobbin. You can't sew with these needles if your bobbin is inserted from the side of the machine.

When multiple needles are used, your sewing machine requires special threading. See "Twin- and Triple-Needle Stitching" on page 15 for more details.

The recommended needles and machine settings in the "Guide to Decorative Threads" table at right are a starting point. Remember that you need to test your stitching and, depending on the fabric, you may have to make additional adjustments including changing the needle, changing the needle or bobbin threads, and increasing or decreasing the tension. Also, most decorative work produces better results when the appropriate stabilizer is used.

Many of the decorative threads listed for use on the serger (see page 34) may be used for bobbin couching (see page 115).

Alternately, it's also possible to use some sewing machine threads on your serger. But whether at the sewing machine or serger, the manner that the thread feeds off the spool is important. If the thread doesn't flow evenly, you will have tension problems.

Parallel-wound thread, seen most often on domestic thread brands, generally feeds more easily from a vertical pin.

Cross-wound thread, commonly found on tubes and cones for serger sewing, usually reels off smoothly from either a horizontal or a vertical pin on a sewing machine.

If you have stitching problems with any cross-wound thread that's mounted on a vertical pin, use a horizontal spool feeder. The reverse is also true, so try switching to a vertical pin if your thread isn't feeding properly when it's mounted horizontally. If you can't adjust your horizontal spool pin to an upright position, use a spool feeder to make it vertical.

Guide to Decorative Threads

Type

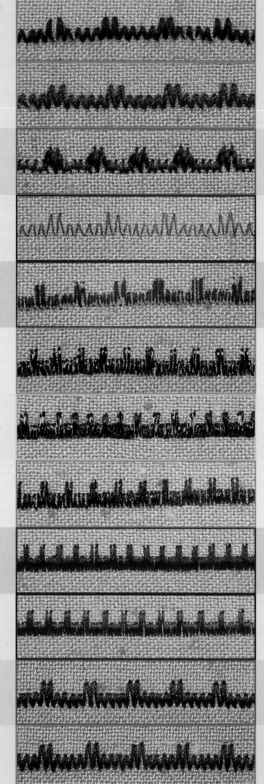

Type
Acrylic/wool (Burmilana; Renaissance)
Blue jean
Designer threads and yarns
Embroidery, acrylic
Embroidery, cotton
Embroidery, hologram (Prizm, Jewel)
Embroidery, lamé/tinsel (Sulky Sliver)
Embroidery, metallic
Embroidery, rayon
Silk
Silk buttonhole twist
Topstitching, buttonhole twist, Cordonnet

Characteristics	Recommended Needle	Special Handling
Looks like fine crewel yarn	Topstitching or jeans, 90/14 or larger	Use cone-thread holder; creates more lint; clean machine more often
Heavy-duty 100 percent spun polyester; cross-wound on cone	Topstitching or jeans 90/14	Rebalance needle and/or bobbin tensions; use cone-thread holder
Assorted thicker decorative threads, cords, and yarns	Will not fit through needle	Use in bobbin for bobbin couching and as cording for needle couching
Antistatic thread with more sheen than cotton but less than rayon	Embroidery 75/11, 90/14, or 80/12	Loosen needle tension; use lightweight cotton in bobbin
Finer than sewing cotton; high luster; stitches lie flat; thicker than rayon embroidery thread	Microtex or embroidery 70/10 or 80/12	Loosen needle tension; use lightweight thread in bobbin
Ribbonlike film with hologram pinpoints of dazzling, light-reflective color	Embroidery 75/11 or 90/14, Metalfil or topstitching 80/12 or 90/14	Place on vertical spool pin or use horizontal thread holder to adapt; do not use with heat-soluble stabilizers
Flat Mylar ribbon; metallized with aluminum for high reflection	Metalfil or topstitching 80/12, 90/14; embroidery 90/14	Place on vertical spool pin or use horizontal thread holder to adapt; loosen top tension; all-purpose thread in bobbin
Metallic foil usually twisted with a core thread of nylon or polyester for added strength	Metalfil or topstitching 80/12 or 90/14; embroidery 75/11 or 90/14	Apply a lubricant such as Sewer's Aid to prevent friction and static electricity; try Lingerie Thread in bobbin
Very smooth, shiny, fine thread; size 30 is thicker for more coverage	Embroidery 75/11 or 80/12; Metalfil, jeans, or topstitching 80/12 or 90/14	Loosen needle tension; try all-purpose, Lingerie Thread, or Bobbin Thread in bobbin
Fine, lustrous thread for special effects	Microtex or embroidery 70/10 or 80/12	Adjust tension for fine thread; try lightweight thread in bobbin
Heavy, lustrous thread for stitch definition in topstitching and buttonholes on heavy fabrics	Topstitching or jeans 90/14	Due to expense, use in needle only; loosen needle tension
Heavier and stronger than all-purpose thread; suitable for seaming heavy leather, canvas, vinyl, and upholstery	Topstitching, jeans, or stretch 90/14	Loosen needle and bobbin tensions and rebalance

If you don't have this handy tool, try a cone spool holder for the sewing machine.

The threads in the "Guide to Specialty Threads" table at right are designed for special fabric types and sewing machine applications, such as shirring, smocking, machine or hand quilting, and machine embroidery.

Sizing isn't always given in this table because some specialty threads are not made and measured in the traditional way.

Workroom Secret

When I think about how many bobbins I've wound, usually mid-seam, I can't believe I didn't figure this one out sooner! During a recent sewing session, short on time, I left the machine threaded and stacked a spool of matching thread on top of the spool that was already threaded on the machine. I wound the bobbin from the second spool. Was I surprised to discover that it worked—and saved the bother of unthreading and rethreading the machine! Try it; it might just work on your machine if it has a vertical spool pin. Laziness often is the real "mother of invention" in my sewing room.

Guide to Specialty Threads

Type	
Basting, such as Wash-A-Way	
Darning or basting	
Elastic	
Fusible	
Indoor/outdoor; home decorating (such as Heavy Duty Super-Tuff; Nymo B)	
Lingerie Thread and Bobbin Thread	
Clear transparent monofilament polyester or nylon, sizes 60 and 80	
Quilting, size 40/3	
Textured woolly nylon or polyester	

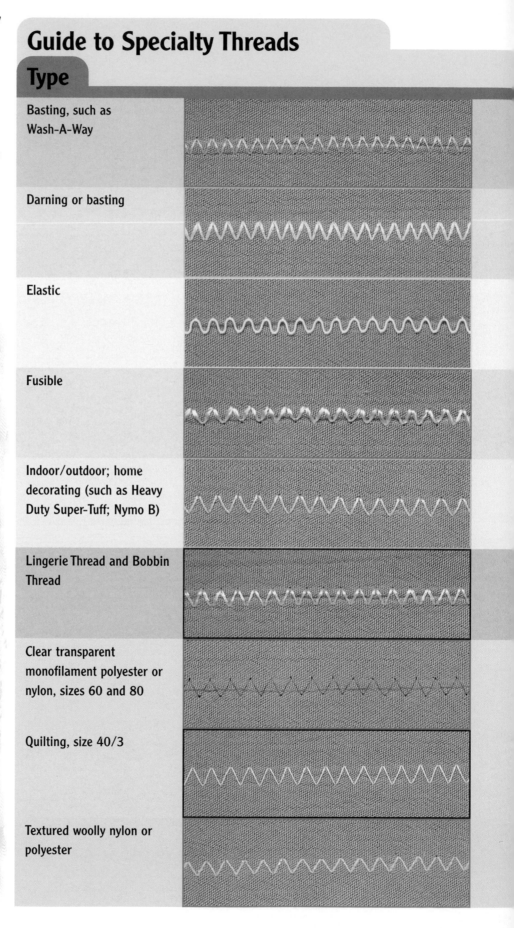

Uses

Special Handling

Uses	Special Handling
Hand or machine basting; strong enough for garment basting for fitting	Use in needle and bobbin with long stitch; shorter stitches take longer to dissolve; keep dry by storing spool and wound bobbin in plastic bag
Free-machine embroidery	Use in bobbin to draw needle thread down for better stitch quality; loosen needle tension so bobbin thread doesn't pull to surface
Shirring and smocking	Use in bobbin only; hand wind firmly for lightweight fabrics, loosely for others; use regular or decorative thread on top; adjust stitch length to 8 spi (3.5 mm)
Fuse-baste a pocket in place; position appliqués; match plaids; secure facings and hems	Use in bobbin with all-purpose thread in needle; loosen bobbin tension if necessary; use press cloth to fuse
Canvas, upholstery, heavy leather, outdoor gear	Loosen bobbin tension if necessary; use 10 spi (2.5 mm); change needle often on large projects
Lingerie fabrics; beadwork; applying elastic; use in bobbin when you need more tension to draw top thread down	Use in needle and bobbin for lingerie; in bobbin for twin-needle pintucks; in needle and in bobbin with wing needle for large-hole hemstitching
Use on top for invisible machine quilting and appliqué, and for invisible stitches when bobbin couching; also for fluted hems, stitching on clear vinyl	Loosen needle tension or tighten bobbin tension; for truly invisible blindstitching, increase needle tension when used in needle and bobbin
Machine or hand quilting	Use on top and in bobbin; do not use waxed hand-quilting thread in machine
Lingerie; twin-needle hems on knits; blend with other threads for decorative work	Use in bobbin with twin needles for knit hems; stitch at a moderate speed to avoid stretching, puckering; use with a Metalfil needle with other decorative thread for thread blending; hand wind onto bobbin to prevent stretching

THREAD BLENDING

Despite all the threads available today, there are times when just the right color isn't available or you need a very special effect. When stuck in this situation, thread blending is the solution. This multicolor result of combining several threads is different than that achieved with variegated threads that your local fabric store stocks.

For machine sewing and machine embroidery, blend lightweight threads of the same or different colors through a single needle to create a heavier topstitching thread. Use a larger topstitching or jeans needle to accommodate the bulk. If three fine threads will work, use the Thread Palette on a cone thread stand to hold the spools. See the diagram at right.

On the serger, route as many as five different threads through the serger's upper (or lower) looper, using a Thread Palette to hold the spools for even feeding.

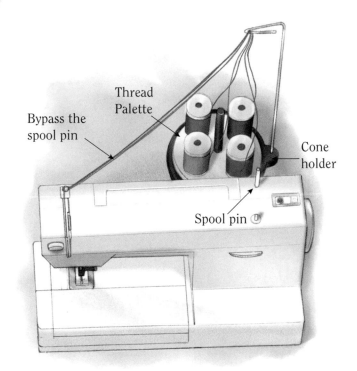

Bypass the spool pin

Thread Palette

Cone holder

Spool pin

Workroom Secret

You don't need a Thread Palette to combine only two threads. Instead, extend your single vertical spool pin with a plastic drinking straw so that you can stack two spools on top of each other. Arrange them so one thread reels off the spool front, the other off the spool back.

Or, use two spool pins, if available, and the threading setup for twin-needle stitching, but insert both threads through the eye of a single needle.

The thread paths for twin-needle stitching are further explained on page 16. Remember that the spools unwind in opposite directions so that the threads don't tangle.

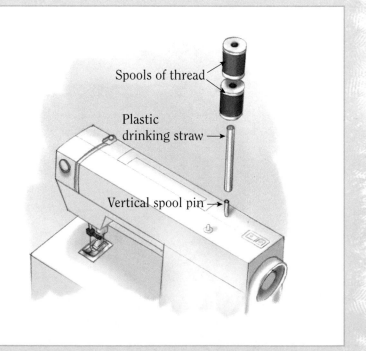

Spools of thread

Plastic drinking straw

Vertical spool pin

Fancy Footwork

Before the zigzag sewing machine was available, the standard equipment for a sewing machine included a straight-stitch presser foot and a zipper foot. Now machines come with a variety of presser feet that are considered essential for daily sewing. As innovative stitchers explore the capabilities of their machines, they also find new and different ways to use these presser feet. Many of the special uses are detailed in this chapter and in "Sewing and Serging from A to Z" (see page 55).

The most obvious variations in a group of presser feet are the width between the toes, the size and shape of the toes, and the size of the needle opening. Turn the feet over, though, and you'll notice one more important difference—the contour of the sole.

This shape varies depending on the task for which the foot is designed. For example, a flat-soled zigzag foot, as shown below, will not glide over the built-up stitches in satin stitching and some embroidery. The embroidery foot, on the other hand, has a wide tunnel on its sole so that these stitches are not flattened or snagged as they flow out from underneath the foot. The pintuck foot, also shown below, has a series of grooves to accommodate tucks as they form.

Other feet have special parts for specific functions. For example, some brands of the blindstitch foot have a metal plate between the toes, or to the side, to ride along the fabric fold so that the stitches are perfectly positioned.

Holes in a multicord presser foot prevent threads from twisting or overlapping as you couch them to your fabric. Before you feed the threads through the presser foot, you may want to insert each length into a small plastic bag for additional control.

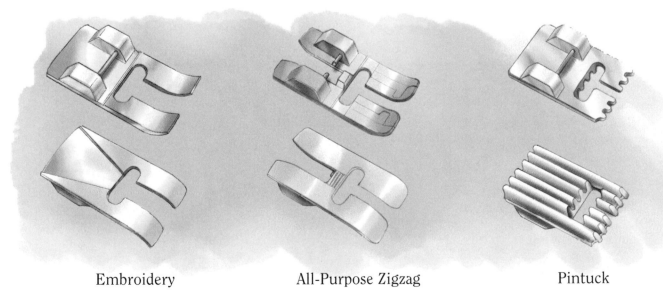

Embroidery   All-Purpose Zigzag   Pintuck

FUN FEET

There are hundreds of presser feet on the market—enough to fill an entire book with illustrations, descriptions, and tips for their use. And, of course, you can do without many of them. But do you want to? If your pocketbook has put the brakes on your desires, you may want to consider only a few additional purchases. To help you hone your list to a manageable size, here's an admittedly opinionated list of my favorites.

Big Foot. This large, clear-plastic darning foot provides more surface contact with, and control of, layers during free-motion quilting. Its unique mushroom-shaped hole assures that the outer edge of the foot is always

¼ inch (6 mm) from the needle, even while stitching straight lines or curved designs. The foot fits most low-shank machines, and Berninas with a special adapter.

Fastube Foot. Sew even-width tubes for cording, straps, belts, and more with this innovative foot with an adjustable guide. It was designed to use with the Fasturn tool for stitching and turning tubing. It fits a low-shank

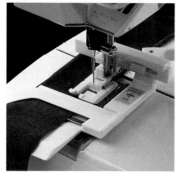

machine, but a high-low adapter is available to make it and other low-shank feet fit high-shank models.

Little Foot. Designed for quilters, this clear plastic foot is nevertheless great for sewing narrow, straight seams. Stitch with the fabric along the right edge of the foot for a perfect ¼-inch (6-mm)-wide seam

allowance or along the left edge of the foot for a perfect ⅛-inch (3-mm)-wide seam allowance. Perfect topstitching is also a cinch with this foot.

Pearls 'N Piping Foot. A deep channel on the bottom of this foot accommodates the cord filler in piping and easily rides over prestrung beads, rhinestones, and decorative cords.

Satinedge Foot. This foot replaces the tedious and often messy two-step process for satin stitching the edge of a heavy fabric: stitching inside the edge, then hand trimming close to the stitches without cutting the stitches. It

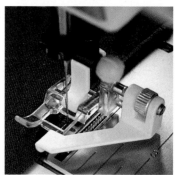

was specially designed to sew a flat, clean, satin-stitched edge on any fabric weight. The foot has an edge guide plus a metal guide finger like the stitch finger on a serger. Unlike the similar overedge or overcasting foot for the sewing machine, the finger on the Satinedge Foot is adjustable and the edge guide adjusts with it.

Sequins 'N Ribbon Foot. Stitch ¼-inch (6-mm)-wide elastic, ribbon, trim, and sequin strings in place while feeding them through the tunnel in the adjustable guide. Two extra guides in the

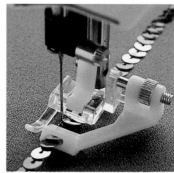

accessory kit accommodate ⅛- and ⅜-inch (6- and 9.5-mm)-wide elastic and trims.

Getting the Most from Your Sewing Machine Stitches

Throughout the "Sewing and Serging from A to Z" section of this book, you'll find a vast array of ways to use the stitches that your machine has to offer, whether the selection is limited to forward, reverse, and zigzag, or it contains a hundred decorative options. In this entry, the basics of creating successful multiple needle and satin stitching are addressed. In addition, the "New Uses for Basic Stitches" table on page 22 offers guidelines for the use of standard stitches.

Stitched pintucks are a surprising addition to the sleeves on this jacket. They were created by sewing multiple rows of twin-needle serpentine stitch to the fabric.

TWIN- AND TRIPLE-NEEDLE STITCHING

Twin- and triple-needle stitching multiply the creative options on your machine. Something as simple as the serpentine stitch turns into an artful addition around a neckline or hem when done with two needles. As you would expect, extra needles means extra threads and that can increase the chance of poor stitch formation. Take the time to thread them correctly, and twin and triple needles will become your first choice for adding an elegant but easy embellishment to special sewing projects.

A twin needle produces a straight stitch on top, and on the bottom the bobbin thread zigzags between the two needle threads. See **Diagram 1.** This results in a stitch that's a bit more flexible than an ordinary straight stitch. It's an excellent choice for knits and can be used for functional and decorative stitching. It's often used to stitch hems in knit garments, for example.

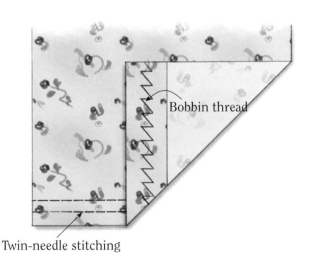

Bobbin thread

Twin-needle stitching

Diagram 1

Threading for Twin-Needle Stitching

1. Position two spools on the spool pins so the threads unwind in opposite directions, to avoid tangles. See **Diagram 2.** If you don't have two spool pins, wind thread onto a bobbin and place it underneath the spool (or place the spool and the bobbin side by side on a horizontal spool pin).

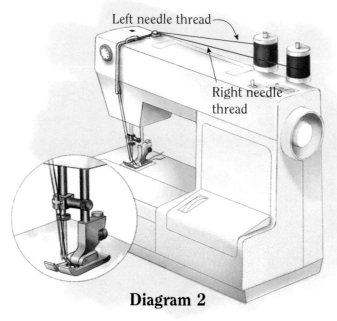

Left needle thread

Right needle thread

Diagram 2

2. For straight stitching, set the stitch width at 0. For zigzag and decorative stitches, you need to look at the distance between the needles and the stitch width. If the needle distance is too wide for your machine, the needles will hit the presser foot or the needle plate, and they will bend or break. For example, if the maximum stitch width on your machine is 4.5 mm and the distance between needles is 1.6 mm, the widest stitch you can use is just under 2.5 mm. After adjusting the zigzag stitch width, slowly move the handwheel to make sure the needles clear the foot and the hole in the needle plate.

3. Adjust the stitch length as desired.

4. Thread the two threads through the machine as one until you reach the tension discs, taking care to keep them from twisting around each other. Place one thread on each side of the disc. If your machine doesn't have a dual thread guide above the needle, leave one thread out to avoid tangling.

Threading for Triple-Needle Stitching

1. Use two spools and a bobbin of matching thread if you have two spool pins. See **Diagram 3.** If your machine has only one spool pin, stack two bobbins on top of the spool.

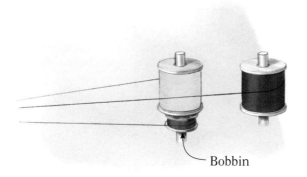

Bobbin

Diagram 3

2. Run the three threads through the machine as one until you reach the tension discs. Place two threads on one side of a disc and the remaining thread on the other side.

3. Continue threading the machine. However, the thread that went through the tension discs by itself doesn't go through the thread guide. Insert this thread in the center needle.

4. Subtract the needle width from the widest stitch width possible on your machine to determine the stitch width setting. If your machine's maximum stitch width is 4.5 mm, and you're using a 2.5 mm needle, the maximum stitch width for your triple needle stitching is 2 mm. Just to check your calculations, slowly move the handwheel to make sure the needles clear the foot and the hole in the needle plate.

Turning When Twin- or Triple-Needle Stitching

1. To turn corners with a double needle, stop with the needles sitting just above the surface of the fabric.

2. Pivot the corner halfway, then manually turn the handwheel, inserting the inner needle in the hole of the previous stitch. Complete the stitch, then complete the pivot. See **Diagram 4.**

3. Reinsert the needle in the same hole and complete the stitch. See **Diagram 5.** You can use the same process to turn corners with a triple needle, taking three small stitches across the corner.

Diagram 5

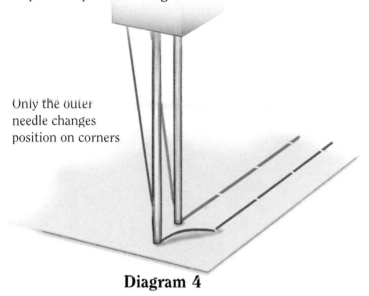

Only the outer needle changes position on corners

Diagram 4

Make It Easy

To hold additional spools of thread, use a Thread Palette placed on a cone thread holder. You can also add a makeshift vertical spool holder by securely taping a short length of plastic drinking straw to the back of your sewing machine.

Don't use the cone thread holder and the plastic drinking straw at the same time. For two spools of thread, stack them on the plastic drinking straw, unwinding in opposite directions. The Thread Palette and cone thread holder work for up to four spools.

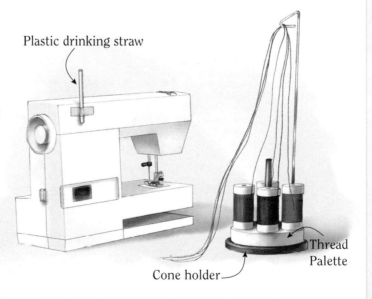

Plastic drinking straw

Thread Palette

Cone holder

SATIN STITCHING

Satin stitching is a key element in a variety of decorative techniques, including appliqué, cutwork, monograms, and needle lace. But it tends to draw up, causing puckering and fabric tunneling under the stitches. To prevent these problems, always use a stabilizer under the fabric.

Use an embroidery or Microtex needle and rayon or cotton embroidery thread for smooth, lustrous stitching. Loosen the needle tension so that the bobbin thread pulls the needle thread to the underside. Adjust for the desired width and a stitch length of about 50 spi (.5 to .8 mm) and use an embroidery or appliqué presser foot.

Once the stitch width, length, and tension are perfectly adjusted, maneuvering around curves, corners, and points is the next challenge. Study the diagrams on this page and the next to learn how to stitch these shapes to perfection. Note that satin stitches are very closely spaced, but for the sake of clarity they are farther apart than normal in the illustrations.

Topstitching doesn't have to be straight and narrow. On this garment, the collar edge is defined by lines of satin stitching.

Satin Stitch Outside Corner

Step 1

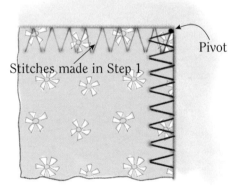

Stitches made in Step 1

Pivot

Step 2

Pivot

Stitches made in Step 1

Step 2 (variation)

Satin Stitch Curves

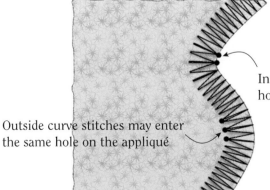

Outside curve stitches may enter the same hole on the appliqué

Inside curve stitches may enter the same hole more than once on the inside edge

Satin Stitch Inside Corner

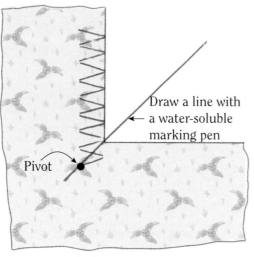

Draw a line with a water-soluble marking pen

Pivot

Step 1

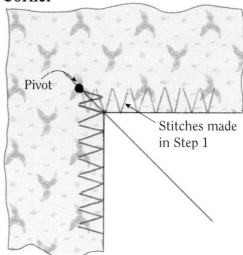

Pivot

Stitches made in Step 1

Step 2

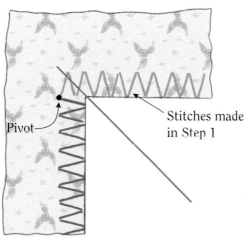

Pivot

Stitches made in Step 1

Step 2 (variation 1)

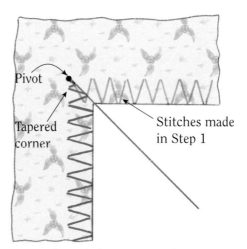

Pivot

Tapered corner

Stitches made in Step 1

Step 2 (variation 2)

Satin Stitch Inside Point

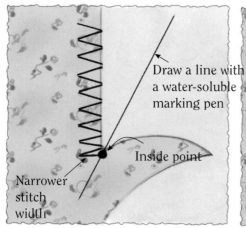

Draw a line with a water-soluble marking pen

Inside point

Narrower stitch width

Step 1

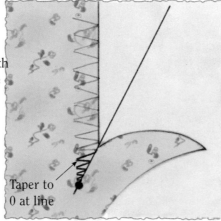

Taper to 0 at line

Step 2

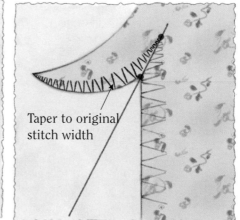

Taper to original stitch width

Step 3

SUCCESSFUL STRATEGIES FOR APPLIQUÉ SATIN STITCHING

Curves first. Begin on a side or in a curve, never at a point or in a corner unless absolutely necessary.

De-fuzz it. Arrange your work so that the left swing of the needle catches the appliqué and the right swing goes over the appliqué edge and into the background fabric. This ensures completely covered raw edges.

Do the bump. To avoid lumps on the wrong side, draw the bobbin thread to the surface of your work, take a few stitches in place to anchor it, and then satin stitch over the beginning stitches.

Get down. Set your machine for the needle down position. Perfect satin stitching relies on lots of stops and starts to pivot and reposition the work.

Make it go away. Use a disappearing ink, like a water-soluble marking pen, to mark guidelines to stitch perfect pivots and tapers.

Stop and go. Take all satin stitches so that they are perpendicular to the appliqué edges. This means stopping to pivot and reposition the work periodically, particularly along curves. This avoids uneven stitches and stitch pile-ups.

Do the twist. Don't satin stitch around curves without pivoting. Otherwise you'll have wavy edges and uneven stitches. Keep the stitches perpendicular to the appliqué edge and pivot often. The tighter the curve, the more pivots you need. Always pivot from the longest edge of the stitching to the tightest part of the curve.

Think shifty. As the illustrations on pages 18 and 19 show, you have to "play" a bit with your stitches to create tapered satin stitching. You'll find this easier if your sewing machine needle can move to the right or left, because shifting the needle position is helpful.

Relax. Let the machine do the work, helping it along only when crossing previous satin-stitched areas. Use your fingertips to coax the fabric under the presser foot while stitching slowly.

Dial down. To tie off, change to a short straight stitch and take several stitches right alongside the satin stitching, gradually adjusting the stitch length to 0.

Shop wisely. Use high-quality thread. Although it is often difficult to see the difference with the naked eye, your stitch quality can be greatly affected. You may be able to see one indicator of less-than-perfect thread, and that is a fuzzy surface. Simply avoiding the spools in the "bargain bin" will reduce problems with tension and thread breakage.

Pretreat. Toss washable fabrics into the washer and dryer to remove sizing that can cause the needle to stick.

Tame dust bunnies. Remove lint in the tension discs and in the bobbin case and bobbin case area. You can blow out the lint with canned air or you can suck out any mess with your vacuum. Hard-to-reach areas are accessible by attaching small nozzles and brushes that are sold in kits available through many sewing shops. Using a vacuum is the best option because you won't force lint into any crevices. There's nothing wrong with using ozone-friendly canned air, just direct the blast away from the interior of your sewing machine. Lint brushes and pipe cleaners are good for daily, routine cleanups.

Do it right. Make sure that your sewing machine is threaded correctly and that the needle is inserted properly.

Select carefully. Choose a needle that matches both your fabric and your thread.

Get help. If balanced tension and regular stitching elude you, have your sewing machine serviced. Skipped stitches can be caused by faulty timing in the stitching mechanisms or a damaged hook in the bobbin mechanism. These are mechanical problems that require the attention of a trained machine technician.

BLINDSTITCHING

A great imitator, the blindstitch can replicate hand stitching, regardless of the make or age of your sewing machine. While specifics vary, all you really need is a blindstitch setting and specialized presser foot. In some cases transparent thread and water-soluble basting thread are a plus.

Although the appearance of blindstitch feet varies from one brand of sewing machine to the next, all of the feet function in essentially the same way. An offset toe on the foot, a center bar, or an adjustable bar on the right side of the foot is positioned next to a fabric fold to guide the work so that the straight stitch goes through a single layer of fabric and the intermittent zigzag stitch just catches a folded edge to the left.

Although the serger has no blindstitch, it does have an optional blindstitch foot, designed for the same purpose. It has an adjustable guide that rides along the fabric fold while stitching—just as it would if you were doing traditional blindstitching on a sewing machine.

There are a variety of ways to use the blindstitch, and you can also use it to slip stitch, create hand-picked topstitching, and baste (see "Zigzag Basting by Machine" on page 71.)

It is easy to think of the sewing machine blindstitch as only a utility stitch. Yet it's versatile enough for decorative applications.

You can use the blindstitch to stitch a pretty shell edge on lingerie straps or hems, or a series of delicate shell tucks at the neckline of a handkerchief-linen blouse. Fold the fabric on the tuck line and stitch along the fold, using the blindstitch foot and the blindstitch. Position the garment so that the zigzag stitch goes over the folded edge, drawing it into little scallops or "shells."

The blindstitch is also great for making delicate elastic button loops. Lay the cord along the edge and bartack the end to the fabric. Position your work so that the zigzag catches the cord on the outer swing of the stitch. You get a button loop between each zigzag. Experiment with the stitch length to adjust the spacing.

Another idea for the blindstitch is to stitch over the edge of a knit collar with a decorative thread to

Aptly named the blindstitch, the needle's left swing catches only a few threads of the folded garment. When the hem (underneath) is folded out, the stitching is barely visible on the right side of the fabric.

imitate the picot edge featured on some ready-to-wear knit collars.

If you're sewing on knits, use the stretch blindstitch. In this case, tiny zigzag stitches replace the straight stitch of a standard blindstitch. Substitute the stretch blindstitch for the traditional blindstitch when doing invisible appliqué. The difference? When you use a contrasting decorative thread in the needle, the stitching adds detail to the appliqué.

STITCH SAMPLER

Have you tried making all the stitches that your machine offers? Just playing with the settings and trying a variety of threads can lead to some innovative stitching that you can use on future garments.

So get out some fabric scraps and experiment. Make every stitch in a contrasting color thread and adjust the stitch length and width about every inch to see the various effects you can achieve with simple adjustments. Check the wrong side, too. You're bound to have a "happy accident"—a stitch that you like better on the back.

Creative sewers hang on to these samples, and note the stitches and settings for future reference.

Basic stitches and their most common uses are shown in the "New Uses for Basic Stitches" table at right. As well as offering a reference guide for your sewing needs, you can use the photographs of the stitches as a launching point for your own creative explorations. You'll certainly find alternative uses for these stitches, alone or in combination with other stitches.

Expand your creative stitching options with presser feet that are not intended for your machine. It may be possible to use presser feet from other brands with the same shank style. I know that I warned you to be careful about using presser feet not intended for your machine, but rules are meant to be broken. Before the ¼-inch (6-mm) patchwork foot and the Little Foot were available, I often attached my Singer Featherweight straight-stitch foot to my Elna, which requires a short-shank presser foot. I loved using it for narrow topstitching. Try a high-low adapter to "change" a high shank to a low shank. If you have more than one sewing machine, it's more than likely that you already have many interchangeable feet at your fingertips.

New Uses for Basic Stitches

Type	
Blindstitch	
Double overlock	
Honeycomb or smocking	
Overlock	
Scallop	
Straight	
Stretch blindstitch or edging	
Super stretch	
Three-step zigzag	
Triple straight (also called elastic straight)	
Triple zigzag or rickrack	
Zigzag	

Uses

Hemming woven fabrics; shell-tucked edges on lingerie; couching; invisible machine appliqué

Overcasting raw edges on knits and wovens; stitching and finishing ¼-inch (6-mm)-wide seam allowances

Finishing ¼-inch (6-mm)-wide seam allowances; decorative stitching; lapped seaming on lacy fabrics; hemming lightweight knits; decorative topstitching

Overcasting raw edges; doing a one-step elastic application; hemming and seaming on fine knits

Decorative stitching and finishing edges

General sewing including seaming, easing, basting, topstitching, edgestitching, understitching, and functional and decorative twin-needle stitching

Hemming knit fabrics; decorative edge finishing; sewing appliqués in place with the look of a blanket stitch; reinforcing buttonholes

Sewing ¼-inch (6-mm)-wide seams on super stretchy fabrics; also for flat-joining seams on terry cloth; fagoting; reverse blanket stitching

Raw-edge overcasting; attaching elastic; decorative stitching with twin needles; understitching facings to flatten the bulk; fagoting; topstitching; couching

Reinforcing areas of stress; topstitching; not recommended for seaming as it is difficult to rip out mistakes

Topstitching and other decorative work

Seam finishing; sewing on buttons; making cord belt loops; couching; making buttonholes; gathering over a cord; satin stitching monograms, appliqués, and embroidered designs; finishing appliqués and monograms

Taming Tension

Perfect stitching. It's the dream of every sewer who battles with her machine when she would rather be sewing yards and yards of pretty ruffles or making her own strips of insertion trim using her machine's embroidery capabilities. Don't assume you know everything about tension. Many sewers never learn the tips in this section until they've sewn for years or their machine goes on strike.

For a balanced stitch, adjust the needle and bobbin tensions so they exert equal pressure on the thread. When you use specialty thread for decorative work, you have to make more tension adjustments because you often use one type of thread in the needle and a different type in the bobbin. Tension adjustments must make up for the weight and strength variations of the two threads for a balanced stitch.

You can make most tension adjustments by loosening or tightening the needle thread tension. If you have a strong or stretchy thread in the bobbin, increase or tighten the tension on the needle thread to obtain a balanced stitch. Otherwise the bobbin thread will pull the needle thread to the underside of the seam. However, if you use a very strong, fine thread in the needle, such as clear monofilament polyester, you'll need to decrease or loosen the needle tension.

As you can see, perfect tension can be elusive. Many variables can affect tension. If you're having trouble, make sure that your machine is properly threaded and also inspect your tension discs for lint buildup.

TEST YOUR TENSION

Mention the word tension to a group of sewers and you're likely to get the same negative reaction. It can be the most nagging challenge of day-to-day sewing. Think of the tension regulator as a problem solver instead of a problem, and give yourself permission to adjust both the needle and bobbin tensions whenever necessary. Even the preset tensions on high-end sewing machines need fine tuning—especially when you start playing with decorative thread combinations.

1. Start with two layers of fabric and all-purpose sewing thread. You'll find it easier to pinpoint problems if you use a thread that's a contrasting color.

2. Set the straight stitch length for 10 spi (2.5 mm). If you're testing the zigzag tension, use a medium-width stitch. Stitch on the bias.

3. Stretch the sample on the bias. Both threads should break. If only the needle thread breaks, the needle thread tension is too tight. If only the bobbin thread breaks, the needle thread is too loose. The loop formed when the needle and bobbin thread interlock should be between the two layers of fabric. You should not see loops on either side. A tiny bit of loop showing on the reverse of zigzagging is acceptable.

BOBBIN TENSION ADJUSTMENTS

"Never touch the bobbin tension," still rings in my ears from my childhood. It's hard to break that old rule, but guess what—it's okay to adjust the bobbin tension, if necessary, for some stitches. Besides, if you accidentally drop the bobbin case, the tension screw might loosen, requiring a tension adjustment. You can do it!

If you have a removable bobbin case, you can make sure the tension on the thread is balanced by holding on to the thread and letting go of the bobbin case like a yo-yo, with your other hand underneath—but not touching—the bobbin. See **Diagram 1.** Give the bobbin a series of little jerks. The bobbin case should drop slowly, once with each jerk. If it doesn't, the tension is probably too tight.

Diagram 1

Loosen the bobbin tension by turning the screw on the bobbin case. See **Diagram 2.** If there are two screws, loosen the one closest to the thread. Adjust the screw counterclockwise, moving it no more than one quarter of a turn at a time.

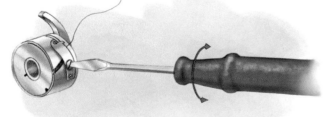

Removable Bobbin Case

Diagram 2

When you pull on the thread in a loaded built-in bobbin case, the thread should feel snug, but it should not be difficult to pull, and it should not break. If it slips or slides easily through the tension mechanism, it's incorrectly threaded or there isn't enough tension on the thread. First rethread it, then test it again. If necessary, tighten the screw by turning it clockwise no more than one quarter of a turn at a time, testing after each adjustment. See **Diagram 3.**

Built-In Bobbin Case

Diagram 3

Treat yourself to an extra bobbin case for decorative work if your machine has a removable bobbin case. Then use the extra one whenever a technique, such as bobbin couching, calls for a bobbin tension adjustment. To easily identify the extra case, mark it with a dab of bright nail polish.

Make It Easy

Put an extra bobbin case and a dozen bobbins on your gift wish list. Remember to specify the brand and model number of your machine so you get the right ones! It's a treat to have an empty bobbin when you need one, and it's essential if more than one person is using the machine.

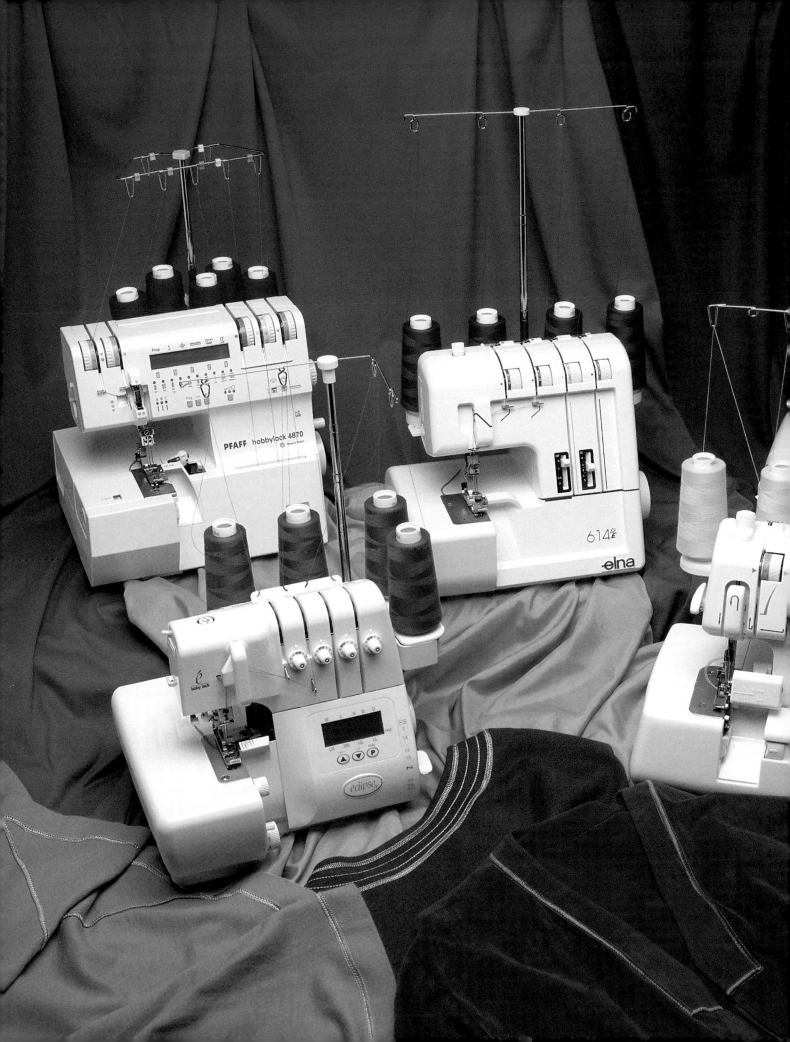

Getting the Most from Your Serger

Hailed for speedy seam stitching and finishing—its most basic talent—the serger is a wonder machine capable of executing many decorative techniques with special threads. With a serger it is truly possible to imitate and duplicate some of the most innovative embellishment and stitching techniques used in ready-to-wear—often with more interesting results and better quality than you'll find in ready-made clothes.

In this section, you'll learn some of the basics of successful serging so that you can execute any of the serger techniques included in the A-to-Z section of this book. Learn to master threading and tension adjustments, and then serge ahead to some of the most gratifying stitching you will ever do.

Anatomy of a Serger

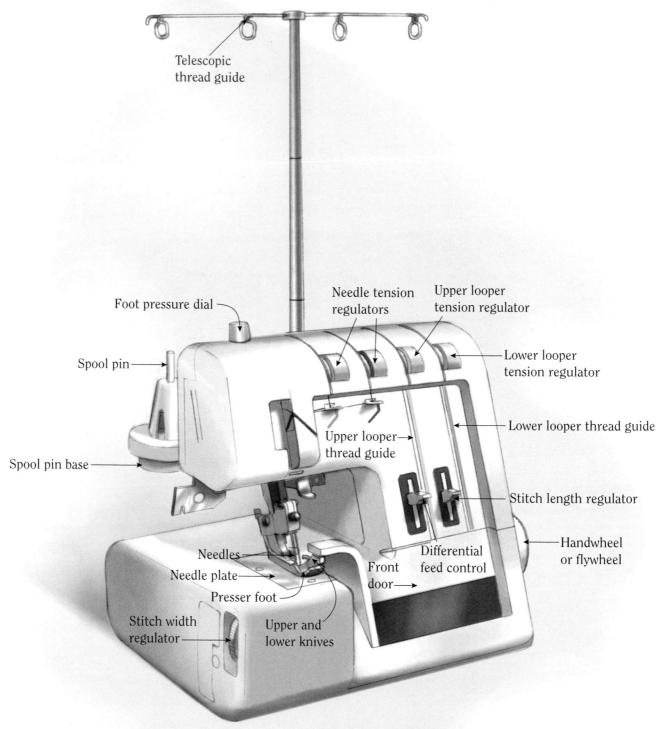

Telescopic thread guide

Foot pressure dial

Spool pin

Spool pin base

Needle tension regulators

Upper looper tension regulator

Lower looper tension regulator

Lower looper thread guide

Upper looper thread guide

Stitch length regulator

Needles

Needle plate

Presser foot

Front door

Differential feed control

Handwheel or flywheel

Stitch width regulator

Upper and lower knives

Getting to know the parts of your machine is the first step to successful serging. Sergers are available with a wide variety of features so the tips in this section are a culmination of many hours of research on a variety of models and brands. Some, like the Baby Lock Éclipse LX (shown in the photograph on page 26) even have air-jet threading systems. The parts identified on the four-thread serger above are common to most.

Differential feed control. Some sergers have two sets of feed dogs, one behind the other, and a knob to adjust them. When set at 1 or N (depending on how the machine is marked), both sets of feed dogs move at the same rate for normal serging on most fabrics. See **Diagram 1.** Increase to 2 and the front feed dogs take in two times as much fabric as the back feed dogs release, causing the fabric to draw up into small gathers, much like using the "ease plus" feature on a sewing machine. Use the longest stitch length for the most gathering. After stitching, you can also use your fingers to adjust the gathers formed by the differential feed. To gather even more, smooth out the thread chain and draw the short needle threads out of the end of the serger chain. Pull them together to draw up the existing gathers for additional fullness. When you set differential feed below normal, the difference in the feed pulls the fabric taut before it reaches the needle so it will not pucker as you stitch.

Setting 1 (N)

Both feed dogs move
at the same rate

Setting 2 (+)

Front feed dogs move
faster to prevent wavy,
stretchy seams on knits

Setting 0.5 (-)

Front feed dogs move
more slowly to prevent
puckering on sheers
and lightweight fabrics

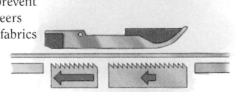

Diagram 1

Foot pressure dial. This keeps the layers of fabric flowing evenly between the foot and the feed dogs. Using the correct pressure (tighter) helps eliminate skipped stitches on heavy fabrics. A somewhat looser pressure controls stretching and seam rippling on knits.

Needle(s). Be sure to use the correct type for your machine. Just because a household sewing machine needle fits, that does not mean it is suitable. See "Serger Needle Savvy" on page 32.

Threading needles and loopers is tough. The work is fine and precise—much like doing dental work! In a fit of frustration, I decided to borrow tools from that profession to see if these would help. Dental-floss holders make threading a breeze! Buy a package of these (colored, not clear) at your drugstore. Place several on a long ribbon to tie to your serger or wear around your neck (even the colored ones are easy to misplace). I also found that needle insertion is easier with a dental mirror.

Presser foot. The standard serger presser foot has a single, long toe. It holds the fabric while it is being cut before the looper stitches form over the cut edge and slide off the short prong (stitch finger) to the right of the needle hole. Before you begin to serge, tuck the threads securely underneath and to the left of the presser foot.

To avoid a messy nest of threads at the start of a seam, chain off 3 to 4 inches (8 to 10 cm) before inserting the thread under the presser foot. Starting with a long

> ## Workroom Secret
>
> I do not need four or five cones of serger thread in every color that I sew. Instead I use matching thread only in the needle, as it is the only one that might show along a serged seamline. I then use whatever threads I have on hand in the loopers rather than buying several cones or spools to match the fabric.

chain ensures that it will not catch under the foot. After chaining off, hand-turn the flywheel in reverse for a half rotation to slip the needle thread out of the lower looper. This prevents needle breakage when you start to serge.

Spool pin. If your thread is not feeding properly, the problem could be caused by the three to five vertical spool pins or, more accurately, the manner that the thread is feeding off the spools or cones on the rods. Thread on serger cones is cross-wound to feed smoothly. If you use thread that is wound in another fashion, your stitch tension won't be balanced and the threads could break frequently. Resolving the problem is as simple as sliding a horizontal spool holder over each of the vertical spool pins. A multiple spool holder, called a thread palette, can be slipped over a spool pin so that you can blend threads feeding through the upper looper.

Telescopic thread guide. This moveable bar behind the serger has loops or slots for the threads. See **Diagram 2**. They are the first of a series of guides that help establish the correct tension. Do not skip these guides when threading. The rod must be fully extended for perfect serging.

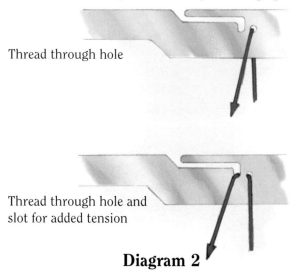

Thread through hole

Thread through hole and slot for added tension

Diagram 2

SUCCESSFUL STRATEGIES FOR USING THE DIFFERENTIAL FEED

Avoid rippled seams. Knits, loosely woven fabrics, and bias-cut edges are prime candidates for rippled seams. Control this by using above-normal settings.

Prevent wavy edges. Set your differential feed above normal to serge around curves and stitch on bias pieces.

Increase gathers. When combined with a maximum stitch length and the differential feed engaged at a maximum setting, the stitching gathers lightweight fabrics to almost double fullness, which is great for ruffles.

Prevent puckers. Rolled hems and pucker-free seams on woven fabrics or single layers are smoother if you use below-normal settings for the differential feed.

Add ripples. A lettuce hem will have even more ripples when you use lower settings.

Create stretch. Add more stretch to swimwear and active wear by using lower differential feed settings.

Reduce excess fullness. Serge-finish the narrow hem edge on a flared skirt or only in the curved section of a shirttail hem with above-normal settings to ease automatically.

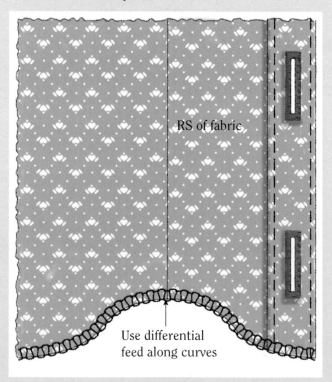

RS of fabric

Use differential feed along curves

Tension regulators. Every serger has one or more dials to control each needle's tension independently as well as a tension regulator for the upper looper and one for the lower looper. If you are stitching with very thick threads and desire a looper tension lower than 0, stitch with the thread removed from the looper tension regulators. See "Successful Strategies for Tension Adjustments" on page 51.

Upper and lower loopers. Every serger has at least two metal looper prongs, each with a large thread hole. They interact like knitting needles to create loops over the cut fabric edge. See **Diagram 3.** The loops connect with the needle thread at the stitching line. The two/four- and five-thread sergers have an extra looper for the chainstitch. It is easier to thread the upper looper before the lower looper because the upper looper thread guides lie behind those for the lower looper.

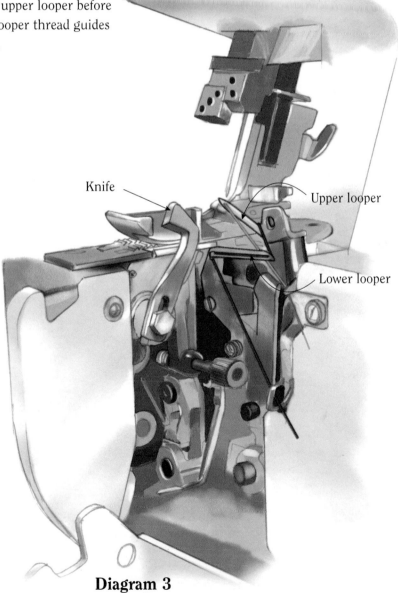

Knife

Upper looper

Lower looper

Diagram 3

> ## Workroom Secret
> Snagged and skipped stitches may be caused by burrs and rough spots on the loopers and needle plate. I buff these away with crocus cloth. Much like a very, very fine sandpaper, this cloth is denim impregnated with jeweler's rouge. It's available from some notions mail-order services.

Serger Needle Savvy

More than any other part on your machine, the needle is often the key to beautiful stitching. Balanced tension and even stitches depend on choosing the right needle for the machine, fabric, and thread.

A needle may fit in your machine, but that does not mean it's the right one to use. Always use the needle type that is recommended for your machine. You may need a household sewing machine needle, a serger (industrial) needle, or a custom needle. The back side of the shank of a household sewing machine needle, labeled 15×1 for example, is flat, while the shank of most industrial needles is round. Industrial needle labels include $DC \times 1$, $BL \times 1$, $DB \times 1$, and $JL \times 1$.

A serger needle is stronger than a household machine needle because it is made to last longer, which is necessary for the high speeds at which sergers run. However, the round shank makes it more difficult to insert it correctly into the needle clamp.

The tricky part of inserting an industrial needle is identifying the back, since the shank is round. The groove and eye face straight forward, and the scarf (the indent at the tip of the needle) is at the back.

Choose a needle in the 70/10 to 90/14 size range. Smaller needles are not strong enough, while larger sizes may not fit and may damage your machine. When appropriate (and if available for your serger) switch to a ball point, stretch, topstitching, embroidery, or Microtex/Sharp needle for special fabrics or threads. (See "Fabric and Thread Guide to Needle Points" on page 5 and "Guide to Specialty Needles" on page 6 for an explanation of these needle types.)

If your serger has more than one needle, use the same brand, type, and size for each position, unless you have an older serger that requires a different needle type in each position. Also keep in mind that multiple needle points may not be even when correctly inserted.

If your machine has multiple needles and you have removed one or more for the stitch that you are doing, set the extra needle aside in a special pincushion to keep slightly used needles separate from your new ones. Insert a new needle after every four to six pro-

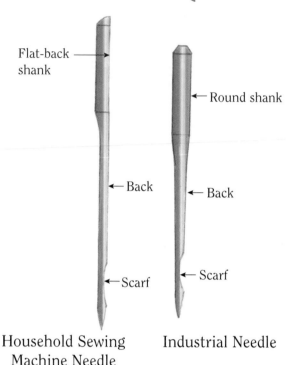

Household Sewing Machine Needle — Flat-back shank, Back, Scarf

Industrial Needle — Round shank, Back, Scarf

jects, or more often if you sew on lots of synthetic fabrics. Throw away your used needles.

When you insert a needle, place a sheet of paper over the needle hole to catch the needle or the set screw in case you drop either one. Push the needle shaft as far up into the needle clamp as it will go. If necessary, move the paper out of the way so that you can lower the needle partially into the needle hole before inserting it into the needle clamp.

Make It Easy

You can magnetize the end of your screwdriver. This is done by placing the tip in a magnetic pin dish. If you unscrew a small set screw too far, it will adhere to the screwdriver rather than drop and roll away.

Serger Thread Smarts

As you experiment on your serger, you will discover that using it for decorative work is exciting—and occasionally a bit challenging. When shopping, be on the lookout for interesting serger thread possibilities, remembering that whatever you use for decorative work must fit through the holes in the loopers, sometimes called the looper eyes. Yarns with heavy, bumplike slubs won't work, but these might be great for sewing machine couching. Buy a sample to try on both machines.

If you can easily thread two strands through the upper looper hole (even though you will use only one), it is probably a good candidate for decorative serging. Remember that the looper thread will show and that it takes quite a bit of thread for a looped edge finish. Threads in small put-ups (yardage) may not be appropriate because you'll run out of thread too often. They are usually more expensive, too.

The threads shown in the "Decorative Serger Threads" table on pages 34 and 35 are the ones used most often for regular serging and decorative work. To stock up your collection, watch for notions sales and buy a spool of each type of thread. Use them to make a stitch sampler for reference, noting the thread name and the appropriate stitch length, width, and tension settings for each of the stitches: overedge, overlock, flatlock, rolled-edge, cover, and chain. This will make choosing thread easier for future projects, and give you lots of practice adjusting tensions and stitch settings.

Make It Easy

You can make an untwisted thread—woolly nylon, for example—easier to thread by adding a drop of liquid seam sealant to the end. Then roll the wet end between your fingers to form a point and let it dry.

Fine serger threads on cones can be used on a sewing machine. But many threads and yarns that work only for bobbin couching on the sewing machine can be used for decorative stitches, seaming, and edge finishing on the serger.

Once you master the basics of serging and move on to working with specialty threads, you will discover exciting new design and sewing options. Add color and texture to fabrics using interesting threads in the loopers so they lie on the surface of the finished garment along seam and hem edges. Stitch with the seam in place to show off your skills. Use rayon embroidery thread to add delicate shine to the rolled edge of a chiffon scarf or feminine skirt. Make tiny rolled-edge tucks with a contrasting decorative thread for added texture in your heirloom sewing project. The "Sewing and Serging from A to Z" section of this book, which explains numerous techniques, will help you explore many of the stitch possibilities that are available for you to explore when you are planning your sewing projects.

All of the decorative threads listed for sewing machines in the "Guide to Decorative Threads" on page 8 can be used on a serger. In addition, the threads shown here are also suitable for decorative serging. Most can be used for edge finishing, seaming, rolled edge finishing, flatlocking, chainstitching, and cover stitching. They can also be used for sewing machine couching.

You may also want to try thread blending. You can obtain thicker, stronger, or more colorful thread by using two or more strands from separate spools in a single location (one of the loopers, for example). Fine, weak threads, such as metallics, can be blended with a strand of woolly stretch nylon for added durability.

The threads shown here are suitable for only the loopers.

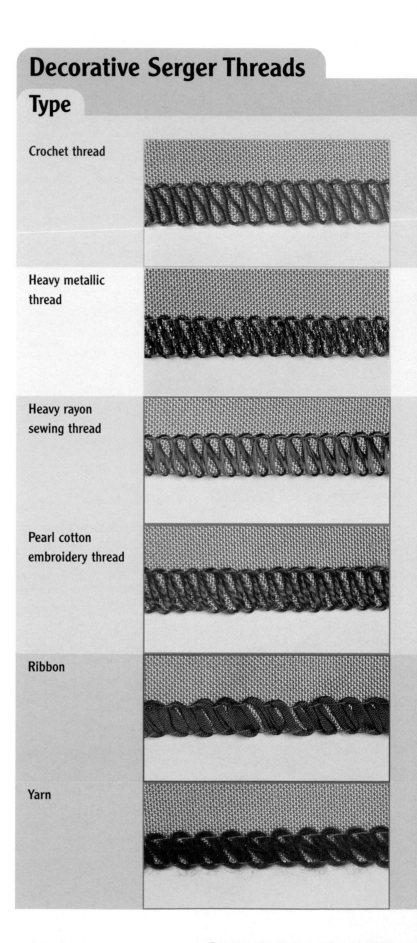

Decorative Serger Threads

Type

Crochet thread

Heavy metallic thread

Heavy rayon sewing thread

Pearl cotton embroidery thread

Ribbon

Yarn

Characteristics	Brand	Stitch and Tension Adjustments
Cotton or acrylic; very strong; tightly twisted; gives good edge coverage	Coats and Clark	Loosen the looper tension and use a longer, wider stitch
Fuller, loftier than metallic embroidery thread; good edge coverage and lots of shine	YLI Candlelight; Madeira Glamour (fine metallic yarns that will fit through the looper eye may also work)	Loosen the looper tension slightly and use a longer, wider stitch
Thicker and heavier than rayon embroidery thread; untwisted versions are more lustrous, but weaker than twisted ones; appropriate for loopers only	YLI Designer 6, YLI Pearl Crown, Madeira Decor 6	Loosen the looper tension slightly and use a longer, wider stitch
Low-twist, shiny cotton embroidery thread; available on skeins and balls	DMC Pearl Cotton, J & P Coats Pearl Cotton	Loosen the looper tension
Regular ribbon, plus ribbon floss, ribbon thread, and ribbon yarn; use 1/16- to 1/4-inch (1.5 to 6 mm) widths; not appropriate for overlocked seams or rolled edges; use narrow silk, rayon, acrylic, and cotton ribbons; avoid nylon and polyester (too stiff)	Kanagawa Silk, Ribbon Floss, Ribbon Thread	Use in the upper looper and loosen the tension considerably; may need to remove ribbon from one or more thread guides and perhaps the tension discs as well; try a longer, wider stitch
Fine, tightly twisted yarns only; machine needle-punch and machine knitting yarns are best; may be cotton, wool, acrylic, silk, or blends; some very fine yarns may fit through the needle	YLI Ultrasheen, Burmilana	Use thicker yarns in the upper looper only and loosen the tension considerably; you may need to remove the yarn from one or more thread guides and perhaps the tension discs as well; try a longer, wider stitch

Workroom Secret

You can insert thick thread through the parts of your machine even when you cannot find your looper threader. This is an instance where special tools aren't really needed, although you can try using a dental-floss threader, if you have one handy. (I usually do, because I often use one to thread sewing machine needles.)

But, in a pinch, place the thicker thread inside the loop of regular serger thread. Then simply thread both ends of the regular serger thread through the hole, drawing the heavier thread through with the "cradle" made by the loop of thread.

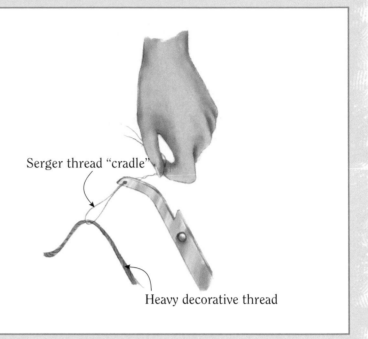

Serger thread "cradle"

Heavy decorative thread

SUCCESSFUL STRATEGIES FOR DECORATIVE SERGING

Test, test, test. Before starting your project, always do a test on the project fabric. Start with a longer stitch and a looser tension than you would use if you were using regular serging thread. Fine-tune the stitch on scraps, adjusting only one dial at a time.

Buy extra. Count on using 8 to 10 yards (7.3 to 9.1 m) of decorative thread per looper for each yard of decorative serging. Buy an extra cone or spool to test stitch length, width, and tension—just in case your calculations were wrong or testing took lots of thread.

Rewind. If the decorative thread is in a skein or on a card, cross-wind it loosely onto an empty cone or wind it into a loose ball, then unwind a large quantity into a "snake" on the table behind the serger. Serge a bit, then stop and snake out more thread. Continue in this fashion to keep the thread feeding smoothly and evenly so it does not suddenly tighten up, causing ugly, uneven stitch formations called "hiccups."

Choose wisely. Heavy decorative threads may work only in the upper looper. The extra thread guides in the lower loopers put more tension on the thread, making breakage more likely. If the stitching will be visible on both sides of the garment edge—such as on a collar—use a thread that will work in both loopers. Another option is to substitute the wrapped stitch for the overlock stitch.

Take it slow. Begin with an attitude of patience and the intention to work at a slower pace. You cannot serge heavy threads as fast as fine ones without thread breakage.

Skip guides. When blending threads in the upper and/or lower loopers, it may be necessary to leave one of the two threads out of one or more thread guides. This will help you obtain even feeding and perfect tension. One nice combination is threading a metallic thread with woolly nylon for extra sparkle, for example.

Visual Guide to Serger Presser Feet

Using the right presser foot for your selected technique takes the work out of serging and turns the stitching into a fun experience. You can make do with the basic foot for your serger—or invest in specialty feet that make it easy to add bead trim, insert elastic, gather fabric layers, or wire an edge for your own inexpensive but beautiful wire-edged ribbon—and more. You are bound to discover some new ways to use the specialty feet as you explore the creative serging techniques in this book.

Some of the currently available feet and attachments are shown here. Not all feet are available for all sergers, but some generic versions are available. You may also be able to mix brands. Take your serger with you to test-fit feet not made specifically for your serger. You may find feet that work on your machine, thus expanding your serging capabilities.

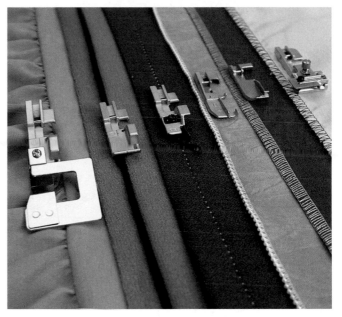

A well-equipped sewing kit will benefit from the addition of the following presser feet, listed as shown from left to right above: gathering, piping, blind hem, beading, basic, and elastic (also called elasticator).

SUCCESSFUL METHODS FOR AVOIDING TANGLES

To avoid tangled cords while stitching, control them with one of these methods before threading them through the foot.

Get guidance. Thread the cords through a multiple cording guide. This small strip of flexible plastic has five holes to guide the cords, tangle-free, to the foot while you stitch.

Improvise. You don't have a cording guide? Then put each spool of cord or thread in its own small, zippered plastic bag and thread the cord through a hole in one bottom corner. Attach the foot and tuck all of the thread bags inside a larger plastic or paper bag that you already attached to the sewing table in front of your machine. You can also use this method with a cording guide for even better cord control.

Make It Easy

Serging with a strip of water-soluble stabilizer on top of some fabrics can give you a cleaner finish. You can see through the stabilizer while you serge and it is easy to remove. Carefully tear the excess plastic film away along the needle stitching and spritz to remove the remainder—or try lifting it out of the stitches with your serger tweezers.

UTILITY PRESSER FEET

The presser foot on a serger is essential to guiding the fabric for smooth cutting and stitching. Each serger comes with at least one standard presser foot but may require additional feet for special stitches. Some sergers have a special foot for the rolled edge stitch. If you have a five-thread machine with cover stitching capabilities, you will need a special presser foot, as well. Begin with the basics, depending on your make and model, then add to your collection as your skills grow and your needs do, too.

Basic presser foot. Usually about twice as long as a sewing machine presser foot, the serger foot securely holds the fabric in place for feeding and cutting before the stitches form. See **Diagram 1.** Some presser feet have needle lines, marks, or notches on the toe that indicate the spot where the needle enters the fabric. Use this as a gauge for feeding the fabric so the seamline is in the right place. You can add needle lines with a permanent marker. If you are using two needles, the left needle line is the seamline.

Blind hem foot. Available for most sergers, it is best used on knits and spongy or highly textured fabrics. This foot has a metal guide that rides along the turned-back hem edge to ensure that the needle bite is consistent. See **Diagram 2.** Try this foot for overlocking, flatlocking, or doing fagoting along a folded edge without trimming. Test it for other applications where stitching accurately along an edge or fold is desirable.

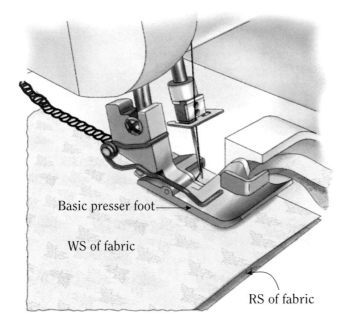

Basic presser foot

WS of fabric

RS of fabric

Diagram 1

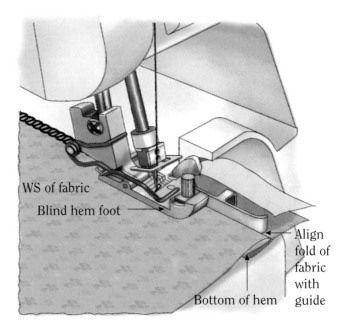

WS of fabric

Blind hem foot

Align fold of fabric with guide

Bottom of hem

Diagram 2

Chainstitch foot. Shorter than a standard serger presser foot, this one is made of transparent plastic so that you can see the chainstitch. This makes it possible to fine-tune and adjust placement while stitching. See **Diagram 3.**

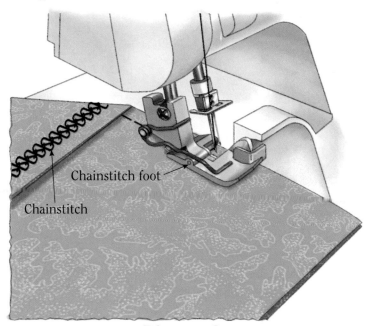

Chainstitch foot

Chainstitch

Diagram 3

Cover hem foot. Use for the cover hem stitch only, with the knives disengaged. See **Diagram 4.**

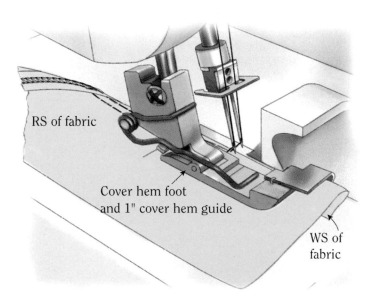

RS of fabric

Cover hem foot
and 1" cover hem guide

WS of fabric

Diagram 4

Elastic foot (elasticator). This foot holds elastic in place without pins. A screw on the toe adjusts the tension on the elastic so that it stretches to fit the fabric edge. You can use the elasticator to apply trim and ribbon, too. See **Diagram 5.**

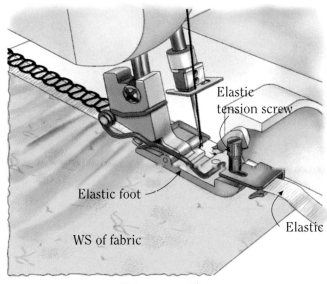

Elastic
tension screw

Elastic foot

Elastic

WS of fabric

Diagram 5

Narrow rolled-hem foot. Required for models without built-in rolled hem adjustments, this foot has a narrow stitch finger for correct-width stitch formation. See **Diagram 6.**

Narrow rolled-hem foot

Diagram 6

SPECIAL-PURPOSE PRESSER FEET AND ACCESSORIES

Shown on these two pages are special feet and accessories that make serging more fun and relaxing. Although it is possible to do most of the serger techniques included throughout this book with only a general-purpose foot, the money you invest in extra feet and accessories will pay off by saving you time and eliminating unnecessary frustration. Invest in those you know you will use a lot, then add the others to your serger foot collection as you need them.

Beading/pearl/sequin foot. Known by various names, this foot has a channel in front and a tunnel at the back to guide three-dimensional trims directly under the stitches while serging them in place along a cut or folded edge. You can use the foot to apply cord, wire, and fishline, too. The multipurpose foot for some models combines this function with piping. See **Diagram 7.**

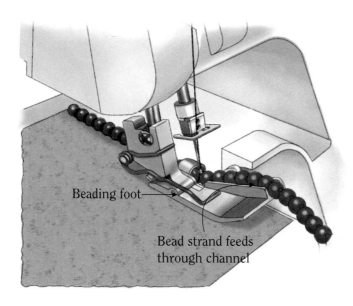

Beading foot

Bead strand feeds through channel

Diagram 7

Bias binder. Attach this to your machine to fold a bias strip over a fabric edge for securing with chainstitching.

Bias tape guide/piping attachment. Put this on your serger to fold bias over a cord for making piping. Also use it to insert piping or a folded bias strip without filler at an edge or between two layers while serging.

Cover hem belt loop foot. This turns under the edges of a 1-inch (2.5-cm)-wide bias strip and secures them with a cover stitch. See **Diagram 8.** Use it with a cover hem guide attachment and wrapped seam guide.

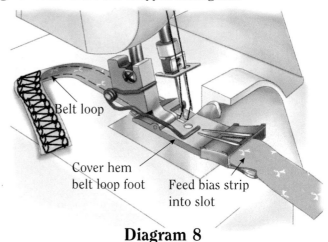

Belt loop

Cover hem belt loop foot

Feed bias strip into slot

Diagram 8

Cording or gimp foot. A hole guides fine cord, wire, gimp, or fishline. Try the tape guide or lace/heirloom foot as a substitute, or check the toe of your basic presser foot for a threading slot. See **Diagram 9.**

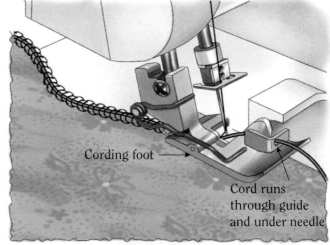

Cording foot

Cord runs through guide and under needle

Diagram 9

Lace/heirloom foot. A guide on the front of this foot keeps fabric in line for narrow seams, pintucks, lace insertion, and lace finishing. See **Diagram 10.**

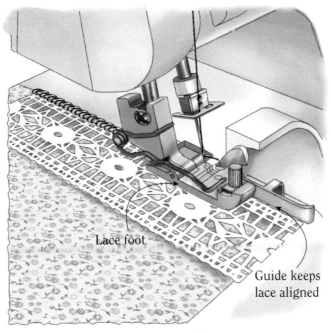

Lace foot

Guide keeps lace aligned

Diagram 10

Ribbon/tape foot. This may be a separate foot with a slot in the front of the toe for guiding ribbon and tape, or there may be a slot in the front of the standard presser foot for this purpose. See **Diagram 12.**

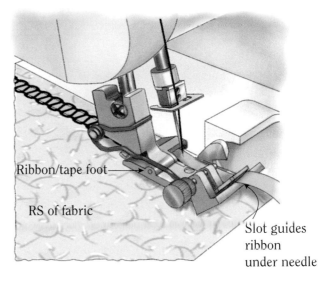

Ribbon/tape foot

RS of fabric

Slot guides ribbon under needle

Diagram 12

Piping foot. The groove on the bottom of the foot, to the left of the needle line, accommodates piping while serging it to fabric. See **Diagram 11.**

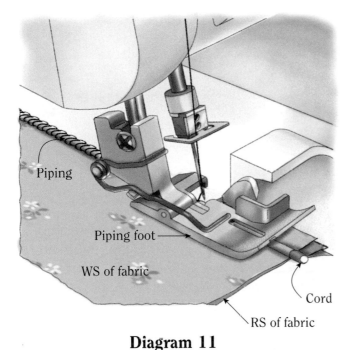

Piping

Piping foot

WS of fabric

Cord

RS of fabric

Diagram 11

Shirring/gathering foot. This foot separates two fabric layers so that it can gather the bottom layer of fabric while stitching it to the flat top layer. Use the foot to gather single layers, too. See **Diagram 13.**

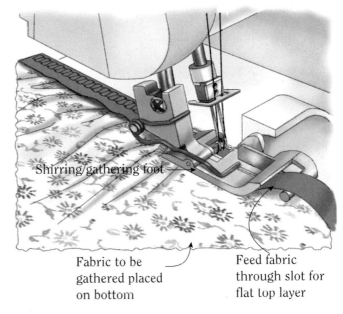

Shirring/gathering foot

Fabric to be gathered placed on bottom

Feed fabric through slot for flat top layer

Diagram 13

Threading Demystified

Threading your serger can be difficult at first, and the best advice I can give you is to thread, rethread, and rethread again—in other words, practice until you've got it down pat.

For those of you who just cannot warm up to threading your machine, take heart! Machines that do much of the work for you, like the air-jet threading system on the Baby Lock Éclipse LX (shown on page 26), will probably become more and more available.

Fear of threading and adjusting tensions often prevents sewers from taking full advantage of their sergers. Practice will give you confidence to set up your machine and adjust tensions for any stitch.

THREADING FROM SCRATCH

It is possible to change threads on an already threaded machine by tying thread ends together (see the opposite page), but you'll eventually have to rethread from scratch. Your manual and the colored thread paths that are probably marked on your machine will guide you. The steps that follow will help you as you work through the positions.

1. Make an enlarged photocopy of the threading illustration in your manual and trace along the threading paths with a colored pencil.

2. The usual threading sequence goes from right to left (lower looper, upper looper, right needle, left needle). You may be able to thread the upper looper first, which is easier since the thread guides for the upper looper lie behind those for the lower loopers.

3. If the spool of your parallel-wound thread has a

notch on one side, place the spool on the spool pin so that the notched end is on the bottom, where it won't catch the thread.

4. Use a dental-floss holder to guide difficult threads through the guides and looper holes.

5. If glare makes it difficult to thread the lower looper, turn off the serger light.

6. For additional visibility, try tipping the serger up and back a bit. At this angle it may be easier for you to maneuver the thread into the lower looper with the looper threader.

7. To make sure that the thread is fully engaged in the tension regulator, tug gently on the thread on each side of the tension knob or dial.

SPEEDY SERGER THREADING

Use this method when you wish to replace threads on a serger that is already correctly threaded. You can also use this technique when one or more threads break while you're serging. However, on some machines you must unthread the needle before rethreading the loopers. Otherwise, the needle and looper threads will tangle and the threads will break when you start to stitch again.

1. Clip all the threads just above the spools. (If you clip them above the tension knobs, they will not be long enough for this threading method.)

2. Remove the spools you wish to replace, and position the new threads on the appropriate spool pins.

3. Lay each set of thread ends (old and new for each spool) side by side and tie an overhand knot. Make sure the knot is secure, and trim the ends, leaving a 1-inch (2.5-cm)-long tail. See the diagram below.

4. Lift the presser foot or touch the release lever to release the thread tensions. Dial down to 0 tension on each disc to eliminate undue wear.

5. Separately pull each looper thread though its guides and tension discs until the knots pass through and come out under the foot. You can also pull through all of the looper threads at the same time, if you prefer.

When using decorative threads, the thicker knot may not pass through the tension discs and/or the looper hole with ease. Loosen the tension or remove the thread from the tension discs. When the knot reaches the looper, pull an extra length of thread through the machine to this point, then clip at the knot and thread the end through the looper hole.

6. Pull the needle thread through the machine in the same manner. Clip the knot when it reaches the needle and rethread as usual. If there is more than one needle, thread the second one in the same manner.

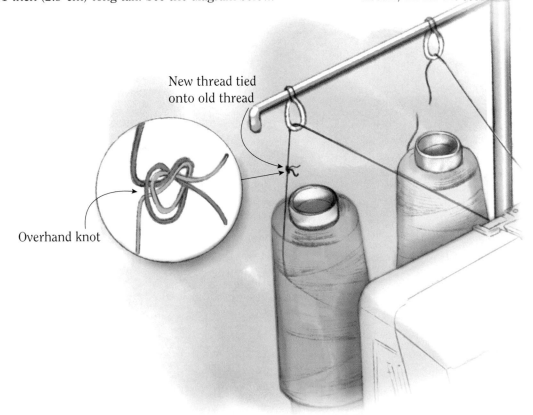

New thread tied
onto old thread

Overhand knot

Getting the Most from Your Serger Stitches

The anthem of many serger owners could easily be "too much to try and too little time to do it!" At first glance serger stitches appear pretty basic—and their uses rather limited. But as more sewers explore the capabilities of their machines they are discovering a wealth of new techniques and fun design options for the chain, cover, and flatlock stitches.

Think beyond utilitarian uses for your serger. Why not use silklike threads and try chainstitching?

CHAINSTITCH APPLICATIONS

Every serger owner will agree that the chainstitch is a great way to sew a sturdy seam. But you can do more with this simple two-thread stitch since it has some interesting decorative options, too. Unfortunately, the chainstitch is generally available on two/four- and five-thread models only.

It's great for embellishing fabric because the knife action is disengaged, so you can sew anywhere you wish. The underside of the stitch makes a chain, so if you stitch with the wrong side of the fabric facing you, the chain appears on the right side of the fabric surface, creating the look of more time-consuming hand embroidery.

For successful stitching, set the stitch length at 3 mm or longer to control thread breakage and jamming. To control puckering, slightly loosen both the needle and looper tensions, or set the differential feed at 1.5 to 2.

Also remember to disengage the knife action so that you can maneuver the fabric to stitch where you wish without cutting into the fabric.

To be safe, begin chainstitching on the fabric. If you can't do that or don't like this starting sequence, place a scrap under the foot and the needle before lowering both of them into position. Then tuck your garment fabric under the serger toe so that it's butted against the scrap. On some serger models the chain will not form when you stitch unless there is fabric under the foot and the needle.

To complete your stitching at the end of the line, knot the needle and looper threads at the fabric edge. Another option is to draw the threads to the underside with a hand-sewing needle and tie off, if necessary. Do not use a liquid seam sealant because chainstitching unravels too easily.

Apply trim. If you want decorative chainstitching to embellish a purchased trim, machine baste the trim in place on the right side of the garment. On the wrong side of the garment, chainstitch along the basting.

Baste seams. This is a great way to join pattern pieces in order to do a fitting, since chainstitching is easy to remove. Simply pull the looper thread from the end where you stopped stitching. See **Diagram 1**.

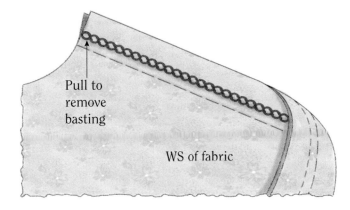

Pull to remove basting

WS of fabric

Diagram 1

Embellish fabric. With the fabric face down, chainstitch along the fabric's printed or woven stripes, to add color and texture. If a bold print fabric shows clearly enough on the wrong side, you can chainstitch the printed motifs to add color and texture along the outer edges and follow design lines within to mimic chainstitched commercial fabrics.

Hem knits. Use a long stitch and stretch as you serge for a flat, ripple-free, and decorative hem.

Imitate couching. Make decorative stitches in a free-form manner to imitate couching (see page 114). Mark the design on the fabric's wrong side or trace the design onto stabilizer and place this on the wrong side of the fabric.

Seam knits. Use woolly nylon thread in the needle and loopers and stretch the fabric while you are serging. Do not use chainstitching for active wear or swimwear, however, because it doesn't have enough stretch.

Seam wovens. Stitch strong, nonstretchy, plain seams on wovens. Press the seams open.

Shirr lightweight fabric. Use elastic thread in the looper, with a long stitch and loose tension (set the differential feed at 2, if available). Serge the fabric with the right side up. If you want fuller shirring, tighten the tension more, if necessary. Make several rows for added detail. See **Diagram 2**.

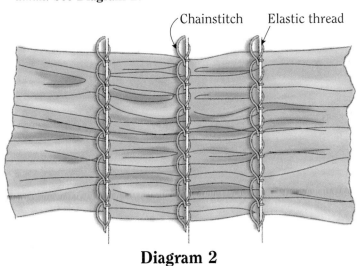

Chainstitch   Elastic thread

Diagram 2

Stitch tucks. Fold the fabric with the right side out and stitch along the length of the tuck using the edge of the presser foot as the guide for the tuck's width. Serge all of the tucks in the same direction and press them to one side to expose the chainstitching. See **Diagram 3**.

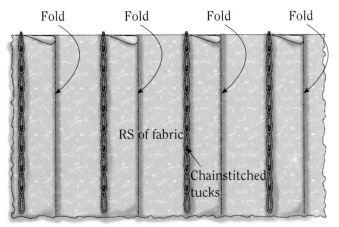

Fold   Fold   Fold   Fold

RS of fabric

Chainstitched tucks

Diagram 3

Topstitch. Stitch with the fabric right side up for straight topstitching or with the wrong side up so that the chainstitching appears on the right side of the garment. Before you start to stitch, mark the stitching line with extra-long basting stitches or with a marking pen or chalk.

COVER STITCH APPLICATIONS

For years sewers have tried to imitate the ready-to-wear look of cover stitching on their own garment hems. Yet it was only recently that this stitch started to appear on sergers for the home sewing market. If your machine has this stitch, you can use it for details just like those featured on designer garments.

The cover stitch is best known for hemming knits, but you may want to consider using it anywhere you want two rows of straight, even topstitching, such as on a pocket or the edge of a collar. It combines two rows of straight stitching on top with a double row of chainstitching on the wrong side. A single looper thread on the underside creates the chains, connecting both rows in much the same way a twin-needle stitch is connected with zigzagging on the underside. Since no cutting is required, you can cover stitch anywhere on the garment.

The width between the stitching rows is determined by the set width between the two needles on the serger, which is just under 3 mm on some sergers and is 5 or 6 mm on others.

Apply elastic. Lap lacy stretch lingerie elastic over the fabric edge and stretch to fit while cover stitching in place.

Add details. In one step you can create two rows of topstitching for decorative work on a pocket or collar edge. See **Diagram 4.**

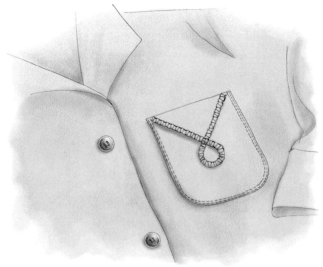

Diagram 4

Texture chainstitching. This technique is almost like bobbin couching on the sewing machine. You can use a decorative thread in the loopers and serge with the fabric wrong side up. The right side of your fabric will feature a double row of decorative chainstitching. See **Diagram 5.**

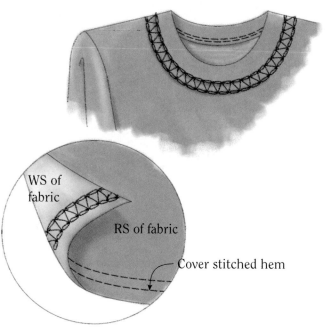

WS of fabric

RS of fabric

Cover stitched hem

Diagram 5

Weave ribbon. Stitch as directed in Texture Chainstitching, then weave yarn, cording, or ⅛-inch (3-mm)-wide ribbon in and out of the stitches on the right side of the fabric. See **Diagram 6**. You can also experiment with weaving patterns to create different looks.

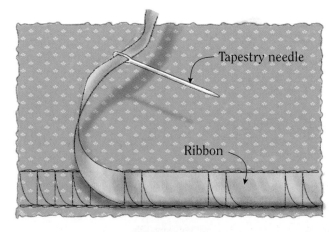

Tapestry needle

Ribbon

Diagram 6

Finish ribbing. Serge ribbing to a neckline or cuff with a three-thread overlock stitch, then turn the seam to the inside and cover stitch through the garment and ribbing to hold the seam smooth and flat inside. See **Diagram 7.**

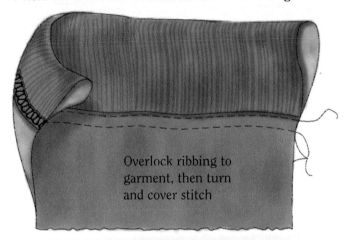

Overlock ribbing to garment, then turn and cover stitch

Diagram 7

Machine quilt. The double rows of topstitching look great in contrasting thread and the chainstitching adds a decorative finish to the lining or backing side of the stitched layers.

Create belt loops. Some sergers have a specialty foot that allows you to make bias belt loops with the cover stitch and also apply bias strips to another layer of fabric. See **Diagram 8.**

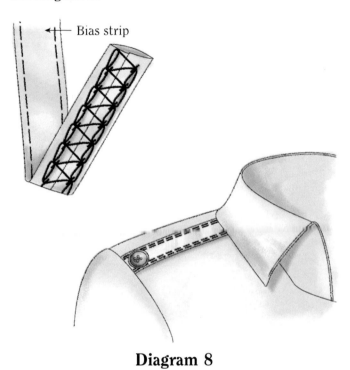

Bias strip

Diagram 8

FLATLOCK STITCH APPLICATIONS

The flatlock stitch offers creative versatility because its finished appearance is so different on each side of the fabric. Loops of thread intertwine and loop in a lacelike manner along the fabric surface on one side, while a more delicate ladder of straight stitches appears on the reverse. See **Diagram 9** on page 48. You can use either the loops or the ladder side to create a variety of creative surface textures—one-of-a-kind looks that can change something quite plain into a stunning garment.

Add spots of color, create tucks, couch a cord or ribbon under the stitches, play with several threads for multicolor effects, show the loops or show the ladders, make a tuck, or create the look of piping. Also try folding the garment along a completed seam, then flatlocking over it to disguise the seamline.

This basic stitch, traditionally used for flat seaming on knits, is serged over two raw edges or over a folded

edge, then opened and flattened. Worked over folded fabric, flatlocking allows the freedom to place straight and gently curving lines of flatlocking anywhere on a garment. To make this possible, it is necessary to position the fabric fold under the foot so that the stitches hang halfway off the fold, leaving room for the fabric to open and flatten under the stitches.

Some sergers are capable of making a two-thread flatlock stitch, often preferred because it uses less thread. However, three-thread flatlocking is possible when your serger does not have two-thread flatlocking capability and some of the decorative flatlocking options are enhanced with the use of three threads. For a three-thread flatlock stitch on three- or four-thread sergers, use one needle and loosen the needle thread tension almost all the way. Then tighten the lower looper tension until it draws the needle thread to the raw or folded edge. You can do most decorative flatlocking variations with a two-thread stitch, but there are some that require three threads for the best stitch definition.

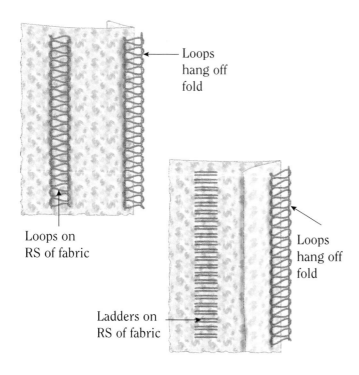

Loops hang off fold

Loops on RS of fabric

Loops hang off fold

Ladders on RS of fabric

Diagram 9

Decorative hemming. Use decorative thread in the needle for a straight or moderately flared hem. Fold and flatlock over the fold created by turning back the hem allowance. Not all sergers have a blind hem foot, but if yours does, you will find it useful for this technique. See **Diagram 10.**

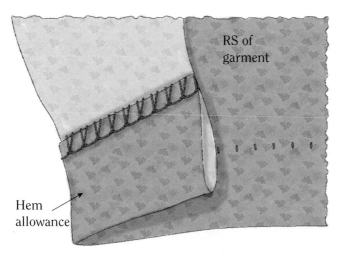

RS of garment

Hem allowance

Diagram 10

Flatlocked diamonds. With the serger set for a wide flatlock stitch and the fabric folded right sides together, serge on and off the fabric's folded edge, in a half-diamond shape. When opened, the ladder stitch creates diamondlike motifs. Allow thread chains to float on the underside, or if they are long enough between the diamonds, clip them and tie them in knots close to the diamond ends. Use flatlocked diamonds when you want to create your own fabric texture or spots of color on a blouse yoke, collar, cuffs, or for added interest on a blouse placket.

Flatlocked filler. With this technique, the filler shows as a decorative element that floats under the open loops. See **Diagram 11.** Narrow cording, ribbon, or yarn all work well with this technique. Use filler that is slightly narrower than the stitch width you are using, which is usually ¼ inch (6 mm) or less. Fold the fabric wrong sides together. Arrange the filler on top of the fold so that the stitch loops go over the filler and hang off the fold. The knives should not cut the fabric or the filler. Use a long stitch and hold the filler taut while serging. When opened flat, the filler floats under the loops.

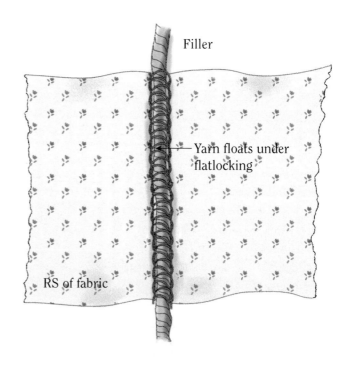

Filler

Yarn floats under flatlocking

RS of fabric

Diagram 11

Flatlocked piping. This is a great way to create the look of piping without cutting a pattern into parts and sewing the pieces back together with commercial piping inserted in the seam. See **Diagram 12**. It's best to stitch the piping on an oversize piece of fabric, then cut out the pattern piece from the embellished fabric. Adjust the serger settings to a very narrow width and short stitch length, testing the stitch to make sure that you can just catch the fabric fold with the needle and still open the stitch over the fabric tuck that forms under the loops. Tighten the needle tension slightly for the characteristic raised appearance of piping. Fold with the fabric wrong sides together.

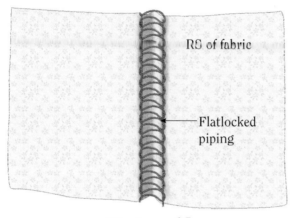

RS of fabric

Flatlocked piping

Diagram 12

Floating flatlocking. Use transparent thread in the needle and the lower looper and decorative thread in the upper looper. This will make the upper looper stitch "float" on the surface. (The ladders always float on the surface.) See **Diagram 13**.

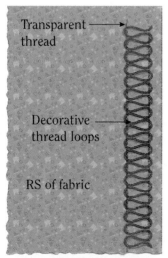

Transparent thread

Decorative thread loops

RS of fabric

Diagram 13

Framed flatlocking. If you are using a two-thread flatlock stitch, use a contrasting thread in the needle. For a three-thread flatlock, use a contrasting thread in the needle and the lower looper. When the flatlock stitch is opened, the upper looper threads will be framed with a line of contrasting stitching. See **Diagram 14**.

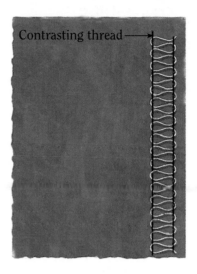

Contrasting thread

Diagram 14

Two-color flatlocked loops. With different-color decorative threads in the upper and lower loopers, adjust for a normal three-thread flatlock stitch. Next, tighten the upper looper and loosen the lower looper until the loops meet in the center when the stitch is pulled flat. See **Diagram 15**.

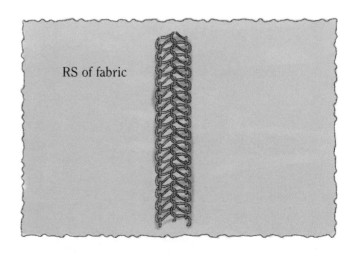

RS of fabric

Diagram 15

Ribbed flatlocking. Choose this technique when you want a ribbed look on the fabric surface. See **Diagram 16.** It is perfect for short sleeves on a linen blouse or jacket, or to add texture to a collar, cuffs, or skirt hem. Draw straight lines on an oversize piece of the fabric, stitch the ribs, then cut out the pattern piece, positioning the ribs where you want them. You will need to allow at least ⅜ inch (9 mm) of extra fabric width for every rib you intend to make. Adjust your serger for a medium to wide, medium-length, three-thread flatlock stitch with a decorative thread in the upper looper. Next, tighten the needle tension a bit to create a slightly raised stitch. Fold the fabric along each marked line and flatlock so the stitches hang slightly to as much as halfway over the folded edge. When you open and flatten the stitch, the fabric tuck inside creates the rib. Open the stitch and press.

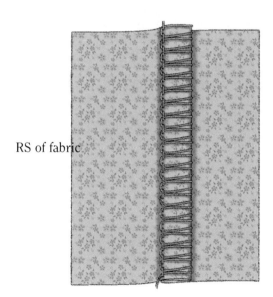

RS of fabric

Fabric tuck inside the stitches

Diagram 16

Scalloped flatlocking. Use a different color thread in each looper and the needle of a three-thread flatlock stitch. Adjust for a short stitch—try 1 to 2 mm. While stitching, periodically use your finger to press tightly against the upper looper thread above the tension dial. Count stitches with and without the finger tension for a uniform scalloped look, or make scallops of random lengths for more free-form results. If you are careful

counting, you will be able to line up side-by-side rows to create your own interesting trims. See **Diagram 17.**

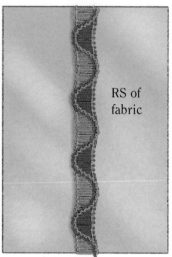

RS of fabric

Diagram 17

Woven ladders. This is a nice treatment for a hem, imitation "tucks" at the shoulder, or to add color to the interior of a garment. See **Diagram 18.** To create flatlock ladders on the right side of your fabric, use buttonhole twist or other strong thread in the needle. Fold the fabric with right sides together and stitch over the fold. Open the stitch, then thread a tapestry needle with ⅛-inch (3-mm)-wide ribbon and weave it through the ladders. You can also try two strands of ribbon floss, alternating the weaving pattern with the second strand. Braiding ribbon through the ladders adds even more dimension.

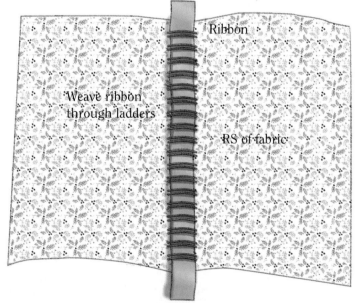

Ribbon

Weave ribbon through ladders

RS of fabric

Diagram 18

Serger Stitch Solutions

The stitches available on your serger depend on the total number of threads (two, three, four, or five) you can use to form a stitch. Each stitch requires tension, stitch length, and stitch width adjustments, depending on the fabric and the desired results. Refer to your owner's manual for setup directions for each of the stitches available on your serger. In some cases, you may need a special needle plate and foot for the rolled edge stitch.

First, thread the serger with serger thread and adjust for the desired stitch, following your manual. After mastering all stitches with serger thread, try again with a lightweight decorative thread, such as top-stitching thread, in the upper looper and then in both loopers. You'll be a fearless tension-adjusting pro before you know it!

Decorative threads offer many exciting possibilities. The secret for really successful stitching with these products is taking the time to adjust the tension.

SUCCESSFUL STRATEGIES FOR TENSION ADJUSTMENTS

Compare tensions. The tighter the needle tension, the tighter the other tensions must be.

Tighten up. Adjust the thread that appears to be the tightest first.

Use woolly nylon. If you cannot get the lower looper tension tight enough for a three-thread flatlock or a rolled edge stitch, use woolly nylon or monofilament thread in the lower looper. This will increase tension on the stitch.

Test the seam. If the seam pulls apart easily, tighten the needle tension; if the seam puckers, loosen the needle tension.

Adjust slowly. Turn only one tension dial at a time. Stitch for a few inches, examine the results, and adjust

a little more if necessary. Continue in this fashion until the stitch is correctly adjusted.

Contrast the colors. You can identify tension problems by using a different color thread in each needle and looper. This is a great help when learning to adjust tension or when struggling to adjust tensions for a new combination of threads because the colored thread immediately "shows" you which looper or needle tension needs to be adjusted.

Check the curl. If the edge curls under (when it shouldn't), the lower looper is too tight or the upper looper is too loose. Remember that in some cases, such as a rolled edge stitch, the stitching should curl under. If the edge curls toward the top (when it shouldn't), the upper looper is too tight or the lower looper is too loose.

TENSION ADJUSTMENTS FOR DECORATIVE THREADS

When you use the same thread in the needle(s) and loopers, begin with a balanced tension setting and fine-tune as necessary. When using a variety of threads together—a different thread in each location, for example—remember that the stitch length and width affect the looper tension. You may need to adjust all three for perfect stitch formation.

Also keep in mind that it's best to test your tension every time that you try a new fabric, since so much can affect stitch quality.

Heavier threads in the looper require more space for loop formation, so start with a longer stitch. If you are down to 0 looper tension on thick decorative thread and it is still too tight, remove the thread from one or more of the thread guides. If that does not help enough, remove the thread from the tension regulator, too. For the heaviest threads, you may end up stitching with them caught only in the telescoping thread guide and the guides in the looper area behind the door on the front of your machine.

Although they are thin, threads such as woolly nylon and monofilament stretch while you serge, automatically tightening the tension by two to three settings without your adjusting the tension dial. That is why you need to loosen the looper tension for these threads.

The "Looper Tension Guidelines" table below should help you analyze tension and make adjustments.

Looper Tension Guidelines

Thread, Stitch, and Fabric	Tension Adjustment
Thin, highly twisted thread	Tighter
Thick thread	Looser
Stretchy thread	Looser
Narrow stitch width	Tighter
Wide stitch width (3 to 5 mm)	Looser
Short stitch length	Tighter
Long stitch length (less than 3.5 mm)	Looser
Thin fabric	Tighter
Thick fabric	Looser

REMOVING SERGER STITCHES

There are several methods that you can use to rip out serger stitching. Choose the technique that is most suitable for the amount of time that you have, as well as the type of fabric that you're working on.

The fastest way to eliminate erroneous stitching is to trim away the mistake along the needle line and serge again. Cut off the line of stitching with scissors or simply remove the needle thread from your serger so no stitches form, and serge off the error. Of course, this will not work if you already serged along the garment seamline and a good fit is essential.

If your garment fabric is smooth, try a whiskers trimmer. The blades will skim over the looper stitches without ruining your fabric. Test first. If this does not work with the fabric right side up, turn it over and try again!

On two-thread stitching, just pull the looper thread. On three- or four-thread overlocking, pull the needle thread or threads. To find the needle thread, use your fingers to smooth out the serger chain where the stitching ended (not where it started).

The needle thread is always the shortest in the chain. Use a pin to lift it out of the chain of stitches and pull gently, pushing the remainder of the chain toward the fabric edge. Pull firmly but gently.

When using both needles on a four-thread serger, clip the right and left needle threads every 3 to 5 inches (8 to 13 cm) on the top side and pull them out. You will be able to remove the looper threads in long pieces.

On chainstitching, pull the looper thread. If this is not effortless you are pulling the wrong end.

The messiest way to remove serger stitching consisting of two-, three-, or four-thread stitches is to rip through the looper thread with a seam ripper. You'll have to pick out lots of little threads.

SUCCESSFUL STRATEGIES FOR OPERATING YOUR SERGER

Plug in. Before you get settled, make sure that the machine is plugged in and all of the connections are secure.

Get a foothold. Check to see that the machine's presser foot is securely and properly positioned.

Follow directions. Be certain the needle is correctly inserted.

Be sharp. Needles and knives work best when they are sharp and correctly positioned. It is best to replace needles after every four to six projects so that you are not sewing with a dull needle. Also, inspect needles frequently for bends and burrs.

Follow the path. Trace the route of the thread through the loopers and needle(s). This will ensure that all of the threads are caught in the appropriate thread guides.

Set it up. Make sure the tension and pressure, plus the stitch length and width, are appropriate for the chosen stitch, thread, and fabric.

Lube it. Make sure the machine is properly oiled. (If your serger is not self-oiling, oil after every eight hours of use.) Oil often but lightly. Too much oil attracts lint and the machine may bind up and stop stitching.

Spring clean. Check the tension guides, knives, and the looper area inside the doors to ensure the machine is lint-free. Every six months (or sooner), remove the throat plate and vacuum out lint in and around the feed dogs.

Inspect evidence. The threads might be puddled off the spool, caught on a spool, or looped under the spool holder at either end. Also, watch for tangles in the telescoping thread guides.

Sewing and Serging from A to Z

This section is dedicated to every sewer who has tried on a ready-to-wear garment and wondered, "How did they do that?" Chances are, you'll find the elusive instructions in the following pages because many of the most popular techniques that you've admired, and perhaps tried to duplicate, are here.

In addition, this section includes machine instructions for techniques that are traditionally done by hand. Battenberg lace. Drawn thread work. Entredeux. Heirloom sewing. Smocking. You can do all of these techniques—and more—on your sewing machine and serger, in less time and with less effort than stitching by hand.

You don't need to read these entries page by page. Each technique is self-contained, with all your machine settings and instructions in one place so you can get to your machines and get sewing.

Appliqué

A great many forms of embellishment are described by the general term appliqué. Several of the best methods, including European, invisible, Madeira, shadow, and soft-edge, are presented in this entry. Appliqué is a great way to add character and dimension to a garment, and the methods are so versatile that a bit of creativity will mold the work into a unique item. The end results depend on the application method and machine stitches that you choose. Shadow appliqué, for example, is best on a delicate collar, whereas the invisible or European techniques are suitable for a jacket, as shown at right.

EUROPEAN APPLIQUÉ

Unlike traditional satin stitch appliqué, this sewing machine method requires no fusing. European appliqué by machine is faster, and the layered area is much softer and a bit more drapable—perfect for intricate layered designs.

Sometimes known as reversible appliqué, this technique is also referred to as upside-down appliqué. Either one of these nicknames is appropriate because you stitch the pieces in place from the wrong side before stitching them permanently from the right side.

This appliqué method is equally attractive whether you use a traditional straight stitch or attach the appliqué shapes with free-motion stitching.

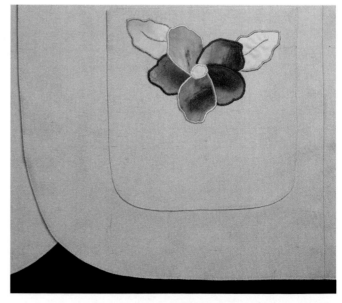

A layer of iron-on, tear-away stabilizer is the secret to the precise design placement and smooth satin stitching characteristic of European appliqué.

Get Ready

	First Pass	Second Pass
Needle	Embroidery, Metalfil, or topstitching	Embroidery, Metalfil, or topstitching
Needle thread	All-purpose	Embroidery cotton, metallic, or rayon
Bobbin thread	All-purpose	Bobbin Thread or machine embroidery cotton
Notions	Pencil or dark pen; iron-on, tear-away stabilizer; appliqué scissors	

Get Set

	First Pass	Second Pass
Presser foot	Appliqué or open-toe embroidery	Appliqué or open-toe embroidery
Stitch	Straight	Satin or zigzag
Stitch length	12 spi (2 mm)	Almost 0
Stitch width	—	Narrow
Needle tension	Lower one or two numbers*	Lower one or two numbers*

You need to lower the needle tension enough to draw the top thread to the underside of the work so the bobbin thread never surfaces.

Sew

1. Make a design sheet by tracing the design onto the nonfusible side of a piece of iron-on, tear-away stabilizer that is larger than the completed appliqué. If the appliqué is asymmetrical, trace the mirror image instead. To do this easily, trace your design onto another piece of paper with a dark pen, then flip the new tracing over and trace this mirror image onto the stabilizer. It will be easier to trace the pattern if you hold it up to a light source, so tape both the traced image and the stabilizer to a window and trace the pattern there.

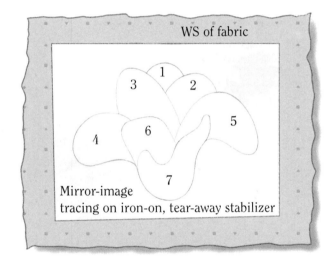

Diagram 1

2. If the appliqué consists of more than one shape, number the pieces in the order that you will appliqué them to the fabric. Do this on your design sheet, then transfer the numbers to the stabilizer to avoid confusion. Unlike traditional appliqué, you must reverse the order, beginning with the piece or pieces that are in the background of the design and progressing in order to the piece on top. Position and apply the stabilizer to the wrong side of the garment fabric. See **Diagram 1**.

3. For each shape, cut a roughly square or rectangular piece of the appliqué fabric at least ½-inch (1.25 cm) larger all around than the finished shape. Pin the fabric shape in place, right side up, on the right side of the garment fabric, over the design area. You may need to hold the fabric up to the light so that you can position it correctly. With the stabilizer face up, straight stitch along the design lines for the shape. If you prefer to attach the appliqué shapes with free-motion stitching, use a darning foot, lower the feed dogs, dial down to a 0 stitch length, and stitch around each appliqué. When lowered, the spring-loaded presser foot exerts no pressure on the work so that you can move it as you stitch, eliminating the need to pivot the work.

4. With the garment right side up, trim the appliqué fabric close to the stitching. Use appliqué scissors to lift the edge and cut closely. Working in numerical order, cut and attach a fabric piece for each remaining shape, as explained in Steps 3 and 4.

5. Change your thread and machine settings as indicated for the Second Pass. After stitching and trimming all of the shapes on the stabilizer side, satin stitch over the edge of each one. Stitch them in the order that you applied them so that you can stitch over areas where your stitches started on the layers underneath for a neat finish. To end, change to a 0 stitch width and take several stitches in place. You can pull each set of threads to the underside and tie them in an overhand knot for added security.

6. Tear away the stabilizer after completing all of the satin stitching.

Sharp Notion

An openwork effect is created with sheer reverse appliqué. Use lace fabric for the appliqué. After satin stitching it to the garment, carefully trim away the garment along the inside edge of the stitches so only the lace remains.

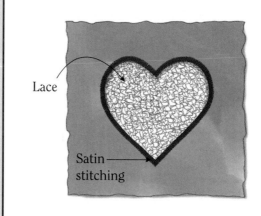

Lace

Satin stitching

INVISIBLE APPLIQUÉ

Appliqué shapes lined with stabilizer or tulle "float" on the surface. They are machine blindstitched in place invisibly with transparent thread. You may need to vary the technique a bit for some fabrics. For example, for nonwovens such as synthetic suede, simply stitch close to the raw edge (no lining is required, unless you want to add texture and dimension to the edge with a zigzag or other decorative stitch).

Get Ready

Needle	Appropriate for fabric and thread
Needle thread	Transparent
Bobbin thread	Machine embroidery
Notions	Pencil; lining (water-soluble stabilizer, for washable fabrics only, or tulle for dry-clean-only fabrics); non-stick pressing sheet; glue stick (optional)
Needle	Universal or Microtex 80/12

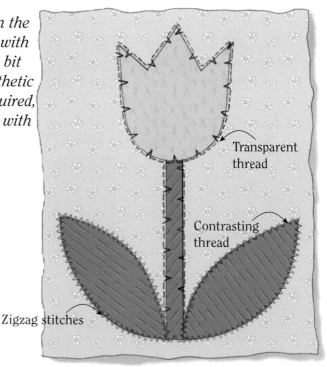

Transparent thread

Contrasting thread

Zigzag stitches

Get Set

	First Pass	Second Pass
Presser foot	All-purpose or appliqué	Blind hem
Stitch	Straight	Blindstitch
Stitch length	5 spi (4.5 mm)	20 spi (1 mm)
Stitch width	—	Narrow
Needle tension	Balanced	Loosen so that the bobbin thread pulls the needle thread to the underside of the fabric

Sew

1. Draw the appliqué shape on the wrong side of the appliqué fabric. Cut out with a ½-inch (1.25-cm)-wide allowance. Sew it, right side down, to the stabilizer or tulle "lining" on the drawn line. Trim ⅛ to ¼ inch (3 to 6 mm) outside the stitching. See Diagram 2.

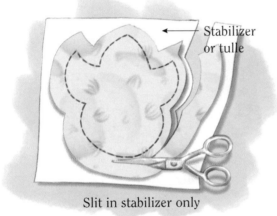

Stabilizer or tulle

Slit in stabilizer only

Diagram 2

2. Turn right side out through a small slit made in the "lining." Place the appliqué right side up on the non-stick pressing sheet on the ironing board. With the iron set for wool, press the edges with the tip of the iron. (Use a press cloth on top of delicate fabrics.)

3. Change your machine as indicated for the second pass. Baste the appliqué on the garment, or use a glue stick to hold it in place. Arrange the appliqué under the presser foot so that the straight stitches of the blindstitching are on the garment fabric, running along the appliqué's finished edge, and the zigzag stitches catch the turned edges of the shape. (If using the zigzag stitch, the right swing of the needle should catch the base fabric, and the left swing should catch the appliqué's edge.)

4. Remove the water-soluble stabilizer. Tulle can remain inside the appliqué.

Sharp Notion

Appliqué can take on a folk art look when you change the stitching. Use a contrasting thread in the needle and substitute a machine blanket stitch, stretch overlock, or feather stitch. You can also edgestitch appliqués in place. Use the edgestitching or blind hem foot to keep sewing an even distance from the edge.

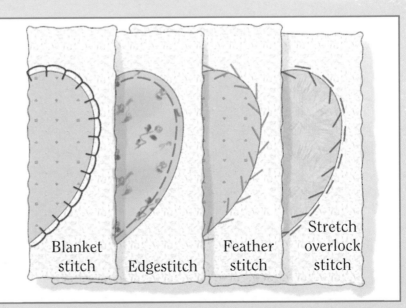

Blanket stitch   Edgestitch   Feather stitch   Stretch overlock stitch

Appliqué

MADEIRA APPLIQUÉ

As the name suggests, this type of sewing machine appliqué originated on the Portuguese island of Madeira. Tiny holes are punched by the needle as it stitches through the sheer fabric, resulting in a delicate, lacy look. Use a wing needle and a decorative stitch, such as the pinstitch, to attach a sheer appliqué.

Get Ready

Fabric	Batiste, linen, organza, or organdy
Needle	100/18 wing or 120/20 conventional
Needle and bobbin thread	Fine cotton or rayon machine embroidery
Notions	Spray starch, water-soluble stabilizer or tulle for the appliqué lining, glue stick (optional)

Get Set

Presser foot	Open-toe embroidery
Stitch	Entredeux, daisy, or pinstitch*

*Try other decorative stitches where the needle goes in and out of the same hole more than once, thus making a large hole. If necessary, stabilize the backing fabric and use an embroidery hoop.

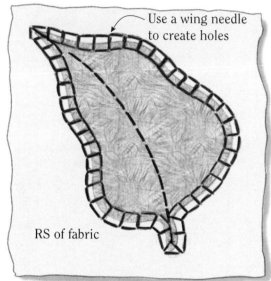

Use a wing needle to create holes

RS of fabric

Diagram 3

Sew

1. Starch the appliqué and background fabrics. Prepare the appliqué shape as directed in Steps 1 and 2 of "Invisible Appliqué" on page 58. If the appliqué has interior design lines that require stitching for definition, do this stitching before positioning the appliqué on the garment fabric.

2. Position the appliqué on the garment and baste it in place, or use a glue stick to hold it in place. Position the appliqué under the presser foot so that you will be stitching along the edge of and into the appliqué. (For decorative stitches that swing to the right only, engage the mirror-image feature, if available, for easiest positioning with the bulk of the work to the left of the needle.) Stitch the appliqué in place. See **Diagram 3**.

3. Rinse the completed work to remove the water-soluble stabilizer.

Make It Easy

Messy knots at the start of your stitching are easily prevented. Carefully make only your first stitch. While holding the top thread, turn the handwheel to bring the bobbin thread to the surface. Holding both threads on top, take a few short stitches. Clip the threads close to the surface or draw them to the underside and tie them off securely.

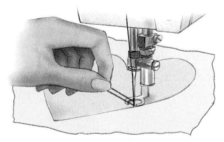

SHADOW APPLIQUÉ

Delicate shadow appliqué made at your sewing machine is the perfect accent on a sheer collar or the neckline edge of a sheer blouse. It is particularly lovely in heirloom sewing projects. True to its name, a colored fabric that is edged in decorative stitching shadows through a layer of sheer fabric on top.

Get Ready

Fabric	Solid-color batiste or broadcloth for the appliqués; handkerchief linen, organdy, or Swiss cotton batiste for the upper layer
Needle	70/10 embroidery
Needle thread	Cotton or rayon embroidery
Bobbin thread	Cotton machine embroidery, size 60
Notions	Pencil, spray starch, water-soluble stabilizer, machine embroidery hoop, appliqué scissors (optional)

Get Set

Presser foot	Open-toe embroidery
Stitch	Satin stitch, zigzag, or other more decorative stitch, such as blanket stitch, pinstitch, or blindstitch
Stitch length	25 spi (0.5 mm) for satin stitch or as desired for other stitches
Stitch width	Narrow for satin stitch or as desired for other stitches

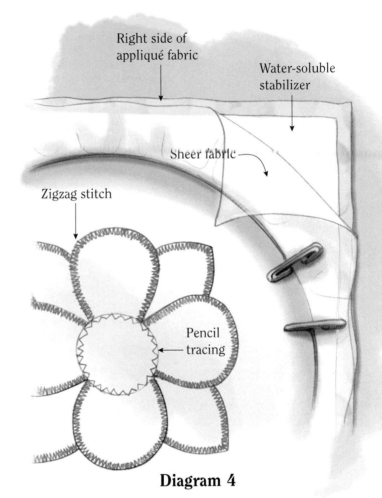

Right side of appliqué fabric

Water-soluble stabilizer

Sheer fabric

Zigzag stitch

Pencil tracing

Diagram 4

Sew

1. Use a pencil to lightly trace the design on the starched right side of a sheer fabric for the garment.

2. Cut a piece of water-soluble stabilizer several inches larger than your hoop and a similarly sized piece of colored fabric for the appliqué. Place the stabilizer under the appliqué design on the wrong side of the garment fabric, then add the colored fabric with its right side against the stabilizer. Put the layers into the embroidery hoop and under the needle and presser foot.

3. On the right side of the sheer fabric, straight stitch along the drawn line. (If you plan to satin stitch the design, substitute a medium length, narrow zigzag stitch for the straight stitching.) See **Diagram 4**.

4. For a satin stitched appliqué, trim the colored fabric layer close to the zigzagging on the underside. Draw the bobbin thread to the surface. Stitch in place a few times, and clip the threads. Satin stitch from the right side, being careful to catch the raw edges in or under the satin stitching. For other stitches,

adjust the machine as required, draw up the bobbin thread, stitch in place, and continue around the design. Position the work so the right needle swing is along the pencil line and the left swing is inside the appliqué design area. Trim the appliqué fabric close to the decorative stitching on the wrong side of the work. See **Diagram 5.** Remove the stabilizer.

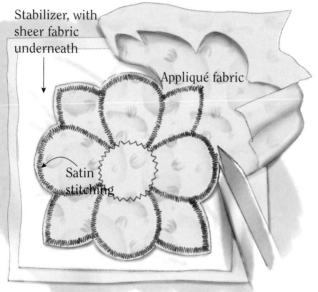

Stabilizer, with sheer fabric underneath

Appliqué fabric

Satin stitching

Diagram 5

Sharp Notion

If you want a sheer appliqué as the lower layer on a sheer or opaque garment fabric, reverse the shadow appliqué layers. After zigzagging around the appliqué shape, trim the garment fabric to reveal the sheer underlayer. The final step for this technique is to satin stitch over the zigzagging, carefully catching and covering the raw edges in the stitching. The sheer fabric appears to float behind the garment. The difference is very subtle, but this may be just the effect you want.

SOFT-EDGE APPLIQUÉ

If you prefer a softer, less defined look along the exposed raw edges of an appliqué, you will like this sewing machine method. It employs free-motion embroidery, which is like scribble stitching or painting with your needle. Such random stitching may seem awkward at first, because sewers are used to stitching with the feed dogs and presser foot controlling the fabric's movement. To develop a feel for this stitching method, practice on scraps first. You'll find it easier if you're relaxed. It also helps if you don't judge your work too critically. Free-motion embroidery looks better at a distance, so up-close inspection may leave you disappointed.

Diagram 6

Get Ready

Needle thread	Embroidery cotton, metallic, or rayon
Bobbin thread	Bobbin Thread, machine embroidery, or transparent
Needle	Embroidery, Metalfil, or Microtex
Notions	Pencil; lightweight, paper-backed fusible web; press cloth

Get Set

Presser foot	Darning, or replace the regular foot and regular needle with a spring needle
Stitch	Straight
Needle tension	Loosen by at least one number so that the bobbin thread pulls the needle thread to the underside
Feed dogs	Disengaged or covered

Sew

1. Draw the mirror image of the appliqué shape on the paper side of the fusible web. Cut it out with a ¼-inch (6-mm)-wide allowance all around.

2. Fuse the shape to the wrong side of the appropriate fabric, and cut it out along the drawn lines. If the appliqué consists of several combined shapes made from more than one fabric, leave a small allowance beyond any appliqué shape edges that will be covered by another shape.

3. Remove the paper backing from the fusible web. Position the appliqués on the garment, one shape at a time, working from the background to the foreground. You may fuse each one or wait until all layers are positioned and then fuse the entire design. When fusing, place the press cloth on top of the appliqué shapes.

4. To sew the edges of the appliqué to the garment fabric, position the appliqué under the needle where you want to begin, and lower the bar for the presser foot. Draw the bobbin thread to the surface and stitch in place several times to lock the stitches.

5. With the machine running quickly, move the fabric slowly to create a series of short stitches inside the raw edge of the appliqué. These stitches are random, and need not proceed in a straight line. See **Diagram 6** on the opposite page.

Sharp Notion

If you prefer an even softer look for your appliqué, do not back it with fusible web. Instead, temporarily position the appliqué with basting stitches or use a glue stick to hold it in place. Now place the work in an embroidery hoop with a stabilizer that is appropriate for the garment fabric underneath. Position and stitch as directed in Steps 4 and 5.

Sharp Notion

Trapunto appliqué is a great way to add areas of dimension to an appliqué shape. For a designer look, cut interesting motifs from printed fabrics to use for appliqués. Follow Steps 1 and 2 of "Invisible Appliqué" on page 58. After turning the appliqué right side out but before positioning it on the fabric, tuck a bit of polyester fiberfill through the slit. Distribute the filling evenly, or only in the areas where you want dimension. Blindstitch the appliqué to the base fabric, adding straight stitching through or around the dimensional areas, to hold the fiberfill in place.

Bartacks

You probably already use bartacking to reinforce areas of strain or to attach buttons. But this feature has some interesting decorative applications that you may want to try. On the neckline and cuffs of the jacket in this illustration, for example, the bartacked rickrack trim is the perfect counterpoint to the houndstooth pattern of the fabric. Also, you can use bartacks to create French knot flower centers or even to embroider daisies. See page 65 for additional ideas for expanding the creative options for bartacking.

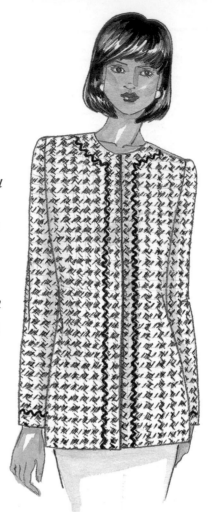

BARTACKED DAISY

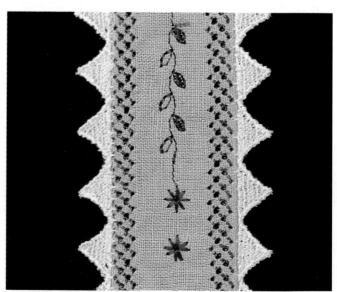

If your sewing machine doesn't have a daisy stitch, you can use bartacking and free-motion stitching to make the flower. This is much easier to do if you can shift your needle position.

Get Ready

Needle	Embroidery or Metalfil/Metallica
Thread	Machine embroidery rayon, cotton, or metallic
Notions	Water-soluble marking pen, machine embroidery hoop

Get Set

Presser foot	None
Stitch	Zigzag
Stitch length	0
Stitch width	Medium to wide, or as desired
Feed dogs	Disengaged or covered
Needle position	Far left

Design your own heirloom trim by combining daisies with other embroidery stitches.

Secrets for Successful Sewing

Sew

1. Mark the center of each flower location on the fabric with the water-soluble marking pen. The bartacks are arranged with the inner points converging at this center.

2. Load the fabric into a hoop and position it under the needle at the inner point of your first bartack. Lower the presser bar, even though you have removed the presser foot, and draw the bobbin thread to the surface.

3. Take several bartack stitches for the first petal and end in the flower center. Note the number of stitches that you made. Rotate the hoop one quarter-turn counterclockwise and make the second petal, perpendicular to the first, using the same number of stitches. Rotate and stitch two more petals in the same manner to make a cross. See **Diagram 1**.

Diagram 1

4. Rotate and stitch a petal between each pair to complete the eight-petal daisy. For a star, make only six petals.

5. Set your stitch length to 0, and stitch in place in the flower center to lock the stitches.

Make It Easy

Higher end and newer machines include one—if not several—bartacking features. But you can still make bartacks if you have an older or less expensive model. Use a zigzag stitch that's medium-width or wider, plus a button sew-on presser foot. Set your machine stitch length to 0 and disengage or cover the feed dogs. The needle tension should be loosened so that the bobbin thread draws the top thread to the underside. Stitch back and forth six to eight times. Change to a straight stitch and sew in place several times. You need to shift your work so that the needle stitches in place at the right or left end of the bartack, not in the center.

SUCCESSFUL STRATEGIES FOR BARTACKING

Reinforce stress points. Bartacks can be positioned at pocket corners, the bottom of a fly front zipper, or the top (release point) of a skirt slit.

Attach items. Use a bartack to machine stitch a button, hook and eye, or a charm in place.

Secure loops. Sew on a belt loop with bartacks at the top and bottom.

Shorten a zipper. Stitch across the coils to stop the slider.

Add dots. Bartacks make good random or specifically placed dots of color in embroidered designs. Use the technique for "Bartacked French Knot" (see page 66) for more defined bartacks.

Attach appliqués. Stitch three-dimensional appliqués in place.

BARTACKED FRENCH KNOT

Just as embroiderers use French knots, you can scatter bartacks across a yoke or pocket to add visual interest and texture to plain fabric. Sewing machine bartacks are also great substitutes for French knots in the centers of flower appliqués. For good stitch definition, try a large topstitching, jeans, or universal needle with heavy decorative thread, a darning or open-toe embroidery foot, and a center needle position.

Get Ready

Needle	Appropriate for fabric and thread
Thread	All-purpose

Get Set

Presser foot	Darning or open-toe embroidery
Stitch	Zigzag, or bartack if your machine has this option
Stitch length	0
Stitch width	Medium (4 mm)
Needle tension	Loosen by one or two numbers so the bobbin thread draws the needle thread to the underside
Feed dogs	Disengaged or covered
Needle position	Centered

Diagram 2

Sew

1. Begin with the machine stitch length and width set at 0 and draw the bobbin thread to the surface. Take several stitches in place.

2. Switch to the bartacking settings and make ten or more complete bartack stitches to build up and form a ball. Thinner thread requires more stitches to achieve this effect.

3. At 0 stitch length and width, take two or three stitches in the center of the tack. Lift the presser foot and lower the needle in front of the bartack to take one stitch. Return to the center and take two more stitches in place. See **Diagram 2**. Tie off the threads on the back of the fabric.

Sharp Notion

Hand sew or machine stitch (see "Bartacked Rickrack Trim" on the opposite page) a pearl or bead at each inner point of the trim. If the trim will be very close to a garment's finished edge, any pearls close to the edge should be added after the garment's facing is attached. Depending on the garment's style, you could substitute dots of fabric paint for the beads.

BARTACKED RICKRACK TRIM

Tired of rickrack edges that curl when you sew the trim down with straight stitching? Bartacking prevents this. The technique works best on jumbo rickrack, but try it on other widths, if you wish. Trim a hemline, decorate a yoke or pocket, or follow a neckline and front edge opening with this easy way to attach the trim. A decorative needle thread adds more visual interest.

Get Ready

Needle	Appropriate for fabric and thread
Thread	All-purpose embroidery
Notion	Jumbo rickrack

Get Set

Presser foot	Button sew-on
Stitch	Zigzag
Stitch length	0
Stitch width	Medium (4 mm)
Needle tension	Loosen by one or two numbers so that the bobbin thread draws the needle thread to the underside
Feed dogs	Disengaged or covered
Needle position	Left, if possible

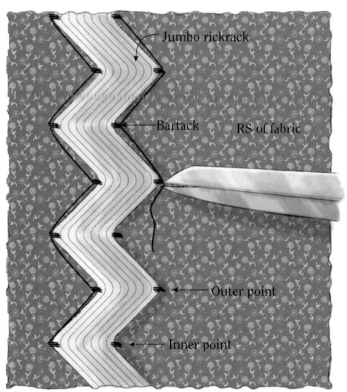

Diagram 3

Sew

1. Position the rickrack on the right side of the garment, and pin it in place.

2. Beginning at one end of the rickrack, bartack the first outer point. Depending on the desired effect, you may take stitches completely inside the trim or across the edge of the trim.

3. If you are making the bartack manually, change to a straight stitch and stitch in place several times. If you could not start with the needle in the left position, you will need to shift your work so the needle stitches in place at the right or the left end of the bartack, not in the center.

4. Without cutting the thread, raise the presser foot, slide the garment to the next inner point of the rickrack, lower the foot, and bartack in the same fashion. Continue in this manner along both edges of the trim. When you are finished, there will be a thread floating on the surface between each bartack.

5. Using sharp scissors, clip the floating threads as close to the surface of the rickrack as you can. See **Diagram 3**. You do not need to cut the threads on the underside of the work, unless you applied the rickrack to a finished edge.

Basting

There's more to basting than dialing a straight stitch and stepping on the foot pedal. You can stretch the capabilities of this versatile stitch by using one of the new wonder threads, as well as by exploring serger-basting. Plus, you can use a blindstitch to baste knits.

Fusible thread is a wonderful product that will help you anchor pockets, hems, and appliqués with the touch of an iron. All you have to do is load the thread into your bobbin or thread it through the lower looper of your serger for slip-free sewing.

This "basting" with fusible thread does double duty on serger-finished pockets and appliqués. For even more interest, add decorative thread to the mix. It adds dimension to an element like a pocket, while the basting thread holds everything in place so that you can easily apply the topstitching.

FAST-FUSE POCKETS AND APPLIQUÉS

Tired of endlessly pinning embellishments, pockets, and other details to your garments? By including fusible basting thread in your serger stitching you will save time and improve the quality of your garments. Using fusible basting thread allows you to skip a step by eliminating hand basting, and it will help you securely position an item on your fabric before topstitching it in place at the sewing machine. You can add dimension to your serger work by using fusible basting thread in the lower looper with decorative thread in the upper looper and needle.

While these instructions are written specifically for pockets and appliqués, you can easily apply the techniques and ideas to other items.

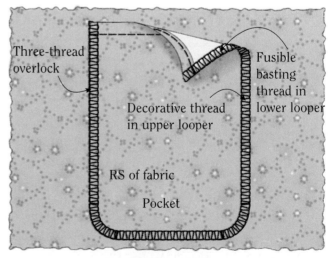

Three-thread overlock

Fusible basting thread in lower looper

Decorative thread in upper looper

RS of fabric

Pocket

Diagram 1

Get Ready

	Serger	Sewing Machine
Needle thread	All-purpose serger	Decorative or all-purpose
Bobbin thread	—	All-purpose
UL thread	Decorative*	—
LL thread	Fusible	—

Get Set

	Serger	Sewing Machine
Presser foot	All-purpose	All-purpose or satin stitch
Stitch	Three- or four-thread overlock	Straight or satin
Stitch width	3 to 5 mm	As desired
Stitch length	Short	As desired

Don't use heat-sensitive metallic thread in the upper looper because it can't be pressed.

Serge and Sew

1. Serge-finish the pocket or appliqué edges from the right side. If the item you plan to attach has seam allowances, cut these off. The fastest way to do this is to serge with the upper knife engaged so that the extra fabric is trimmed away as you stitch.

2. Position the pocket or appliqué on the garment. Fuse-baste by pressing for several seconds. See **Diagram 1.**

3. Topstitch or edgestitch around the pocket or appliqué edges.

4. You can position an appliqué using only your sewing machine. Zigzag around the edges with fusible thread in the bobbin, fuse, then satin stitch in place.

Make It Easy

To baste with a serger, simply loosen the needle tension and use a long stitch. To remove the serging, tug gently on the needle thread (the shortest one in the thread chain tail) to release the looper threads.

SUCCESSFUL STRATEGIES FOR FUSE-BASTING

Baste to place. Transfer trim placement lines. Trace the design onto iron-on, tear-away stabilizer and apply it to the fabric wrong side. With fusible thread in the needle, machine baste on each placement line. Stitch again $\frac{1}{16}$ inch (1.5 mm) inside of each line. Remove the stabilizer. Position the trim on the fabric right side, on top of the stitching, and fuse. Stitch the trim permanently to the garment.

Save face. Use fusible thread in the bobbin when understitching facing edges. Turn the facing to the inside and press to hold the facing in place. This is particularly helpful if you plan to topstitch the facing.

Lap it up. Fuse-baste a lapped seam before topstitching it in position.

Baste in haste. Create serger braid that you can fuse in place before stitching.

Sew zippy. Position a zipper before stitching.

PERFECT POCKET APPLICATION

Like the procedure for "Fast-Fuse Pockets and Appliqués" on page 68, this technique will also save you time because fusible basting thread is used at the sewing machine to attach the fabric pieces. You won't need to hand baste the pocket in position and, if you cut and basted accurately, the pocket will be perfectly shaped.

If you're looking for creative options, you may want to use a decorative, rather than straight, stitch for the topstitching.

Get Ready

Needle thread	All-purpose
Bobbin thread	Fusible

Get Set

Presser foot	All-purpose
Stitch	Straight
Stitch length	6 spi (4.5 mm)
Stitch width	0

Sew

1. With the fabric right side up, machine baste ¼ inch (6 mm) from the raw or pinked edge of the seam allowance.

2. Stitch again, still in the seam allowance but closer to the seamline. If you have a ⅝-inch (1.5 cm) seam allowance, your second row of stitching is about ⅛ inch (3 mm) away from the line of stitching that you made in Step 1. The long stitch length and two rows of basting provide more thread "surface" for a better bond when the fabric is fused.

3. Turn under the seam allowance and fuse-baste it in place, pressing for several seconds. See **Diagram 2.** Press the fabric for a longer length of time if you would like to have a more permanent bond between the two pieces of fabric.

4. Machine topstitch through all of the layers of fabric from the right side of your garment.

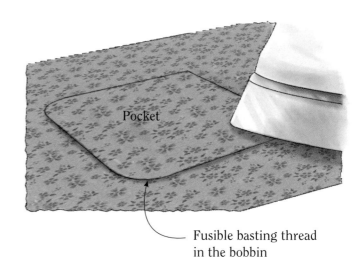

Pocket

Fusible basting thread in the bobbin

Diagram 2

Make It Easy

It's a lot easier to remove machine basting if you loosen the top tension a setting or two and take a few minutes to clip the bobbin stitches every inch or so. To remove the basting, pull on the top thread. It will come out with ease, leaving small sections of bobbin thread to remove on the other side of the seam.

ZIGZAG BASTING BY MACHINE

In a couturier workroom, the people who hand sew the garments are called the "mains," and they have an extensive repertoire of stitches. Among these is zigzag basting. Rather than spending hours perfecting the hand stitch, why not spend a few minutes learning to do it on a sewing machine? The time will be well spent if you sew knits because you'll be able to speed-baste your seams.

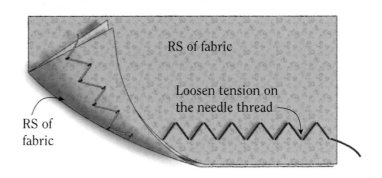

Diagram 3

Get Ready	First Pass	Second Pass
Needle	Appropriate for fabric and thread*	Appropriate for fabric and thread*
Needle thread	All-purpose	All-purpose
Bobbin thread	All-purpose or water-soluble basting	All-purpose
Notion	Dressmaker's chalk	

Get Set	First Pass	Second Pass
Presser foot	All-purpose	All-purpose or zigzag
Stitch	Zigzag	Straight
Stitch length	6 spi (4.5 mm)	10 to 12 spi (2.5 to 2 mm)
Stitch width	Medium (4 mm)	—
Needle tension	Loosen 1 or 2 settings	Balanced

For knits, use ball point or stretch, size 60/8 to 90/14, depending on the fabric's weight.

Sew

1. Don't forget to loosen the upper tension to make it super easy to remove the basting. Zigzag-baste the seams with the fabric wrong sides together. See **Diagram 3.** Even though the machine is set for a wide, long zigzag, guide the seam edge along the desired seam width marking on the throat plate.

2. Try on the garment and adjust the seams if necessary. Chalk-mark the seamlines along the basting on the fabric right side. Remove the basting, trim the seam allowances to a standard width, if necessary, and take the garment back to the sewing machine to do the permanent stitching. Adjust your machine for the second pass and sew.

Battenberg Lace

While it has long been popular for lingerie, pretty blouses, and heirloom sewing, Battenberg lace can also be used to grace the point of a collar or the edge of a pocket, or to add character along a hem.

Battenberg lace is characterized by delicate bars of stitching that form lace patterns inside tape loops. You can make this lace at a sewing machine using a stabilizer, rather than stitching by hand. In addition to saving time, free-motion embroidery on the machine adds more texture and dimension than handmade versions.

Get Ready

Needle	Machine embroidery, size 70/10
Thread	Machine embroidery cotton
Notions	Battenberg tape, paper, pencil, long straight pins, water-soluble stabilizer, machine embroidery hoop, water-soluble marking pen, mounting board,* embroidery scissors, glue stick, purchased design (optional)

Get Set

Presser foot	Darning
Stitch	Straight
Stitch length	0
Stitch width	—
Feed dogs	Disengaged, covered, or 0 stitch length

*You can make a mounting board by covering a piece of foam core board or an empty fabric bolt with a layer of batting topped with a layer of muslin.

Sew

1. Preshrink the tape in hot water and air dry. Trace a purchased design onto a sheet of white paper or sketch your own, and pin the paper to the mounting board.

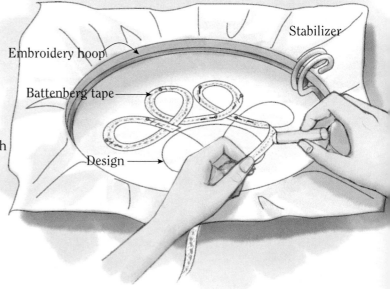

Diagram 1

2. Cut two pieces of water-soluble stabilizer, each 2 to 3 inches (5 to 8 cm) larger than the embroidery hoop's diameter. Place both pieces of stabilizer in the hoop and adjust them so that they are taut. Position the hooped stabilizer on top of the design sheet on the mounting board, and anchor it to the board with pins. Trace the design onto the stabilizer using the water-soluble marking pen. Remove the pins and the design sheet, then replace the hoop (with the stabilizer still in it) on the mounting board.

3. Cut a piece of tape long enough to follow the outer curves of the design, plus 6 to 12 inches (15 to 30 cm), or more for large, complex designs. Draw up 15 to 20 inches (38 to 51 cm) of the gathering thread on one edge of the tape for designs with inside curves. For designs with inside and outside curves, repeat on the other edge. The first several inches of the tape should be flat.

4. Beginning at a loop intersection, arrange the Battenberg tape, right side up, on the hooped stabilizer. Shape one loop at a time, pinning it to the mounting board and working the gathers along the inside and outside curves as needed. See **Diagram 1** on the opposite page. As each loop is completed, remove the pins carefully, apply glue to the underside of the tape, and adhere and pin it to the stabilizer. Where any cut ends cross under the tape, allow a small extension beyond the finished tape edge to be sure it gets caught in the stitching. Trim it later. Remove the pins when the glue has set.

5. Place the work under the sewing machine needle, lower the presser foot, draw the bobbin thread to the top of the work, and machine stitch in place a few times to anchor the threads. Clip the threads close to the work. Stitch at the outer and inner tape edges, beginning and ending with backstitching. Stitch the tape layers together where they cross each other at intersections. Trim any raw edge extensions close to the finished tape edge. Where the loops touch, stitch across both finished edges with three or four stitches by moving the hoop from side to side. See **Diagram 2.**

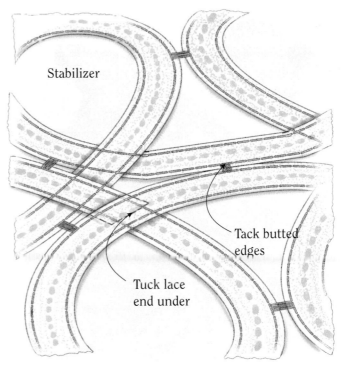

Stabilizer

Tack butted edges

Tuck lace end under

Diagram 2

6. Draw stitching lines for the connecting bars in each loop on your original design sheet. Choose from those shown in **Diagram 3** on page 75. Remove the prepared Battenberg shape from the embroidery hoop and place it over the design sheet. Use a water-soluble marking pen to make dots on the inner edge of the tape to indicate the starting and stopping points for the Richelieu bar stitching lines.

7. Make Richelieu bars by connecting the inner edges of each loop from dot to dot. See **Diagram 3** under "Richelieu Embroidery" on page 75. For further instruction on making the bars, see page 74.

8. After completing the bars, remove the work from the hoop and tear away the stabilizer. Immerse the work in cool water for five minutes to remove any remaining stabilizer. Let dry, then press.

RICHELIEU EMBROIDERY

Bars of stitching that create the "lace" between the loops of Battenberg tape are often called Richelieu embroidery. The effect of the completed bars is very striking and feminine.

*The most common types of bar pattern configurations that can be made on the sewing machine for Richelieu embroidery in Battenberg lace are shown in **Diagram 3** on the opposite page.*

There are commercial patterns available for these configurations, but you can create your own patterns by placing the dots as desired on your Battenberg tape (see Step 6 in "Battenberg Lace" on page 73).

If you're feeling particularly creative, you can also make these bars on a serger, using a flatlock or narrow rolled hem stitch. See "Cutwork Appliqué" on page 124.

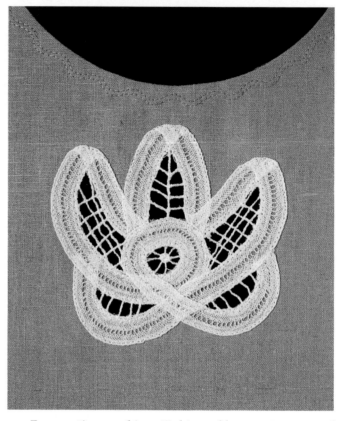

Free-motion machine stitching adds more texture and dimension than there is in the handmade version of the "leaf" pattern used for these Richelieu bars.

Get Ready

Needle	Machine embroidery, size 70/10 or 80/12
Thread	Machine embroidery cotton*
Notions	Embroidery scissors, long straight pins, machine embroidery hoop

Get Set

	First Pass	Second Pass
Presser foot	Darning or none	Darning or none
Stitch	Straight	Zigzag
Stitch length	0	0
Stitch width	0	Narrow (1 mm)
Feed dogs	Disengaged, covered, or 0 stitch length	Disengaged, covered, or 0 stitch length

For heavier stitching, use pearl cotton, size 8 or finer, in the bobbin.

Sew

1. Make your design by sewing together the Battenberg tape loops as described in "Battenberg Lace" on pages 72–73. Select the pattern for your Richelieu bars. The most common are shown in **Diagram 3.**

Fill-In Patterns

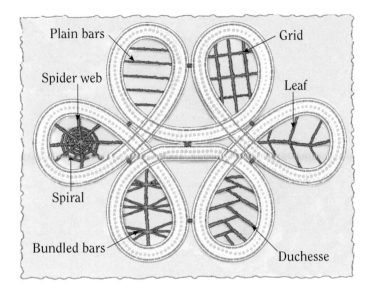

Plain bars
Spider web
Spiral
Bundled bars
Grid
Leaf
Duchesse

Diagram 3

2. Draw stitching lines for the connecting bars in each loop on your original design sheet.

3. Remove the prepared Battenberg shape from the embroidery hoop and place it over the design sheet. Use a water-soluble marking pen to make dots on the inner edge of the tape to indicate the starting and stopping points for the Richelieu bar stitching lines.

4. With the Battenberg lace still attached to the stabilizer and remounted in the embroidery hoop, make a slit in the stabilizer and carefully tear it away inside one loop of the lace motif. Place the work under the sewing machine needle at one of the dots marked on the tape's inner edge. Draw the bobbin thread up to the top of the work. Anchor the thread

with a few stitches in place, and clip the threads close to the surface of the work.

5. Moving the hoop quickly and stitching from dot to dot as indicated in **Diagram 4**, stitch to the opposite side of the tape loop for the first bar. A chain of stitches will form between the tape edges. Catch the tape edge, take one small stitch into the tape, and stitch quickly back to where you started. Stitch again to the opposite tape edge.

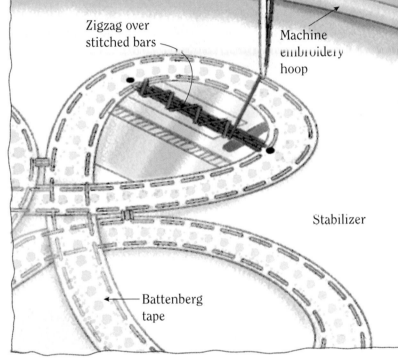

Zigzag over stitched bars
Machine embroidery hoop
Stabilizer
Battenberg tape

Diagram 4

6. To complete the bar, change to a narrow zigzag stitch or move the hoop from side to side and toward you quickly as you zigzag over the bar of stitches. See **Diagram 4**. Do not let the stitches build up in thick clumps.

7. Change back to a 0 stitch width and stitch along the inner edge of the tape to the next bar location. Repeat Steps 3 through 6 for the next bar and each remaining bar in the loop. Stitch the remaining loops in the same way or fill with one of the other Richelieu patterns.

Beading

Yes, it's possible to attach beads, sequins, charms, and large decorative stones by machine. Just use free-motion sewing or a special presser foot and zigzag stitching. At your serger you can try edge applications, as shown on the collar in this illustration. The strings are couched in the interior.

Beading adds life to any garment. For example, machine stitch single beads to a simple black jersey dress. Start with a dense application on the bodice and upper sleeve, then scatter the beads as you move down the skirt. Or apply vertical rows of prestrung sequins down a silk tank tunic. Outstanding!

COUCHED STRINGS OF BEADS OR SEQUINS

You can imitate some of the most expensive garments available using this sewing machine technique to attach cross-locked or molded plastic beads or strands of sequins. This is faster than attaching individual beads to the surface of your fabric, and the effect can be just as striking when the goal is to create a "line" of beads or sequins on the garment. Special presser feet guide the beads so you can concentrate on maneuvering the fabric.

Get Ready

Needle	Appropriate for fabric and thread
Thread	Metallic embroidery,* transparent, or all-purpose polyester
Notions	2-mm-diameter prestrung plastic or cross-locked beads or sequins

Get Set

Presser foot	Pearls 'N Piping, piping, or Sequins 'N Ribbon†
Stitch	Zigzag or blind
Stitch length	16 spi (1.5 mm)
Stitch width	Medium (2.75 mm)

*Match the metallic thread to the sequin color that sparkles, if you can't find an exact match.
†You can use some piping feet, depending on the size of the beads and the size of the tunnel on the bottom of the foot.

Sew

1. Prestrung beads on cotton thread must be transferred to a stronger thread before you attach them to your garment. See "Make It Easy" on page 80.

2. Position the beads or sequins through the tunnel and under the groove in the appropriate foot at the start of the marked design line on the garment.

3. Turn the flywheel by hand for a few stitches to make sure the needle will not hit the beads. Adjust the stitch width and length so the stitches go between each bead or across a flat sequin. If the beading design line has tight curves, try using the blindstitch.

4. Stitch the beads in place. To sew strings to a turned or finished edge, position the string next to the edge and zigzag in place with the left swing of the needle catching the fabric edge and the right swing catching the beads. See **Diagram 1**.

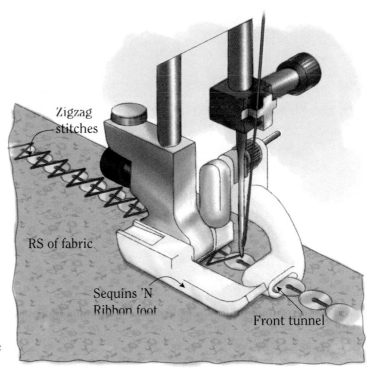

Diagram 1

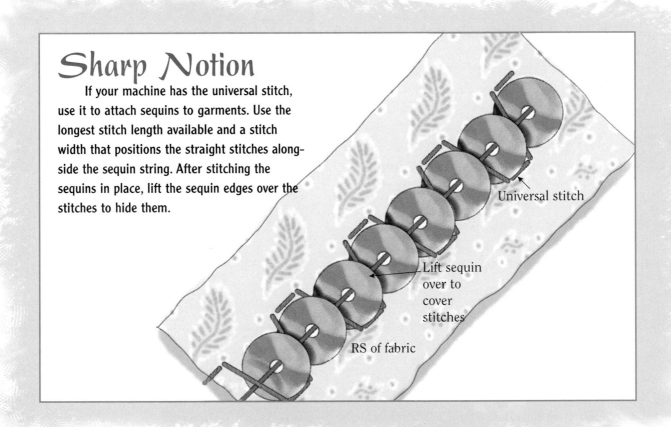

Sharp Notion

If your machine has the universal stitch, use it to attach sequins to garments. Use the longest stitch length available and a stitch width that positions the straight stitches alongside the sequin string. After stitching the sequins in place, lift the sequin edges over the stitches to hide them.

FLATLOCK BEADING

Even without a special beading foot you can serge strings of beads. You have your choice of several stitches. Use flatlocking to stitch beads to the fabric interior. The Sharp Notion on the opposite page suggests the balanced three-thread stitch for beading along a finished edge and a rolled hem stitch to apply fine beads along a raw edge while hemming.

Get Ready

Needle	Appropriate for fabric and thread
Thread	All-purpose serger or transparent
Notions	2-mm-diameter prestrung plastic or cross-locked beads

Get Set

Presser foot	Standard or beading
Stitch	Flatlock
Stitch length	Longer than ⅛ inch (2 mm)*
Stitch width	Wider than ⅛ inch (2 mm)*
Tension	Loose
Upper knife	Disengaged

*The stitch length and width are determined by the size of the bead. If you use beads that are larger or smaller than 2 mm, the rule of thumb is to make your stitch longer than the bead's diameter and wider than the bead's width.

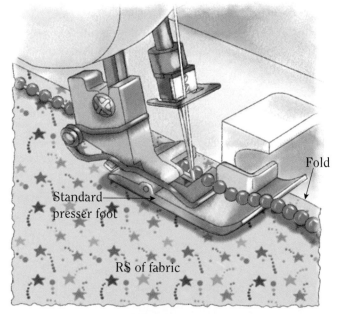

Use flatlocking to stitch beads to a fabric surface in straight lines or free-form shapes.

Sew

1. Transfer prestrung beads on cotton thread to a stronger thread before you attach them to your fabric.

2. Mark straight or gently curving design lines on the garment right side. Fold along a design line with the wrong sides together, and place the fold under the presser foot.

3. Place the end of the beads under the presser foot with a few beads extending beyond the back of the foot. Bring the string of beads up over the top of the foot between the needle and the edge of the fold. See **Diagram 2.** While holding the beading and the thread tails, lower the needle and take a few stitches by hand-turning the flywheel. If there isn't enough

Standard presser foot

Fold

RS of fabric

Diagram 2

room for the beads underneath the back of the presser foot, you can serge without a presser foot. Just hold the string of beads and the fabric slightly taut, and guide the string of beads between the needle and the fabric edge.

4. Serge slowly. Position your fabric so that the flat-lock stitching is extending beyond the folded edge and the string of beads. You'll find it easier to do this stitching if you hand-guide the beads over the foot, ensuring that they're always to the right of the needle. Continue stitching in this manner until you reach the end of the design line to which you are attaching the string of beads. End your stitching, cut the threads, and tie them off on the wrong side of the fabric or at the edge (if the design line ends at a seam allowance).

5. Flatten the fabric so that the beads pop up between the stitches.

Sharp Notion

You can make a beautiful rolled edge and attach a string of beads with one procedure. With the upper knife engaged and the rolled edge settings and presser foot, position the beads as described in Step 3 of "Flatlock Beading." Serge slowly and guide the beads between the needle and knives. You can attach strings of sequins in the same manner, but make sure that the overlapping edges of the sequins are facing you as they're stitched.

You can attach beads or sequins to an edge without adding a rolled hem. Just switch the rolled edge settings to a balanced three-thread overlock stitch. The looper stitches meet at the fabric edge.

FREE-MOTION BEADING

For ultimate sparkle and shine, don't secure every single bead or sequin to your fabric; you want them to move so they catch and reflect light. The stitching for free-motion beading lies alongside, instead of over, the beads. The results are similar to couching (see page 76), but each item isn't captured by an individual stitch.

Get Ready

Needle	Appropriate for fabric and thread
Thread	Metallic embroidery, transparent, or all-purpose polyester*
Notions	2-mm-diameter prestrung or cross-locked beads or sequins, machine embroidery hoop

Match the metallic thread to the sequin color that sparkles, if you can't find an exact match.

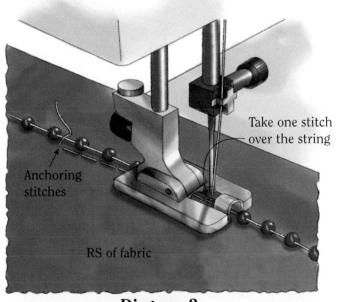

Take one stitch over the string

Anchoring stitches

RS of fabric

Diagram 3

Get Set

Presser foot	Piping, bulky overlock, Pearls 'N Piping, or Sequins 'N Ribbon
Stitch	Straight
Stitch length	16 spi (1.5 mm)
Needle tension	Slightly decrease
Feed dogs	Disengaged, covered, or 0 stitch length

Sew

1. Prestrung beads on cotton thread must be transferred to a stronger thread before you attach them to your garment. See "Make It Easy" below.

2. Load the fabric right side up into the embroidery hoop. Remove a few beads or sequins from the end of the string. Place the start of the string on the fabric, under the presser foot. Stitch on the string end several times to secure it. If the beads can't be removed, stitch across the string between two beads several times.

3. Take four or five stitches alongside the string of beads. Stop with the needle up and swing the string to the other side of the needle. Take four or five more stitches alongside the beads, stop with

the needle up, and shift the string to the other side of the needle. See **Diagram 3** on page 79. Continue until the entire string is stitched. End by stitching around the last bead or sequin or across the string several times.

4. For a simple variation, pull a loop of beads to one side of the stitching line. Take a stitch over the string at both ends of the loop. See **Diagram 4.** Pull the string to tighten the loop. Continue stitching the string of beads as before.

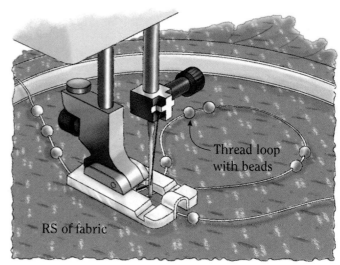

Thread loop with beads

RS of fabric

Diagram 4

Make It Easy

Beads that come prestrung on cotton thread must be transferred to a stronger thread before you attach them to your garment. Here's a nifty way to accomplish this on your sewing machine. You won't find yourself chasing after loose beads that escape your needle as you would when trying the same maneuver with a hand needle and thread.

Set up the machine as described in "Free-Motion Beading" on page 79, using all-purpose or transparent thread. Draw out a length of thread

from the needle long enough for all of the beads. Pull it to the front of the machine. Tie the end of the cotton bead string onto the needle thread. Slide the beads from the cotton string over the knot and onto the needle thread. Don't clip the thread. Position the garment or fabric under the presser foot and needle where the beading starts. Move the beads out of the way and take a few short stitches in place to begin. Sew the string of beads to the fabric using the free-motion beading technique.

SCATTERED FLAT BEADS AND GEMS

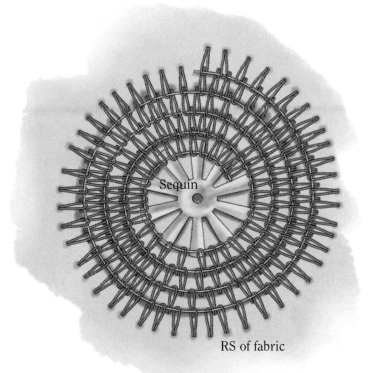

Capture single sequins, flat-backed beads, gemstones, and even shisha mirrors on the surface of your fabric with this free-motion method. The bobbin stitch loops are visible on the surface because they lie over the edge of the bead. Indulge in a novelty bobbin thread for a dynamic effect, or use clear monofilament and your beads will "float" on the fabric.

Get Ready

Needle	Appropriate for fabric and thread
Needle thread	All-purpose or transparent
Bobbin thread	Decorative embroidery
Notions	Flat-backed beads, gems, single sequins, or shisha mirrors; glue stick; machine embroidery hoop; seam sealant

Get Set

Presser foot	None
Stitch	Straight
Needle tension	Very tight
Bobbin tension	Very loose
Feed dogs	Disengaged, covered, or 0 stitch length

Sequin

RS of fabric

Diagram 5

Sew

1. Glue the selected embellishment in place on the garment, load the fabric in the embroidery hoop, and place it under the needle.

2. Draw the bobbin thread to the surface close to one of the embellishments, and take a few short stitches to secure. Trim the threads close to the fabric.

3. Free-motion stitch around and close to the embellishment. The bobbin thread loops should come up and over the edge, capturing and securing the piece. Stitch slowly around the piece, then switch directions and stitch around again. See **Diagram 5**. Clip the thread, leaving tails long enough to tie off on the underside. Treat the knot with seam sealant for added security.

Sharp Notion

A free-form eyelet or flower is made by omitting the bead. You just stitch around and around in a tight circle several times with the bobbin tension set very loose.

SINGLE BEAD STITCHING

At the sewing machine, place single beads or sequins exactly where you want them: alone, in lines, or in clusters. While this may be awkward at first, you'll develop speed with practice. The results are definitely more professional and permanent than gluing.

Get Ready

Needle	70/10*
Thread	Strong polyester or transparent
Notions	Machine embroidery hoop, beads†

Get Set

Presser foot	None
Stitch	Straight
Tension	Slightly decrease the needle tension
Feed dogs	Disengaged, covered, or 0 stitch length

Make sure you can easily slip the bead up the needle shaft.

†*The bead can be no thicker than the distance from the bottom of the needle bar to the needle plate when the needle is lowered as far as possible. See Diagram 6.*

Sew

1. Place the fabric in the embroidery hoop and under the needle. Even though you removed the presser foot, it's necessary to lower the bar that controls the position of the presser foot. Draw the bobbin thread to the surface, and take a few stitches in place close to the first bead position. Clip the thread tails. Take four or five short stitches and stop with the needle up.

2. It's easy to accidentally step on the floor pedal that controls your machine. To prevent this from happening, take your foot off the pedal for this step. Slide a bead up the needle and hold it in place with your left hand. Pull just a little slack in the thread above the needle, then hand-turn the flywheel to lower the needle into the fabric. See **Diagram 6.**

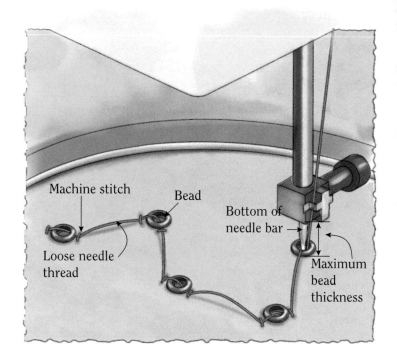

Diagram 6

Complete the stitch by turning the flywheel or, if this feature is available on your machine, tap the foot pedal once to complete the stitch.

3. Let the bead fall over and take a second stitch next to it. See **Diagram 6.**

4. Add the next bead in the same manner. Don't cut the threads if the next bead is nearby. To end after a row of beads or a single bead, stitch in place several times to secure the threads. Cut the loose needle and bobbin threads between each bead.

SINGLE BEADS AT A CORNER OR EDGE

A single flat bead, charm, or gemstone can be sewn to a garment edge or corner in a similar manner to the way that an item is attached anywhere else. Free-motion sewing machine stitching is the key, and this method incorporates tear-away or water-soluble stabilizer.

Get Ready

Needle	70/10*
Thread	Strong polyester or transparent
Notions	Machine embroidery hoop, tear-away or water-soluble stabilizer, single beads†

Get Set

Presser foot	None
Stitch	Zigzag
Stitch length	0
Stitch width	Medium to wide
Needle tension	Slightly decrease
Feed dogs	Disengaged or covered

*Make sure you can easily slip the bead up the needle shaft.
†The bead can be no thicker than the distance from the needle bar to the needle plate when the needle is lowered as far as possible. See **Diagram 6** on the opposite page.*

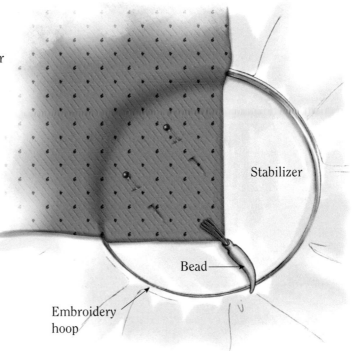

Diagram 7

Sew

1. Load the embroidery hoop with tear-away or water-soluble stabilizer. Place the garment edge or corner on top of the stabilizer. Pin it in place.

2. Draw up the bobbin thread and stitch in place through the fabric edge at the bead location.

3. Make a few a straight stitches with the stitch length close to 0, then change to the zigzag stitch and catch the bead in the stitching. Catch the garment edge with the left swing of the needle and the stabilizer with the right swing. See **Diagram 7.**

4. Switch back to a straight stitch and stitch in place through the garment. Clip the threads, tie off securely on the underside, and remove the stabilizer.

Make It Easy

Having trouble selecting beads that fit your presser foot? If you have a beading foot, take it with you to the store. If the bead you choose fits in the guide channel on the foot, you can use the foot to apply it.

Binding

Binding is one of the simplest structural details on a garment, but it can be one of the most elegant or decorative features as well. It's a striking contrast for any edge on a garment, particularly when another, complementary fabric is used. A multicolor binding, for example, adds instant style to an otherwise plain bound edge.

In addition to sewing machine techniques that include an elastic binding, several serger methods for binding are included here. The braid binding is worth trying because it allows you to copy the ready-to-wear look of color-matched trim.

Braid Binding

A serger makes it possible to create the color-matched trims that are so hard to find. Now you can custom design your own trims using one or more decorative threads. Knit tops and dresses are perfect candidates for this treatment, but lightweight wovens benefit when you want just a hint of color at an otherwise plain neckline or hem edge.

Get Ready	Serger	Sewing Machine	Serger
Needle	Appropriate for fabric and thread	Appropriate for fabric and thread	Appropriate for fabric and thread
Needle thread	All-purpose serger	All-purpose	All-purpose serger
Bobbin thread	—	All-purpose	—
UL thread	Decorative	—	Decorative
LL thread	Fusible or all-purpose serger	—	All-purpose serger

Get Set	Serger	Sewing Machine	Serger
Presser foot	Standard or blind hem (optional)	All-purpose or ¼-inch (6 mm) patchwork	Standard or blind hem (optional)
Stitch	Three-thread overlock	Straight	Three-thread overlock
Stitch length	Short	12 spi (2 mm)	Very short
Stitch width	Wide	—	Half of the first serging
Differential feed	1.5 to 2, if available and necessary	—	Normal

Serge and Sew

1. Prepare the garment edge for a bound-edge finish. See the "Workroom Secret" below.

2. Cut bias strips 1¼-inches (3-cm)-wide for ¾-inch (2-cm)-wide finished braid binding. For woven fabric, cut the strips on the true bias. For knits, cut the strips across the fabric width (the stretchiest dimension). Turn under and press ¼ inch (6 mm) along one long edge of the binding strip.

3. Satin overlock the folded edge of the strip, taking care not to cut the fold. If the edge has a tendency to ripple, engage the differential feed or use the ease-plus sewing technique. See Differential Feed Control in "Anatomy of a Serger" on page 29.

4. With raw edges even and the binding right side against the garment wrong side, at the sewing machine (or serger), stitch the two layers together ¼ inch (6 mm) from the raw edges, taking time to ensure seam width accuracy.

5. At the seamline, turn the binding to the outside over the serged seam to encase it. Press carefully to fuse it in place (or baste), then topstitch just inside the looper threads of the overlocking for added durability.

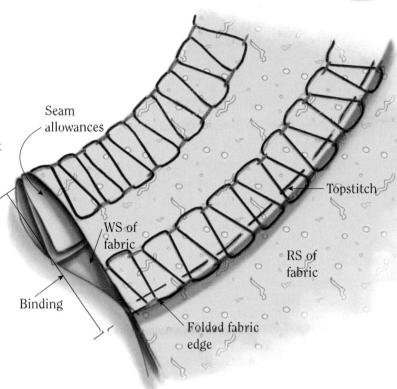

Seam allowances

WS of fabric

Binding

Topstitch

RS of fabric

Folded fabric edge

Diagram 1

6. Change your thread and machine settings as indicated for the second serger pass. Serge over the folded edge, taking care not to cut the fold. See **Diagram 1.**

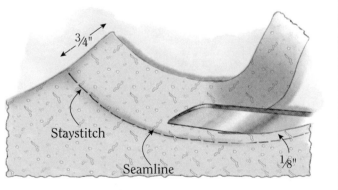

Workroom Secret

Unless your pattern is specifically designed for a bound-edge finish, you need to remove the seam (or hem) allowances before attaching the binding. Staystitch ¾ inch (2 cm) from the garment raw edge—this is ⅛ inch (3 mm) above the hemline or away from the seamline, inside the garment. Trim all but ⅛ inch (3 mm) from the seam allowance.

¾"

Staystitch

Seamline

⅛"

ELASTICIZED BINDING

Sewing on super stretchy fabrics, such as Lycra spandex, to make a tank top, a sundress, exercise clothing, and swimwear requires a few special notions and techniques. The most interesting is the inclusion of elastic serged inside the binding for a snug but flexible fit. Twin-needle stitching by machine adds a decorative touch to the finished binding without interfering with the stretch. Use woolly nylon thread because it won't scratch your skin; however it does stretch with the fabric as you move.

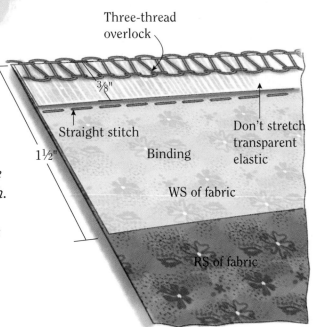

Diagram 2

Get Ready	Sewing Machine	Serger	Sewing Machine
Needle	Ball point or universal 65/9 to 80/12	65/9 to 80/12	Twin (Stretch) ball point or universal, 65/9 to 80/12
Needle thread	Woolly nylon or all-purpose polyester	Woolly nylon	Woolly nylon or all-purpose polyester
Bobbin thread	Woolly nylon or all-purpose polyester	—	Woolly nylon or all-purpose polyester
UL thread	—	Woolly nylon	—
LL thread	—	Woolly nylon	—
Notion	⅜-inch (1-cm)-wide cotton/spandex braid or transparent elastic		

Get Set	Sewing Machine	Serger	Sewing Machine
Presser foot	All-purpose	Standard	All-purpose
Stitch	Straight	Three-thread overlock	Straight
Stitch length	10 spi (2.5 mm)	Medium	10 spi (2.5 mm)
Stitch width	0	Medium	0
Upper knife	—	Disengaged (if possible)	—

Sew and Serge

1. Cut the binding strip the length of the binding pattern piece and 1½ inches (4 cm) wide (four times the width of the elastic). Cut the binding strip with the greatest stretch along the length. Cut a piece of the elastic the same length as the binding strip. Trim the garment's ⅝-inch (1.5-cm)-wide seam allowance to ⅜ inch (1 cm).

2. With right sides together and raw edges even, straight stitch the binding strip to the garment edge, stretching both layers as you sew. Use a ⅜-inch (1-cm)-wide seam allowance.

3. Place the elastic on top of the binding strip and serge it to the seam allowances. See **Diagram 2** on the opposite page. If you are using clear elastic, don't worry if you nick it because this won't affect long-term stretch. Don't stretch the fabric layers or the elastic.

4. Wrap the binding around the seam allowance and elastic. Pin the binding in place on the wrong side with the binding raw edge extending past the serger stitching.

5. At the sewing machine, twin-needle stitch along the folded edge on the right side, through all layers. On the inside, trim the excess binding close to the stitching. If you prefer a finished inside edge rather than a trimmed edge, you can turn under the raw edge of the binding and baste it in place prior to topstitching.

Make It Easy

Bindings and facings are beautiful ways to finish a curved neckline edge, but not if your seams don't lie flat. When serge seaming a facing or binding to a curved neckline edge, engage the differential feed at a plus setting only in the most curved areas to control rippling.

SUCCESSFUL STRATEGIES FOR BEAUTIFUL BINDING

Be true. Take the time to cut woven fabric strips on the true bias. Even a slight variance can cause rippling later.

Avoid wrinkles. Bias strips are easily stretched out of shape. After joining the strips but before you attach the bias to a garment, steam, then press it. Don't handle the bias strip until it is completely dry.

Bounce back. Press the bias on a grid-printed grain board, aligning the bias edges with the lines. This immediately shows you the stretched areas (where the bias narrows). Coax the bias back to the correct width with your fingertips before steaming.

Control curves. Clip the seam allowance of the bias strip when sewing binding to an outside curve, rather than stretching the bias. Then stretch the garment slightly as you sew the bias in place. When you release the garment, it will relax into the bias.

Snuggle up. On inside curves, try clipping the garment edge so you can straighten it to match the bias raw edge. Stretch the bias slightly as you stitch it to the garment so that when it relaxes, the curve will lie snug against the body.

Stitch in time. When sewing bias to another cut edge with lots of bias give, staystitch the edge first.

Make samples. When binding a garment with a different fabric, first sew a test on scraps. This way you can work out any stitching challenges and make sure you like the results.

FAST-FUSE BINDING

No more basting! No more hand stitching! Combine the best of sewing, serging, and fusible thread to attach a single-layer binding. Serge-finish one edge of the binding for a smooth, flat, nonbulky finish that you can then fuse to the garment.

Get Ready

	Serger	Sewing Machine
Needle	Appropriate for fabric and thread	Appropriate for fabric and thread
Needle thread	All-purpose serger	All-purpose
Bobbin thread	—	All-purpose
UL thread	All-purpose serger	—
LL thread	Fusible	—

Get Set

	Serger	Sewing Machine
Presser foot	Standard	Open-toe embroidery
Stitch	Three-thread overlock	Straight
Stitch length	2.5 to 3 mm	10 spi (2.5 mm)
Stitch width	Medium	—
Differential feed	1.5 to 2 or "+," if available	—

Serge and Sew

1. Prepare the garment edge for a bound-edge finish. See the "Workroom Secret" on page 85.

2. Cut ¾-inch (2-cm)-wide true bias strips from woven fabric or cross-grain strips from knits.

3. Serge-finish one long edge of the binding with the right side up. Use the differential feed to control rippling or stretching.

4. When applying binding to a complete circle, turn under the beginning end of the binding strip at a 45 degree angle, press, and trim to ¼ inch (6 mm).

5. With right sides together, serge the binding to the garment, overlapping and trimming where you started the circular application. (You can straight stitch by machine, using a ¼-inch foot.)

6. Turn the binding to the inside, snugging it against the seam allowances. Fuse in place.

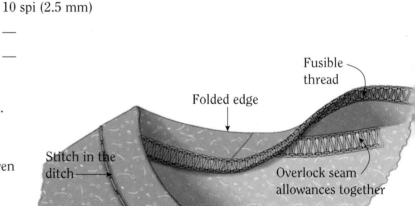

Diagram 3

7. At the sewing machine, stitch in the ditch from the right side to secure the inner edge of the binding. See **Diagram 3**. For a novel approach, you can secure the inner edge of the binding with one of the decorative techniques in the "Gallery of Binding Stitches" on page 90.

PIPED BINDING

Beautiful thread is a nice touch for a silk shell or classic jewel neckline. Choose a decorative thread for the upper looper of your serger and roll-edge finish the edge of the bias strip before attaching it. Consider this binding method for a hem edge treatment, too. You'll need your sewing machine set up for straight stitching in only the first and last steps.

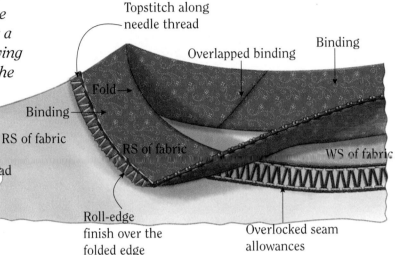

Diagram 4

Get Ready

Needle	Appropriate for fabric and thread
Needle thread	All-purpose serger
UL thread	Decorative
LL thread	Fusible

Get Set

Presser foot	Standard or rolled edge*
Stitch	Rolled edge
Stitch length	Short
Stitch width	Narrow
Upper knife	Disengaged, if possible

Try using a blind hem presser foot for Step 3, if desired.

Serge and Sew

1. Prepare the garment edge for a bound-edge finish. See the "Workroom Secret" on page 85.

2. Cut your bias strips 1¼ inches (3 cm) wide for ½-inch (1.25-cm)-wide finished binding or 1 inch (2.5 cm) wide for ¼-inch (6-mm)-wide finished binding. Turn under and press ¼ inch (6 mm) along one long edge of the binding strip.

3. Roll-edge finish the folded edge of the strip, taking care not to cut the fold. This is a super place to use your serger blind hem foot for absolutely straight, no-trim serging.

4. Change to a medium overlock stitch. With raw edges even and the right side of the binding against the wrong side of the garment, serge the two layers together, using the blind hem foot for a perfectly even seam allowance.

5. Turn the binding strip to the outside over the serged seam to encase it. See **Diagram 4**. Press carefully to avoid stretching. Pin or baste in place.

6. At the sewing machine, sew along the needle stitching of the rolled edge. See **Diagram 4**. For better stitch visibility, try an open-toe embroidery or zipper foot.

GALLERY OF BINDING STITCHES

By now you're probably familiar with the standard procedure for joining binding to the edge of a garment. In most cases the raw edges of a bias-cut strip of binding fabric and the garment are stitched together with right sides facing. Then the binding is folded to the inside of the garment, wrapping the seam allowances. The final step is securing the bias in position by stitching in the ditch of the seamline.

Binding attachments are available for many sewing machines. The Viking foot holds the binding and fabric layers with the edges even. A guide on the right side of the foot adjusts to accommodate different prefolded bias widths so that it wraps around a fabric edge. There is also an adjustment knob for positioning the stitching.

Other bias binders have a funnel through which you guide the binding so that it folds around the fabric edge as it is fed through a slot on the front of the foot. You may not be able to use a zigzag stitch with it.

In many cases stitching in the ditch can be replaced by a broad array of fancy sewing. This is particularly appealing when the binding is folded along the seamline, entirely to the outside—or inside—of the garment, depending on whether it's attached wrong-side-to-right-side or right-side-to-wrong-side.

What a great opportunity to explore the creative stitches stored in your machine. (Even if you have a very basic machine, don't stop reading—this gallery of stitches includes several ideas for you as well.) A tri-motion zigzag stitch, for example, is available on most machines and creates a bold, sporty look. The picot finish, on the other hand, is especially pretty on delicate blouses, children's wear, and lingerie.

Twin-Needle Topstitching

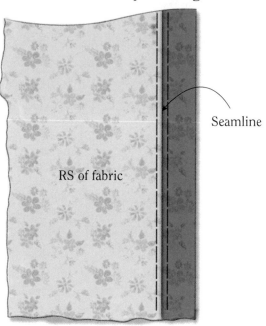

Seamline

RS of fabric

Twin-needle topstitch through the binding and the garment.

Tri-Motion Zigzag Stitch

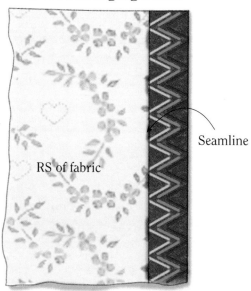

Seamline

RS of fabric

Use tri-motion zigzagging (rickrack stitch) over the binding in a contrasting color thread for a more folk art finish.

Blindstitch

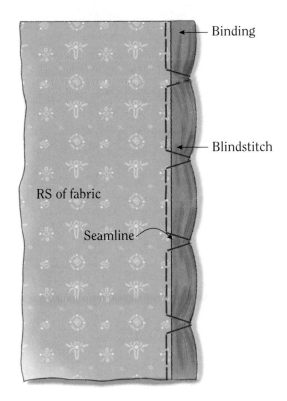

For a scalloped binding, blindstitch or shell stitch over the binding edge using transparent or woolly nylon thread in the needle.

Single- and Twin-Needle Stitch

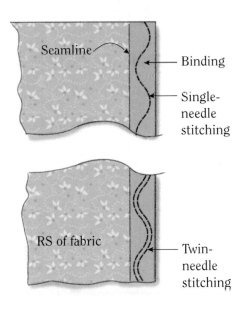

Serpentine stitch with a single or double needle and cotton or rayon machine embroidery thread to add delicate detail.

Decorative Stitch

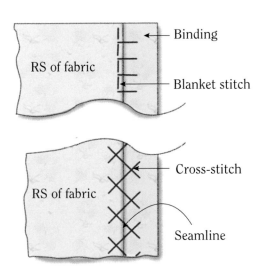

Sew a decorative pattern stitch through the binding.

Overlock Stitch

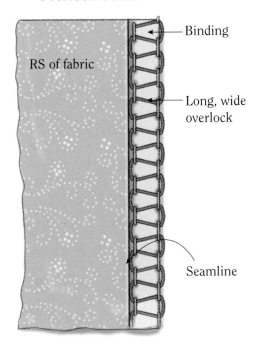

Overlock the binding with decorative thread and a medium-long three-thread stitch. The needle stitches go in the ditch with the looper stitches locking at the edge.

Braid

Custom-designed braid is easy to create with serging and free-motion stitching. The directions in this section include multicord, customized serger, twice-stitched serger, and stretch versions. Consider combining methods for truly unique garment trim that you can couch to clothing and accessories. Try stitching through the center of the braid with contrasting thread or a stitch variation like the scallop or three-step zigzag. Thick or thin, the braid trims will be unique designer touches for your garments.

DECORATIVE SERGED BRAID

In addition to serging a braid that suits your color scheme, you can also adjust its weight to suit the fabric's hand (the way that it drapes). Serging over soft, flexible knitting yarn or ribbon floss will result in a more flexible trim than using a woven ribbon base. Or use fusible thread in the lower looper to baste-fuse the trim in place to make it easier to topstitch.

Get Ready

Needle	Appropriate for fabric and thread
Needle thread	Lightweight rayon
UL thread	Heavy decorative rayon
LL thread	All-purpose serger or fusible
Notion	⅛-inch (3-mm)-wide satin ribbon or other narrow, flat braid

Get Set

Presser foot	Standard foot with tape guide or elastic applicator foot with the screw loosened
Stitch	Three-thread overlock
Stitch length	3 mm
Stitch width	2.5 mm

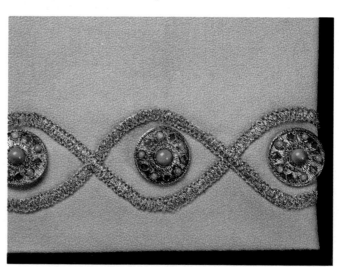

For added glitz, curve braided trim around buttons; large, flat beads; or gemstones, as done on this cuff. Use flexible trim (instead of ribbon) as your base, so it wraps easily around tight curves.

Serge

1. Insert the braid in the tape slot at the front of the presser foot, or try the elastic applicator. Loosen the screw on the elastic applicator to eliminate any tension on the braid. Adjust the stitch length if necessary for more or less coverage of the ribbon as desired. Serge over the braid. See **Diagram 1.**

    If you do not have a presser foot with a slot or a special elastic foot, you can improvise. Raise the presser foot and insert the cut end of the braid under the back of the foot. Then bring it toward you up over the top of the foot so that it lies to the right of the needle along the lip on the edge of the presser foot. This position keeps it between the needle and the knives so it will be caught in the stitches without getting cut by the knife.

2. Position as desired. Fuse the braid onto your garment if you used fusible thread in the lower looper. Machine stitch through the center or along each edge of the braid.

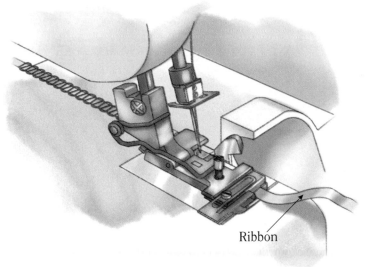

Ribbon

Diagram 1

Workroom Secret

    Avoid the "low-end pitfall." Garments sold in low-end and discount department stores are often embellished only on the front, to save on production and materials costs. But on a well-designed garment, trims and embellishments always carry over to the back for a more unified look, even if this is as simple as circling a complete neckline with trim rather than using it only on the front. The garment in this photograph is a perfect example of a nicely placed braid. The trim stitched to the collar isn't visible only from the front—it continues around the entire neck.

MULTICORD BRAID TRIM

Multicord braid trim is a clever disguise for hemline edges that show (but shouldn't) and as a camouflage for crease lines left after alterations. Apply this camouflage at your sewing machine and be sure to add braid elsewhere on the garment so it doesn't look like an afterthought. A pocket, yoke, or sleeve hem, for example, are all nice spots for additional detailing. Be careful not to overdo it, though, to avoid a spotty look.

Get Ready

Needle	Appropriate for fabric and thread
Needle thread	All-purpose or decorative thread to match or contrast with the decorative braid material
Bobbin thread	Embroidery or Bobbin Thread
Notions	Decorative cords or threads that fit through the clips or holes in the presser foot; plastic cording guide (optional); tear-away or water-soluble stabilizer; large-eyed needle

Get Set

Presser foot	Multiple braid or cord foot (see Step 1 before attaching)
Stitch	Regular or rickrack (tri-motion) zigzag stitch, or experiment with decorative stitches that will leave cording exposed in areas
Stitch length	As desired
Stitch width	Adjusted to accommodate the width of the braid or cords

Sew

1. Thread each cord or braid through the presser foot, and tie them together in an overhand knot behind the foot. You may want to also use a plastic cording guide in front of the presser foot. Attach stabilizer to the wrong side of the garment fabric in the area to be embellished with braid. If you are using a pre-determined pattern, trace it onto the fabric.

2. Stitch the cords to the fabric surface by following a pattern, outlining the garment edges, or applying a

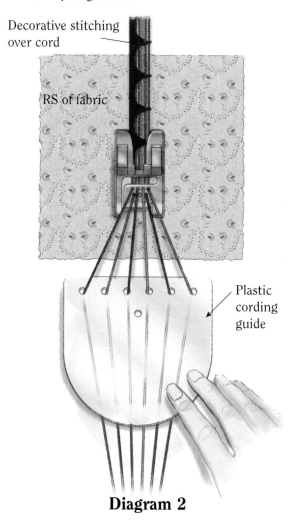

Decorative stitching over cord

RS of fabric

Plastic cording guide

Diagram 2

free-form design. See **Diagram 2**. For variety you can stitch several groups of trim in parallel rows using several pattern stitches.

3. Remove the stabilizer. Cut the cords at the fabric edge or, if the corded design ends in the garment interior, thread a cord end into a large-eyed needle and pull it to the wrong side. Repeat with the remaining cords. Tie them off securely.

STRETCH BRAID TRIM

When working on a knit, do you want a trim that will "give" with the fabric? Try serging on clear elastic. Don't worry if the knife cuts away a little elastic as you serge. It won't weaken this "plastic" elastic, which is perfect for lingerie, knits, and swimwear.

Get Ready

Needle	Appropriate for thread
Needle thread	Woolly nylon or all-purpose serger
UL thread	Woolly nylon
LL thread	Woolly nylon
Notion	Clear elastic in desired width

Get Set

Presser foot	Standard, ribbon, or tape*
Stitch	Balanced three-thread overlock
Stitch length	2 mm
Stitch width	As desired†
Differential feed	0.7 or lower, if available

* *Ensure that the foot has a slot wide enough for the elastic width.*

† *The clear elastic must be wider than the stitch width.*

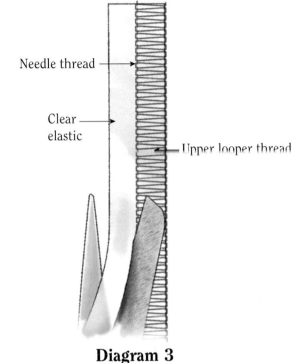

Diagram 3

Serge

1. Adjust the tension for a balanced stitch. (If desired, use all-purpose thread in the needle.)

2. Cut a 24-inch (61-cm)-long strip of elastic to test the stitch. If you do not have differential feed, insert the elastic under the presser foot and begin serging. When a few inches emerge behind the presser foot, hold the elastic taut, but not stretched, in front of and behind the foot. Continue serging for 5 to 6 inches (13 to 15 cm). If you do have differential feed, it is not necessary to hold the elastic taut. Stop and stretch the elastic behind the foot. If the stitches break, the needle thread tension is too tight.

3. Serge the length of elastic braid. Trim the excess elastic close to the stitching. See **Diagram 3**. Because it is transparent, extra elastic at the edge won't show on the finished garment.

4. Position the trim as desired and machine stitch it in place along each edge, stretching the elastic as you serge.

Make It Easy

If you have trouble getting the elastic to feed smoothly under the presser foot even though the differential feed is engaged, use a layer of water-soluble stabilizer under the elastic while stitching. When you're done, tear away the stabilizer next to the needle stitching, then use serger tweezers to pull away the thin strip of stabilizer caught under the stitching. You don't even have to get the elastic wet!

TWICE-STITCHED BRAID

Rich passementerie braid trim that is serged with rayon or glittery metallic thread adds an elegant note to a dressy suit or the bodice of a wedding gown. Made with pearl cotton, it is a beautiful but subtle complement on a linen suit. Play with thread combinations on this twice-stitched braid to design a one-of-a-kind trim that will be sure to garner compliments.

Get Ready

	Serger First Pass	Serger Second Pass	Sewing Machine
Needle	90/14	90/14	90/14
Bobbin thread	—	—	All-purpose
Needle thread	All-purpose serger or lightweight decorative	All-purpose serger, transparent, or lightweight decorative	All-purpose or transparent (optional)
UL thread	Medium to heavy decorative	Medium to heavy decorative	—
LL thread	All-purpose serger	All-purpose serger or fusible	—
Notions	⅝- or 1¼-inch (1.5- or 3-cm)-wide tricot or Seams Great; rotary cutter, ruler, and mat (optional); water-soluble stabilizer (optional)		

Get Set

	Serger First Pass	Serger Second Pass	Sewing Machine
Presser foot	Standard or rolled edge	Standard	Open-toe embroidery
Stitch	Rolled edge	Three-thread overlock	Straight
Stitch length	Short	Short	10 spi (2.5 mm)
Stitch width	Narrow	Widest possible*	—

*For the widest braid possible, use the widest stitch setting on your serger. However, the wider the finished braid, the less flexible it will be. Narrower braids follow curved designs more tightly than wider ones. The rolled edge of this trim is less flexible than the other finished edge.

Serge and Sew

1. Cut a strip of tricot or Seams Great to the desired length of the braid.

2. Pull on the strip to determine the direction in which it curls. Place the curling side against the bed of the serger with stabilizer underneath, if desired.

3. Adjust your thread and machine settings as indicated for the Serger First Pass. Roll-edge finish one long edge of the strip. Allow the knives to trim just a little tricot or Seams Great from the strip as you serge. See **Diagram 4**.

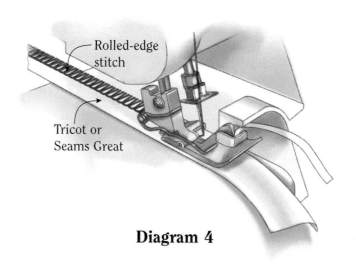

Rolled-edge stitch

Tricot or Seams Great

Diagram 4

4. Adjust your thread and machine settings for the Serger Second Pass. Position the strip under the presser foot so the needle will stitch right next to the rolled edge. This is tricky and will require practice, plus slow, steady stitching with your eye on the needle. Serge, trimming away any excess tricot or Seams Great (and stabilizer). See **Diagram 5**.

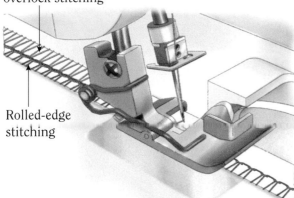

Three-thread overlock stitching

Rolled-edge stitching

Diagram 5

5. If you used stabilizer, immerse the trim in cool water (not hot), massage gently, and air-dry. If you used fusible thread in the lower looper, do not try to press the braid dry.

6. Position the finished braid on the garment as desired, shaping it to follow the large loops and swirls typical of traditional passementerie designs. Pin it in place or fuse it if you used fusible thread in the lower looper.

7. Adjust your thread and machine settings as indicated for the Sewing Machine. Sew the braid in place, stitching in the ditch between the rolled edge and the overlocking. If you don't want the machine stitching to show, you can use transparent thread in the needle. The easiest way to stitch in the ditch is to use an open-toe embroidery foot for better visibility. This type of presser foot also makes it easier to feed the braid. Stitch close to the remaining braid edge, placing the row of stitching just inside the looper thread loops.

Sharp Notion

Straight edges on some garments, like the hem and front opening of a bellboy-style jacket, can benefit from a wider, nonflexible braid. Start with twice as much twice-stitched braid as required. Cut it into two equal lengths. For all but metallic braid, rotary-cut a strip of paper-backed fusible web $\frac{1}{16}$ inch (1.5 mm) narrower than twice the width of the finished trim.

At the ironing board, butt the rolled edges of the trim or the overlocked edges together on top of the exposed side of the fusible web. Fuse. Remove the paper backing.

Position the trim on the garment and fuse. Edgestitch in place. If desired, further embellish the applied braid by zigzagging in a contrasting thread over the butted edges at the center of the braid. See the diagram. Try other pattern stitches for even more dimension.

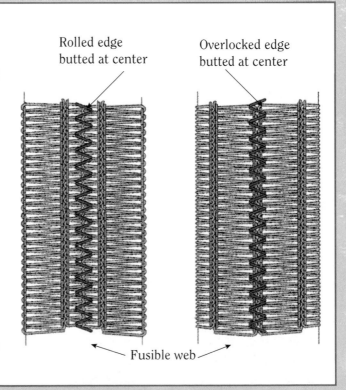

Rolled edge butted at center

Overlocked edge butted at center

Fusible web

Buttonholes

Whether utilitarian or decorative, the keys to the perfect buttonhole are selecting the right shape, width, and length, and then executing it to perfection. A challenge? Not really, when you use the right accessories and methods.

In this entry you'll learn a number of secrets for making the best buttonholes, and you can also try some unique methods. Instructions include imitating a hand-worked buttonhole on your machine, as well as adding decorative bound buttonholes using your serger to embellish the buttonhole "lips."

You may even want to try serger button loops. These loops are a great alternative to the self-fabric ones that you're probably used to making for your garments.

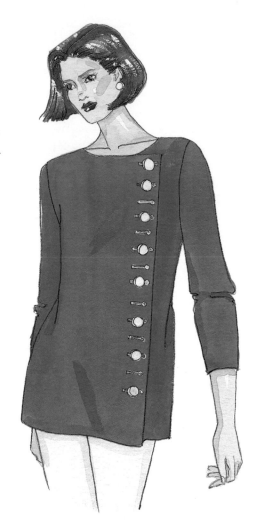

DECORATIVE BOUND BUTTONHOLE

You can make the look of this buttonhole treatment as dramatic or unobtrusive as you desire by simply changing the serged decorative thread that peeks out of the window opening on the "lips." Match the thread to the color and texture of the garment fabric for subtle, less obvious buttonholes, or use a contrasting thread to draw attention to the garment details on your work.

Be sure to use a bit of decorative serging elsewhere on the garment for an integrated look. For example, use the same thread to do a serged-edge finish on the hem, sleeves, front edge, collar, and lapels. This looks particularly striking on a tailored tweed jacket.

A glamorous version of the traditional bound buttonhole, this closure is suitable for a garment with an attached facing.

Get Ready

	Serger	Sewing Machine
Fabric	Fashion fabric and matching lightweight lining	
Needle	Appropriate for fabric and thread	Appropriate for fabric and thread
Thread	Decorative	All-purpose
Notions	Strips of paper-backed fusible web, each ¼ inch (6 mm) wide; pencil; lightweight fusible, nonwoven interfacing; press cloth	

Get Set

	Serger	Sewing Machine
Presser foot	Standard	All-purpose zigzag
Stitch	Wrapped or three-thread overlock	Straight
Stitch length	Varies*	20 spi (1 mm)
Stitch width	Varies*	—
Upper knife	Disengaged, if possible	—

Adjust for thread and desired coverage.

Serge and Sew

1. Cut a 2-inch (5-cm)-wide strip of fabric twice the finished buttonhole length plus 2 inches (5 cm). Press the strip in half lengthwise with the wrong sides together.

2. Serge over the folded edge with the desired stitch and decorative thread, being careful not to cut the fold. Cut the strip in half, then butt together the serged edges of the two lengths and bartack the ends together ⅛ inch (3 mm) beyond the ends of the desired buttonhole length.

3. Trim this "buttonhole patch" into an oval. On the right side, fuse a ¼-inch (6-mm)-wide strip of paper-backed fusible web just inside each row of serging, only from bartack to bartack. See **Diagram 1.** Set aside.

4. Measure the total width of the serger stitching across both "lips" (the two rows of serging) to determine the finished buttonhole width. Pencil a rectangle of the finished length and width on the wrong side of the interfaced garment front.

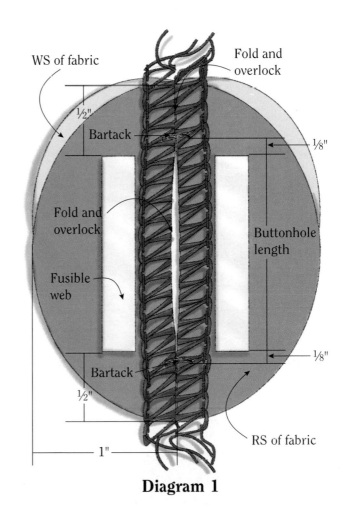

Diagram 1

5. Cut a rectangle of lining 1 inch (2.5 cm) longer and 2 inches (5 cm) wider than the buttonhole. Center the lining patch and pin it over a buttonhole location, face down on the right side of the garment. From the wrong side and sewing through all thicknesses of fabric at 20 spi (1 mm), stitch a rectangle of the buttonhole's finished width and length. Cut open the rectangle through both the lining and the fabric, clipping to but not through the corners. Push the lining to the wrong side, and press it so it's not visible at the opening edges.

6. Remove the backing paper from the fusible strips on the buttonhole patch. Center the buttonhole patch under an opening. Fuse, using a press cloth. See **Diagram 2**. Edgestitch around the opening.

7. Make a window in the facing under the buttonhole. This opening won't be visible from the right side of your garment, so a simple finish is suitable. As explained in Step 5, make a lining patch, sew it to the right side of the facing, and turn it to the inside. Hand sew or fuse the window in place on the wrong side of the buttonhole.

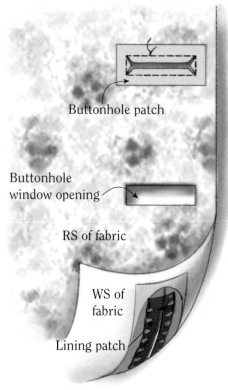

Buttonhole patch

Buttonhole window opening

RS of fabric

WS of fabric

Lining patch

Diagram 2

STRETCHY BUTTON LOOPS

The secret to a button loop that holds its shape is a bit of elastic. While you can insert elastic into a fabric loop, it's easier and faster to serge a cord using elastic thread in the lower looper and a heavy decorative thread in the upper looper. This turns a serger chain into button loops with give.

Get Ready

Needle	All-purpose
UL thread	Decorative
LL thread	Elastic

Get Set

Presser foot	Standard or rolled edge
Stitch	Rolled edge
Stitch length	Short
Stitch width	Narrow to medium
UL tension	Balance or tighten
LL tension	Balance or loosen

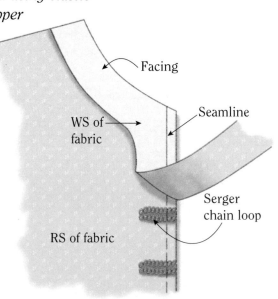

Facing

Seamline

WS of fabric

RS of fabric

Serger chain loop

Diagram 3

Serge

1. Lower the presser foot and serge off 12 inches (30 cm) or more of serger chain. You need enough to make the required number of button loops, plus two seam allowances for each loop.

   Each loop needs to fit around the button as snugly as possible, but make sure that the loop isn't excessively tight. It needs enough room to slip easily over the surface of the button. This is especially important if your button has a rough surface that can wear out the loop. The elastic helps in this method because the loop closes up around the

button after being stretched a little to get around it.

2. Cut a piece of chain the required length for each button, plus two seam allowances. Baste each loop in place and catch the seam allowances in the facing stitching. Backstitch over the loop ends when you reach each one, for added security. See **Diagram 3** on the opposite page.

3. Sew the buttons in place on the left edge, opposite the loops.

TAILORED BUTTONHOLE

Imitating the classic look of a handworked, corded buttonhole involves little more than using the right stitch on your sewing machine and manually pivoting the fabric instead of selecting a built-in buttonhole.

You can use one of several stitches, and this technique is ideal if your zigzag machine doesn't make buttonholes or you'd like more control over the quality and appearance of your buttonholes.

Get Ready

Needle	Appropriate for fabric and thread
Thread	All-purpose
Notions	Water-soluble stabilizer; filler cord (#8 pearl cotton, gimp, silk twist, topstitching thread, or yarn or thread raveled from the cut edge of the fabric); needle threader; seam sealant

Get Set

Presser foot	Buttonhole
Stitch	Rickrack or overlock*
Stitch length	Varies
Stitch width	Varies†
Feed dogs	Lowered, covered, or 0 stitch length for Step 3
Needle position	Left, if possible

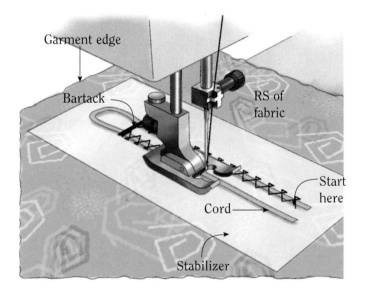

Diagram 4

*This forward and reverse action stitch is also known as the double overlock or overedge stitch.
†Adjust for a stitch that's wide enough to bartack over a double width of the cord.

Sew

1. Mark the start and end of the buttonhole on a strip of water-soluble stabilizer. Pin or baste it to the garment right side. Beginning at the end farthest from the garment edge, sew one side of the buttonhole, stitching over the cording. (You can also use a satin stitch.) Stop with the needle down.

2. Lift the presser foot and pivot the fabric 180 degrees. Pull the cord around to position it under the left side of the foot, leaving a loop of cord.

3. Lower the presser foot, raise the needle, and lower the feed dogs. (If you can't lower the feed dogs, dial down to 0 stitch length or cover them.) Bartack over both halves of the cord. Secure with three or four stitches.

4. Raise the needle and feed dogs. Return the machine to the previous settings. Lower the needle and stitch the second side of the buttonhole. See **Diagram 4** on page 101. Bartack to the remaining end.

5. Pull the cord so the loop is snug against the bartack but the fabric isn't puckered. Pull the threads to the wrong side and knot. Use a needle threader to draw the cord ends between the garment and facing. Tie off the ends and treat the knot with liquid seam sealant.

SUCCESSFUL STRATEGIES FOR BUTTONHOLES

Start fresh. Start with a new machine needle and a full bobbin. To avoid thick, lumpy buttonholes, use a lightweight cotton machine embroidery thread in the needle and the bobbin.

Channel with tunnels. Always use a buttonhole foot so that the satin-stitched buttonhole "legs" move easily under the two stitch tunnels.

Add stability. For washable garments, particularly knits, draw the buttonhole placement lines, plus stop and start lines, on a strip of transparent water-soluble stabilizer. Pin it in place on the right side of the garment. Make the buttonholes, then tear away the stabilizer and spritz with water to remove any remaining traces of the stabilizer.

Loosen up. Reduce the needle tension slightly (or place the bobbin thread through the hole in the bobbin-case stitch finger, if available) so that the satin stitching on top is smooth and even without any visible bobbin loops.

Test drive. Always make a buttonhole sample using the same number of fabric layers and interfacing that you will use for your finished garment. Check the buttonhole length.

Use knit knack. To reinforce a buttonhole in knits, cut a piece of ½-inch (1.25-cm)-wide or wider transparent elastic that's 1 inch (2.5 cm) longer than the length of the buttonhole. Center and baste the elastic over the buttonhole marking on the facing side. Make the buttonhole. Trim the excess elastic close to the stitching.

Blow a fuse. For a stronger buttonhole in ravel-prone fabric, intentionally fuse in the "wrong" order. Cut an oval of fusible web larger than the buttonhole and baste it in place between the garment and facing at the buttonhole location. Fuse after making the buttonholes, to meld the layers and stitches.

Check the fray. For fray-free buttonholes, apply a thin line of seam sealant between the stitched rows, and allow it to dry before cutting the buttonhole.

Stop short. After stitching, place a straight pin across the inside stitch of the end bartacks so you won't slice the buttonhole too far.

DECORATIVE BUTTONHOLE SAMPLER

How many times have you looked for a project to showcase some special stitches and been disappointed because you couldn't find a suitable garment, or just too much work was involved?

Embellished buttonholes offer the perfect opportunity to try out new stitches without spending a lot of time at the machine, and so many garments are suitable for decorative buttonholes. Here's the perfect opportunity to use all of the fancy stitches on your machine.

Don't fret if you don't have a top-of-the-line model, because you can do some really dynamic work with little more than a satin stitch, bartack, or zigzag.

But for those of you with a cache of stitch patterns and motifs stored in the memory of your sewing machine, you'll be delighted with the buttonholes that you can create.

The stitch that you choose to embellish your simple buttonhole with can drastically alter the mood of the garment. Go feminine by adding delicate eyelets, or turn on the funk with geometric shapes.

A few of the endless possibilities for eye-catching buttonholes are shown here, and the starting point is the standard buttonhole.

Also consider using contrasting or decorative threads and combining stitches. For a purely decorative element, don't cut the buttonholes. After all, no one said buttonholes have to work! Make a row of buttonholes around the edges of a collar and cuffs, for example, using a variety of colors and decorative threads. Don't cut them open—they're just for fun. Or march a battalion of colorful buttonholes down a blouse front, cutting only those that must function. Each one can be the same—or entirely different from the next. It's your call because you're the designer!

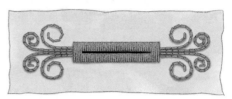

The baroque drama of satin-stitched swirls are perfect for an elegant dinner jacket or romantic dress.

Dynamic, attention-grabbing, geometric shapes are the best way to accent a garment with clean design lines that's sewn in primary colors.

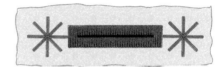

A stitched daisy at each end of a buttonhole adds a playful look.

Ethnic-influenced garments never really go out of style. So make a skirt from an "earthy" print and wear a blouse with southwestern-look buttonholes stitched to match.

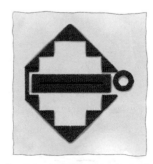

Don't limit your stitching to just the ends of the buttonhole—let the motif wrap its way around.

Charted Needlework

Use your sewing machine to create the look of petit point or fine counted cross-stitch, depending on the stitch density that you select. The technique and supplies are simple: free-motion satin stitching over special needles. The needles hold the stitches for a slightly rounded, "hand-worked" appearance while also keeping your stitching straight and closely aligned.

Get Ready

Needle	Embroidery
Needle thread	Machine embroidery
Bobbin thread	White Basting Thread
Notions	Iron-on, tear-away stabilizer; charted design; lightweight tracing or tissue paper, or water-soluble stabilizer; five or more chart needles; extra bobbins

Get Set

Presser foot	None
Stitch	Zigzag
Stitch length	0
Stitch width	Wide enough to clear the width of the charted needle
Feed dogs	Disengaged or covered
Needle tension	Loosen slightly

If you don't want to change thread colors, consider making your motif with variegated thread.

Sew

1. Although you may stitch on completed garments, when making a garment it's best to work on a piece of fabric that is slightly larger all around than the pattern piece you're embellishing. Mark the grainline for future reference. Fill several bobbins with Basting Thread. Apply the iron-on, tear-away stabilizer to the fabric or garment wrong side.

2. Transfer the design outline to a sheet of lightweight tracing or tissue paper or onto water-soluble stabilizer, and draw lines around each area of color. These lines will act as guides so you'll be able to see where to change the color of your thread on each needle. Pin this stabilizer "design sheet" right side up to the right side of the garment fabric. If you wish to use charted needlework on clothing and don't want the added stiffness of the stabilizer and paper trapped under the stitches, try transferring the design to a water-soluble stabilizer or a starch-stiffened piece of sheer fabric. Remove the stabilizer or trim the sheer fabric close to the completed stitching.

3. Place the fabric under the needle. Even though you removed the presser foot, still lower the presser bar, and bring the bobbin thread to the surface. Sew three or four stitches in place to lock the stitching, and trim the bobbin thread close to the design sheet.

4. Place a chart needle on top of the design in one color area and, holding it behind and in front of the foot, free-motion zigzag the needle in place within the color area, drawing the work toward you slowly. See **Diagram 1.** When you reach the end of the color area on the needle, free-motion satin stitch over the needle to fill in the color area. If an area is interrupted by another color, simply move the work over that area without stitching or cutting the threads and begin stitching again.

5. You can substitute a regular satin stitch for the free-motion stitching, but you will need to work with the feed dogs engaged. Guide the chart needles between the toes of an all-purpose or open-toe embroidery presser foot or under a groove in a three- or five-groove pintuck foot. You may need to reduce the pressure on the presser foot to achieve success with this alternate stitching method.

6. As you complete all colors on a needle, place the next needle as close as possible to the first so that the background fabric will not show. When all the needles are in use, remove the first needle and continue. See **Diagram 2.** (You must always have a needle next to the one you're stitching over, except for the first needle you stitch over.) Continue stitching in the same manner, completing one color at a time.

   When you're ready to change to the next thread color, lock the first thread by changing to a straight stitch and stitching in place several times.

Diagram 2

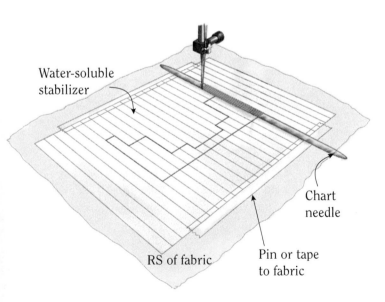

Water-soluble stabilizer

Chart needle

RS of fabric

Pin or tape to fabric

Diagram 1

7. With an unthreaded needle, straight stitch around the completed design to perforate the paper for easy removal. Tear away the paper and stabilizer around the outer edges of the design.

Circular Stitching

 *Piping, couching, twin-needle stitching, decorative stitching—you can do them all in perfect circles, even if your sewing machine doesn't have a special attachment. The technique is so simple that you can easily use it for straight or decorative stitching.*

Perfectly stitched circles have many applications, from basting a fabric circle for covering a button to satin stitching deep, elegant, half-circle scallops along the hem of a linen dress.

Get Ready

Needle	Appropriate for fabric and thread
Thread	Appropriate for fabric and needle
Notions	Pencil eraser, sharp household tack, sturdy tape, water-soluble marking pen

Get Set

Presser foot	All-purpose, or appropriate for decorative stitching
Stitch	Straight or decorative
Stitch length	As desired
Needle tension	Loosen one or two settings

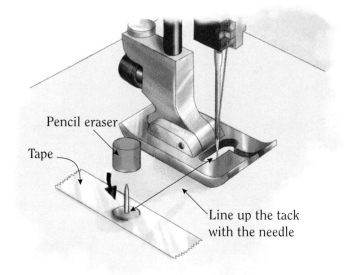

Pencil eraser

Tape

Line up the tack with the needle

Sew

1. Mark the center of the circle on the right side of the fabric in the intended location.

2. Measure and mark the desired circle radius (half the diameter) from the needle to the left or right on the bed of the machine. Tape a tack, point up, at the mark. For perfect circles, the tack point must be exactly in line with the needle. To make half-circles, mark complete circles along a straight edge with a compass, then stitch only halfway around each one.

3. Place a pencil eraser on the point to protect yourself and your fabric from scrapes and snags. See the diagram above.

4. Take the pencil eraser off the tack. With the fabric right side up, position the center dot over the tack and push the fabric into place. Replace the eraser. Take a few short stitches in place to secure your threads.

5. Adjust for the desired straight or decorative stitch and sew around the circle, using your hands to lightly guide the fabric and allowing the feed dogs to do most of the work. Stitch at a consistent speed, especially when using a decorative stitch. Stop stitching when you reach the starting point, and leave a long thread tail to tie off on the wrong side of the fabric.

Cord and Cording

Decorative cord adds visual interest and appeal, but sometimes it's difficult to find exactly what you need. With the variety of decorative threads and interesting trims and yarns available today, you can now make your own one-of-kind cord.

Choose from several machine and serging methods featured here to dress up the simplest garment or embellish an existing one.

Machine techniques for attaching ready-made and custom-made cord are discussed in "Braid" on page 92 and "Couching" on page 114.

BASIC CORDED EDGE

To strengthen a wide satin-stitched edge, sew cord along the already-stitched edge and zigzag it in place. If you use a contrasting cord and a contrasting thread, the results are even more decorative. It's a pretty finish for a hem edge where you don't want the added bulk of a hem allowance, making it a great treatment for single-layer collars, pockets, and cuffs.

Get Ready

Needle	Appropriate for fabric and thread
Thread	All-purpose
Notions	Water-soluble stabilizer; one or more strands of pearl cotton, cord, or gimp

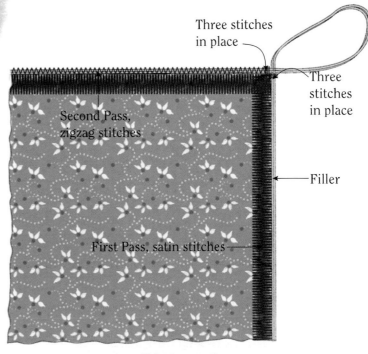

Three stitches in place

Second Pass, zigzag stitches

Three stitches in place

Filler

First Pass, satin stitches

Diagram 1

Get Set

	First Pass	Second Pass
Presser foot	Satin, Satinedge, or open-toe embroidery	Braiding
Stitch	Satin	Zigzag
Stitch length	50 spi (0.5 to 0.8 mm)	15 spi (1.5 mm)
Stitch width	Medium (3 mm)	Narrow (1 mm)

Sew

1. Satin stitch ⅜ inch (9 mm) from the fabric's raw edge and trim the fabric close to the stitches. Use a water-soluble stabilizer underneath to prevent tunneling, or use the Satinedge foot and stitch over the edge instead.

2. Change your thread and machine settings as indicated for the Second Pass. With the start of the fabric under the presser foot, insert the pearl cotton or other filler through the braiding foot, and encase the filler in the stitching.

3. To turn a corner, stop at the corner, disengage the feed dogs, take three stitches in place, and pivot the fabric. Pull out a large loop of the filler, and take three stitches in place. See **Diagram 1** on page 107. Engage the feed dogs and continue to stitch, pulling on the cord to remove the loop. Adjust the corner stitches to cover the cord.

Make It Easy

Very thin fabrics like the sheer tricot used to make Seams Great are sometimes difficult to get started on the serger. The problem disappears when you machine baste a 1 × 2-inch (2.5 × 5-cm) piece of tear-away stabilizer at the beginning of the strip and start serging on the stabilizer. The stubborn fabric has to follow.

BLINDSTITCHED CORDED EDGE

You can add stability, durability, and dimension to the finished edges of collars, cuffs, tucks, and hemlines by using a sewing machine decorative pattern or utility stitch to catch the cord along an edge.

Get Ready

Needle	Appropriate for fabric and thread
Thread	Transparent or all-purpose if you want the stitching to show
Notions	Four to six strands of embroidery floss, fine cord, fine yarn, or pearl cotton for the trim

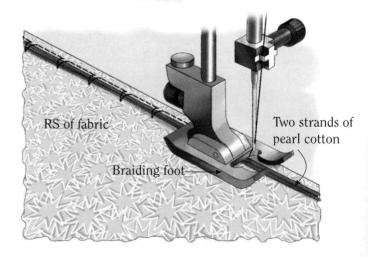

RS of fabric

Two strands of pearl cotton

Braiding foot

Diagram 2

Get Set

Presser foot	Cording, braiding, or open-toe embroidery
Stitch	Blind or picot
Stitch length	10 spi (2.5 mm)
Stitch width	Adjust to suit trim width

Sew

1. Place the trim along the finished edge of the garment or garment part. You can use single or multiple lengths for the trim, as desired.

2. Arrange the garment under the machine and adjust the stitch width so that the needle straight stitches into the fabric along the garment edge and it swings all the way over the trim. Stitch in this position, catching the cord inside each zigzag stitch. See **Diagram 2** on the opposite page.

Workroom Secret

If you have difficulty preventing the cord from catching in the stitching, switch to another type of presser foot. Improvise and experiment, keeping in mind that you can try using a presser foot for a purpose that wasn't originally intended. A piping foot, such as the Pearls 'N Piping or other presser foot that has a round "tunnel" on the bottom, is quite suitable. The foot tunnel keeps the cord in line while you feed and stitch over the cord. Just make sure that your cord flows smoothly under the presser foot that you select. One less worry!

MONK'S CORD

If your sewing machine has an exterior bobbin winder you can use it to twist favorite threads and yarns into eye-catching trim commonly called monk's cord. Use monk's cord for decorative accents, couching, corded belts, drawstrings, tassels, and tassel loops.

Get Ready

Bobbin thread	Decorative thread, such as metallic or heavy rayon and assorted lightweight yarns; mix two or more for interesting effects
Notion	Bobbin with a hole on one side*

Get Set

Stitch	Set up to wind a bobbin

*This technique only works with bobbins that have at least one hole on one side, and you're limited to the number of strands that will fit through the hole. If the bobbin for your machine doesn't have a hole, test bobbins from other machines. They may work on your machine's winder.

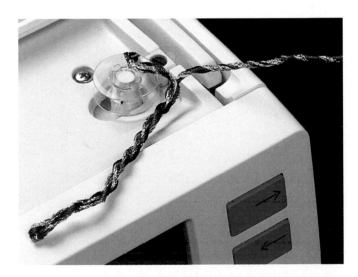

Your monk's cord will only be about 18 inches (46 cm) long unless a sewing buddy steps on the foot pedal while you hold on to longer twisting strands.

Sew

1. Cut 2-yard-long strands of the desired decorative thread, serger chain, or yarn, combining as desired. Fold the group of strands in half and thread the loop through a bobbin hole, then bring the free ends through the loop and tighten. See **Diagram 3.**

Bobbin

Diagram 3

2. Place the bobbin on the bobbin winder, and seat it properly for winding.

3. Holding the decorative strands taut and at an angle, step on the foot pedal to spin the bobbin until the strands are firmly twisted together. They're twisted tightly enough when you release tension on the strands and they kink back on themselves.

4. Holding the twisted cord at the center and at the bobbin, allow the cord to twist back on itself, carefully working out any kinks. While still holding the twisted strands together at the bobbin, tie a knot in the twisted cord as close to the bobbin as possible. Cut the cord from the bobbin.

PUFFY CORD

Fat, puffy serger cord makes great button loops, decorative belt loops, frog closures, and couching trim. It has strength and volume. If you couch the finished cord to attach it to your garment, it will flatten somewhat.

Get Ready

Fabric	Lightweight jersey or sheer tricot knit*
Needle	Standard
Needle thread	All-purpose
UL thread	Heavy decorative thread, such as Decor 6 rayon
LL thread	All-purpose

Get Set

Presser foot	Standard or beading
Stitch	Three-thread overlock
Stitch length	Short†
Stitch width	Wide enough to stitch over the fabric tube without catching in it
Tension	Tighten the lower looper so stitches roll slightly

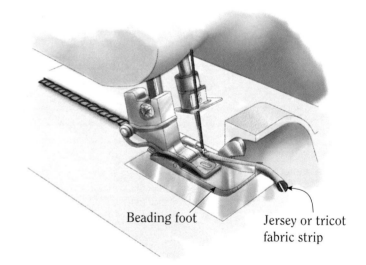

Beading foot

Jersey or tricot fabric strip

Diagram 4

*For finer cord, substitute ⅝-inch (1.5-cm)-wide Seams Great or Seams Saver tricot.
†Use a satin stitch length, which will vary according to the thread and fabric thickness.

Serge

1. Cut a 1-inch (2.5-cm)-wide strip of tricot or jersey knit across the fabric width (the stretchiest direction of the knit), or use sheer tricot for finer finished cord.

2. Stretch the fabric strip so it rolls into a tube.

3. Place the fabric tube in the beading foot, take a few stitches to get it started, then pull the fabric tube taut while you serge to cover it with stitching. Take care not to catch the fabric with the needle. See Diagram 4 on the opposite page. If a beading foot isn't available, place the fabric tube between the needle and the knife, over the foot, then under the back.

Sharp Notion

Even if you don't own a serger you can make puffy cord, although the stitch coverage won't be as good. Use ¾-inch (2-cm)-wide strips of lingerie tricot cut on the crosswise grain. Set the sewing machine for a medium width zigzag stitch (about 3 mm) and 6 spi (4 mm). Attach the open-toe embroidery foot or try the Pearls 'N Piping foot. Zigzag over the strip while continuing to stretch it, with one hand in front and the other behind the presser foot.

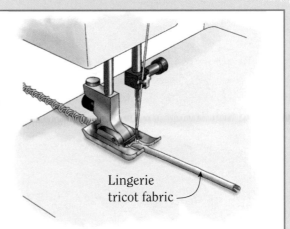

Lingerie tricot fabric

ROLLED CORDED EDGE

Like the "Blindstitched Corded Edge" on page 108, this technique also adds stability, durability, and dimension to a finished edge on a garment. Yet the rolled corded edge is fascinating because it's created on a serger. It's also great because it's a fast way to finish an edge, such as a hem, since you're making a rolled edge at the same time that you're cording it. If you like attaching your cord with heavier decorative threads, this is the technique to use.

You'll find it much easier to make a rolled corded edge if you use the differential feed on your serger. However, it's still possible to achieve nice stitching even if your machine doesn't have this feature.

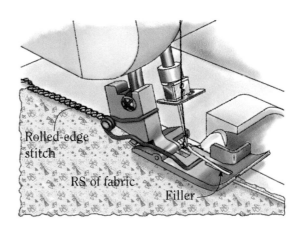

Rolled-edge stitch

RS of fabric

Filler

Diagram 5

Get Ready

Needle	Appropriate for fabric and thread
Needle thread	All-purpose serger
UL thread	Decorative or all-purpose serger
LL thread	All-purpose serger
Notions	One or more strands of pearl cotton to use as a filler

Get Set

Presser foot	Beading, cording, or standard with a tape slot
Stitch	Narrow rolled-edge
Stitch length	Short, adjusted for good cord coverage
Stitch width	Narrow
Differential feed	0.07, lower on stretchy edges

Serge

1. Position one or more strands of pearl cotton filler along the garment edge. For easier stitching, it's best to use a specialized presser foot. Guide the filler into a beading or cording foot, or through the tape slot in the toe of a standard foot.

2. Adjust the stitch so that there's enough thread to cover the cord and roll the fabric edge correctly. Serge over the filler. See **Diagram 5** on page 111.

Make It Easy
Rolled edges that won't roll can often be tamed with the right thread choice. Try woolly nylon, transparent polyester, or nylon thread in the lower looper to encourage a better, tighter rolled edge.

STITCH-WRAPPED CORD

Akin to couching, stitch wrapping at your sewing machine is a nifty way to encase cord in multilayered colored thread. After covering plain cord with colorful, decorative thread using free-motion zigzagging, use the cord to embellish your garment, shaping and couching it to the fabric surface. Imagine it couched onto a rough-and-ready denim jacket.

Get Ready

Needle	Embroidery or topstitching, 90/14
Thread	Embroidery cotton; metallic and rayon in assorted colors
Notions	Water-soluble stabilizer; piping cord or solid-color round cord; fine wire, #28 or #32 (optional)

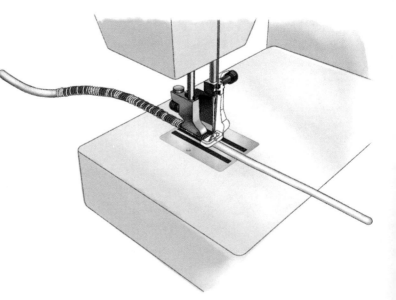

Diagram 6

Get Set

Presser foot	Darning
Stitch	Zigzag
Stitch length	0
Stitch width	Medium or wider, to clear the cord width
Feed dogs	Disengaged or covered

Sew

1. Fill the bobbin with metallic thread and use rayon or cotton thread in the needle.

2. Place water-soluble stabilizer under the cord and take a few stitches in the cord, to anchor the thread. Hold the cord taut behind the presser foot with your left hand and in front of the foot with your right hand, resting it on the sewing machine table. Feed the cord with your fingers. Stitch fast and feed quickly for free-motion zigzagging. Stitch fast and feed slowly for satin stitch coverage. Zigzag over the cord once, then change the needle thread color and stitch again. Continue in the same manner with several more

> # Sharp Notion
> Free-motion satin stitch over finer cord for a softer trim than the one you get with stitch-wrapped cord. Use a decorative needle thread to match the filler and a contrasting thread in the bobbin.

thread colors. See **Diagram 6** on the opposite page.

3. To build up spots of color, free-motion satin stitch (closely spaced zigzagging) where desired with matching thread in the needle and bobbin. If you want more of the bobbin thread to pull up along the cord edges, try tightening the needle tension a little. Sew the cord to your fabric.

4. If desired, catch a fine wire under the stitches with the cord to create a flexible trim that you can shape into buttons, pins, earrings, or free-form, three-dimensional embellishments.

Make It Easy
When blindstitching cord around a pocket that is already attached, place the pocket to the left of the needle so that the straight stitches go into the garment next to the pocket edge and the zigzag stitch goes over the cord and into the pocket.

When working on a collar, place the work to the right of the needle, so that the straight stitches go into the collar and the zigzag stitch goes over the cord. For easier handling, you can place the collar to the left of the needle and substitute a picot stitch—or engage the mirror-image function so the zigzag in the blindstitch swings to the right.

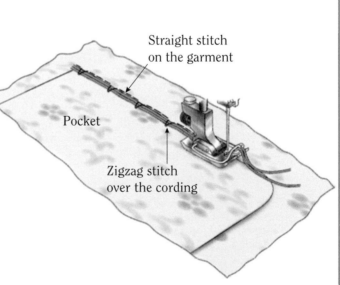

Straight stitch on the garment

Pocket

Zigzag stitch over the cording

Couching

You may know this age-old stitching technique as passementerie or scrollwork.

While couching is traditionally done on the right side of the garment with a straight or zigzag stitch, today's machines and special presser feet make it possible to use a wide variety of stitches to attach trim to a fabric surface. You can also stitch from the wrong side, with the couching material in the bobbin. This allows you to machine stitch thick threads that won't fit through the eye of a needle.

BLINDSTITCH COUCHING

Blindstitch couching has an array of applications. For a distinctive look, capture pearl cotton or other fine cord or yarn at the hemline of a tailored garment. In this sewing machine technique, the cord is fed onto the fabric through the "scroll" of the rolled hem presser foot or a braiding foot while stitching.

Get Ready

Needle	Appropriate for fabric
Needle thread	All-purpose or transparent
Bobbin thread	All-purpose
Notions	#3 or #5 pearl cotton, six-strand embroidery floss, or other fine cord or yarn; water-soluble basting thread (optional); tapestry needle or fine metal crochet hook; seam sealant (optional)

Get Set

Presser foot	Rolled hem or braiding
Stitch	Blindstitch
Stitch length	Short
Stitch width	Narrow
Needle tension	Loosen to balance

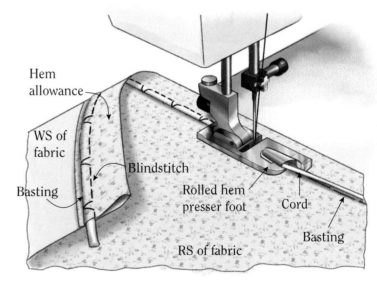

Diagram 1

Sew

1. Experiment with the stitch settings to make sure that the zigzag stitch clears the cord. If desired, machine-baste a placement line with water-soluble basting thread in the needle. For a hem application only, press up the hem allowance and machine baste the hem in place, stitching from the inside of the garment.

2. Insert the cord into the scroll between the toes of the rolled hem foot or into the clip of a braiding foot. Stitch on the fabric right side so that the cord lies next to the basting placement stitches and the zigzag swings over both, making slight indentations in the cord. See **Diagram 1** on the opposite page. It will look as though the cord were in the needle for a row of stitching.

3. To turn corners, stop with the needle down at the end of the left swing of the zigzag. Raise the foot, pivot the fabric, pull the cord toward you, and continue.

4. At the end of the stitching, cut the threads and the cord, remove the work from the machine, and use a tapestry needle (or a fine metal crochet hook on sheer fabrics) to draw the cord ends to the wrong side of the garment. Take several hand stitches through the hem allowance to secure and hide the tails, or tie them in an overhand knot and treat the ends with a seam sealant.

5. Remove the basting thread. Since it's water-soluble, you can do this by spritzing the stitches with water.

BOBBIN COUCHING

Simulate the look of couching on your sewing machine without using a special foot. Wind your couching material onto the bobbin, then stitch with the fabric wrong side up. You can use materials that won't fit through the needle's eye.

Get Ready

Needle	Appropriate for fabric and thread
Needle thread	Transparent or decorative
Bobbin thread	Fine knitting yarn, narrow silk ribbon, pearl cotton, or ribbon floss
Notions	Pencil (optional); water-soluble or iron-on, tear-away stabilizer; machine embroidery hoop (optional); tapestry needle; seam sealant

Get Set

Stitch	Zigzag
Stitch length	8 spi (3.5 mm)
Stitch width	Medium
Tension	Loose (see Step 2)
Presser foot	Open-toe embroidery, appliqué, or zigzag

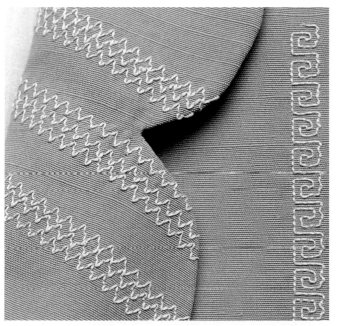

Bobbin couching with a decorative stitch setting is an easy way to embellish anything from a jacket lapel to a sleeve cuff.

Sew

1. Hand-wind the couching material onto the bobbin (or wind slowly and carefully by machine). To machine-wind the couching material onto the bobbin, bypass the tension post for the bobbin-winder and pinch the thread between your thumb and forefinger instead. If you can't put the thread on the spool pin, hold it on a pencil. See **Diagram 2.**

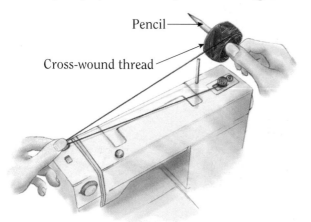

Pencil

Cross-wound thread

Diagram 2

2. Loosen the bobbin tension to allow the heavier threads to pass through the case and flow easily. For thicker materials, you may need to bypass the tension spring. Built-in bobbin cases may have either an adjustable tension screw or a tension bypass hole. Loosen the tension screw in a separate or a built-in bobbin case enough to allow the heavier bobbin thread to pull through the tension spring as easily as normal thread does with balanced tension. When you thread through the bypass hole, there's no tension on the bobbin thread. If the bobbin tension is too loose, the couching material can form unsightly loops that catch and snag. Adjust the needle tension if necessary.

3. Draw your design on the stabilizer. If the design is asymmetrical and the chosen stabilizer is opaque, take the stabilizer to a light source and retrace along the design lines on the reverse side of the stabilizer to create a mirror image.

4. Pin or baste the stabilizer on the fabric's wrong side. Slip both layers under the presser foot with the stabilizer side up. (You may want to use an embroidery hoop to keep the fabric taut.)

5. Lower the presser foot and hand-turn the flywheel to draw the couching material through the fabric. If necessary, thread the couching material into a tapestry needle and bring it through the fabric.

6. Machine sew a few stitches. Stop and check the bobbin-side of the work to make sure you like the results. Stitch the design. See **Diagram 3.**

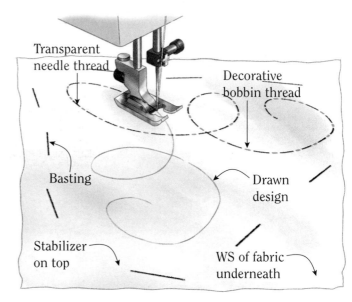

Transparent needle thread

Decorative bobbin thread

Basting

Drawn design

Stabilizer on top

WS of fabric underneath

Diagram 3

7. Remove the stabilizer. Thread the couching material into a tapestry needle and draw it to the wrong side. Knot it securely, treat it with liquid seam sealant, and trim it ½ inch (1.25 cm) from the knot.

Make It Easy

If you really hate adjusting the bobbin tension for specialty threads, treat yourself to an extra bobbin case. Set aside the extra case for use only with difficult threads. You can play with the tension adjustment on the case at will, without worrying about returning to the correct setting for regular sewing. (This works only if your machine has a removable bobbin case.)

FLATLOCK COUCHING

You can use the versatile flatlock stitch to couch narrow trims in straight or gently curving lines. The couching material appears to float on the fabric surface under a "ladder" of needle threads.

Unlike traditional couching, there are no stitches through the couching material. This makes it possible to capture yarns that are too thick to be wrapped around a bobbin for bobbin couching. (See page 115.) The sew-and-serge process is simple: Machine-baste the couching material to the fabric, fold the fabric around it, and flatlock over the fold.

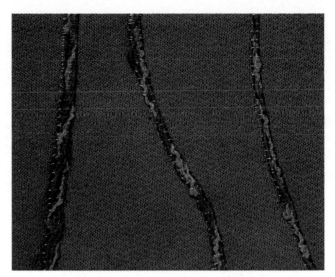

Use transparent thread so that your couching material will "float" on the fabric surface even though it's securely anchored.

Get Ready

	Sewing Machine	Serger
Needle thread	All-purpose or water-soluble	Transparent or decorative*
Bobbin thread	All-purpose, water-soluble basting, or fusible	—
UL thread	—	All-purpose serger
LL thread	—	All-purpose serger
Notions	Water-soluble marking pen; transparent tape; couching material (braid trim, cord, narrow ribbon, or yarn)	

Get Set

	Sewing Machine	Serger
Presser foot	All-purpose	Standard
Stitch	Straight†	Flatlock
Width	—	6 mm
Length	6 spi (4 mm)	6 mm

*If you want the ladder stitches to be visible on top of the couching material, use a decorative thread in the serger needle.

†You can substitute a long, narrow zigzag with a loosened needle tension.

Sew and Serge

1. Select a couching design with only straight or gently curving lines. Trace the design onto the right side of your fabric pattern piece.

2. Tape the couching material on the design lines and machine baste it in place. Fuse-baste difficult couching materials, like thick yarns, in position.

Trace your design on the wrong side of a washable fabric. (Fusing may flatten the couching material a bit.) Thread your machine with fusible thread in the bobbin and water-soluble basting thread in the needle. Machine baste along the design lines on the fabric wrong side. On the right side, fuse the couching material on the stitched lines.

3. Fold the fabric, right sides together, along one of the basted lines of couching material. Serge the fold so that the stitches hang off the fold and the couching material is caught inside the needle stitching. See **Diagram 4.** On curved lines, stop periodically to refold along the basted line.

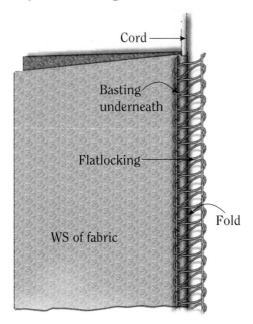

Diagram 4

4. Open the flatlocking. See **Diagram 5.** The couching material appears to float on the surface, held by the transparent ladder of flatlock stitches on top. Remove the basting.

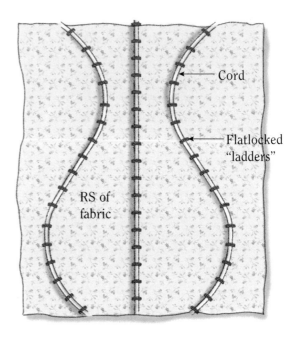

Diagram 5

Make It Easy

You can bobbin couch with a long straight stitch and the needle offset to the right. This is especially effective when working with narrow ribbon. Open decorative stitches, like feathers, waves, and scallops are also appealing.

You may want to experiment with the presser feet. For example, you can do bobbin couching with the darning foot and free-motion embroidery.

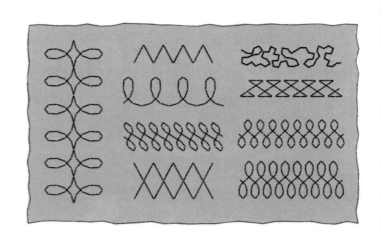

COUCHING BY DESIGN

The appearance of your couching can be dramatically different if you vary the type of stitch you use. And you may be able to use several other types of presser feet for easier positioning. Depending on its thickness, you may be able to substitute any number of other feet.

If you're attaching a thick couching material, try the blindstitch and a sliding (adjustable) zipper foot. Very narrow cord, on the other hand, can be placed under one of the grooves on the bottom of an invisible zipper presser foot. You may also want to try a ¼-inch presser foot, also called a patchwork foot. Set up the couching material so that it rides between the toes of the foot, and use a very narrow zigzag stitch.

Hassle-free alignment is also possible with either a rolled hem or all-purpose zigzag presser foot, or even transparent tape. If you want to use the rolled-hem presser foot to guide your cord, fit the yarn or cord into the scroll. On the zigzag presser foot, the cord might ride between the toes. If you own neither of these feet, place transparent tape across the toes of an open-toe presser foot. Pierce it with the needle, then enlarge the hole to fit the cord diameter.

These suggestions for alternative uses for presser feet aren't all-inclusive because there are hundreds of presser feet on the market. When you have a few minutes to experiment at your machine, but not enough time to start a project, you may want to explore the other presser feet and stitches available for your sewing machine.

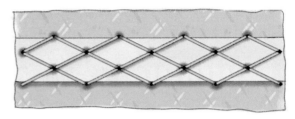

Select narrow ribbon that's the same width as your honeycomb stitch, then secure the ribbon to the fabric by stitching across and through it.

A bolder effect is achieved by stitching across your couching material with a rickrack stitch, also known as a tri-motion zigzag stitch.

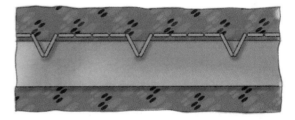

The blindstitch is an effective method for attaching rounder material to a fabric. Let the zigzag stitch just catch the couching material, stitching through it and the surface underneath.

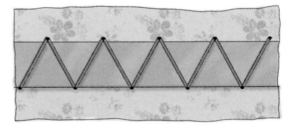

Almost any couching material can be secured with the workhorse of sewing—the zigzag stitch. The couching is flashy with decorative thread in the needle or practically invisible with monofilament thread.

Creases

Permanent creases are a nice way to finish garments made of natural fiber fabrics that lose creases in the laundry. They also add a finished touch to polyester knit or gabardines. To make permanent creases, you can use either the serger or sewing machine.

Superb imitation umbrella pleats can be made with both pintuck and tuck crease techniques. For this accordion-style effect, stitch every second crease on the wrong side of the fabric.

PINTUCK CREASE

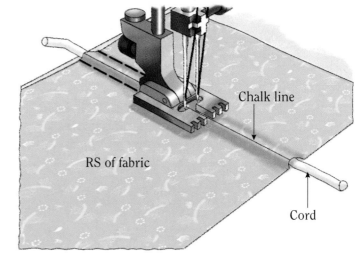

Here's a really practical use for twin-needle stitching on your sewing machine. Stitch extremely tiny tucks to make permanent creases wherever you want them in a garment. Adding permanently stitched creases to trousers is a great way to prevent the dry cleaner from pressing creases in the wrong place. Adjusting the stitch length and adding a cord intensifies the stitching for a more pronounced crease.

Get Ready

Needle	Twin*
Thread	Appropriate for fabric, match color to garment
Notion	Gimp or pearl cotton cording

Get Set

Presser foot	Pintuck†
Stitch	Straight
Stitch length	12 to 20 spi (2 to 1 mm)
Tension	Tighten

*Needle size and distance between the needles depend on fabric weight. Use wider-spaced needles for heavier fabrics.
†If you don't have a pintuck foot, use a buttonhole foot and a half-right or right needle position so the crease will form under the right channel on the bottom of the foot.

Sew

1. Chalk-mark the desired crease line. (For pants, line up the outer leg seam and inseam on the ironing board and press lightly, ending at the bottom of a dart or blending into the fold of the front pleat in trousers.)

2. Insert cording into the crease on the underside of the fabric.

"TUCK" CREASES

Serging along a folded edge creates a tuck. When you use the narrowest rolled edge stitch or a very narrow flatlock stitch in this manner, the result is permanent. To create a textured fabric, use decorative thread in the upper looper, then make side-by-side rows, spacing them as desired.

Get Ready

Needle	Appropriate for fabric and thread
Thread	All-purpose serger

Get Set

Presser foot	Standard or blind hem
Stitch	Narrow rolled edge
Stitch length	Medium
Stitch width	Narrow
Tension	Balanced
Knives	Disengaged, if possible

Serge

1. Press the crease with wrong sides together.

2. Adjust for a narrow rolled edge, testing on scraps to determine the desired length and width.

3. Serge over the fold, being careful not to cut it if you can't disengage the knives. Or, use the blind hem foot to guide the fold to avoid cutting it.

3. Stitch, centering the chalk line between the two needles. See the diagram on the opposite page. The pintuck rides under a channel in the sole of the foot. (Without the channel, you get only two rows of evenly spaced topstitching.) For a pronounced tuck, use a shorter stitch length.

A rolled-edge crease (left), has a more rounded shape than one created with a narrow flatlock using a tightened needle tension (right).

Sharp Notion

To flatlock a crease, adjust the machine for a normal, but narrow, stitch. Then tighten the needle tension slightly so that the flatlock stitch does not open completely flat, but instead creates a tiny tuck, or crease.

Cutwork

Cutwork is a traditional needlework technique, originally done by hand, to create delicate detailing on household linens and blouses. Bars of fine stitching connect "cut out" sections of the design to the remaining fabric.

Now, with the help of your machine, you can add cutwork to a cuff, collar, pocket, skirt hem, or the upper part of a bodice using one of the speedier methods included here. You can even use your serger to simulate the look of cutwork on your garment.

CHEATER CUTWORK

Celebrate the tradition of cutwork without all the fuss by indulging in a faster version of this technique. The secret is stitching over the design lines in a printed motif. Choose a bold print to outline with sewing machine stitching, then cut away negative spaces between the motifs. If the negative spaces are small, you probably don't need to fill them. Embellish the area surrounding simple cutwork shapes with decorative machine stitches for added interest. This is a great opportunity to play with the decorative stitch options on your machine.

Why design a motif when you can take a shortcut? A printed fabric was the starting point for the cutwork on this blouse.

Get Ready	First Pass	Second Pass	Third Pass (optional)
Fabric	Closely woven, with a bold print design	—	—
Needle	Appropriate for fabric and thread	Appropriate for fabric and thread	Appropriate for fabric and thread
Needle thread	White cotton embroidery	White cotton embroidery	Rayon embroidery
Bobbin thread	White cotton embroidery	White cotton embroidery	Rayon embroidery
Notions	Tailor's chalk or water-soluble marking pen; water-soluble or iron-away stabilizer; machine embroidery hoop; embroidery or appliqué scissors; iron-on, tear-away stabilizer (optional)		

Get Set	First Pass	Second Pass	Third Pass (optional)
Presser foot	Darning	Darning	Appliqué or open-toe embroidery
Stitch	Straight	Zigzag	Satin stitch
Stitch length	15 spi (1.5 mm)	15 spi (1.5 mm)	12 spi (2 mm)
Stitch width	—	Narrow	Wide*
Needle tension	Looser	Looser	Looser
Feed dogs	Disengaged, covered, or 0 stitch length	Disengaged, covered, or 0 stitch length	—

Make the stitching wide enough to cover the previous stitching.

Sew

1. On your print fabric, mark the motifs that you want to outline with stitching. Since cutwork has open spaces, you next decide which stitch-outlined motifs will have open spaces. Place a mark on the fabric in the spaces that you'll be cutting away after they're outlined with stitching. If you plan to make Richelieu bars, mark their locations on the fabric, but don't draw the lines for the bars.

2. Use two layers of a water-soluble or iron-away stabilizer underneath the fabric, and place the layers in the embroidery hoop.

3. Place the hoop under the presser foot, lower the foot, and use free-motion stitching to straight stitch along all the design lines, except the lines for the Richelieu bars.

4. Change your thread and machine settings as indicated for the Second Pass, and free-motion zigzag over the straight stitching. See **Diagram 1**. If you don't plan to add Richelieu bars, remove the stabilizer, and cut away the marked fabric. Your cutwork is finished. If you do plan to add Richelieu bars, continue with Steps 5 through 7.

5. Remove the hoop from the machine. With the fabric and stabilizer layers still in the hoop, cut away the fabric in one of the open areas that you plan to fill with bars, leaving the stabilizer behind.

6. Draw the lines for each Richelieu bar on the

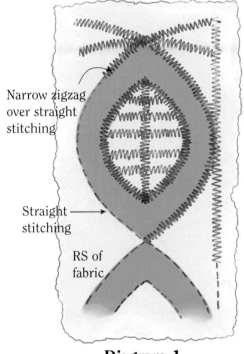

Narrow zigzag over straight stitching

Straight stitching

RS of fabric

Diagram 1

exposed layer of stabilizer, adjust your machine settings, and make the bars by referring to "Richelieu Embroidery" on page 74. Repeat for each open area where you want bars.

7. Adjust for the Third Pass, and finish the cut edges by satin stitching on top of the previous stitches to enclose all the raw edges. Remove the stabilizer.

8. If you plan to cut along the print lines for the bottom edge of a yoke or flap, back the cut edge with iron-on, tear-away stabilizer and satin stitch over the edge. Remove the stabilizer.

Cutwork Appliqué

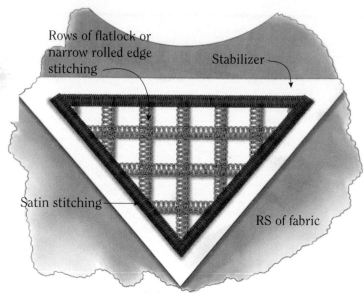

Rows of flatlock or narrow rolled edge stitching

Stabilizer

Satin stitching

RS of fabric

Diagram 2

Richelieu bars made on a serger? You bet! It's fast and easy thanks to the arrival of water-soluble stabilizer. The stabilizer acts the part of the appliqué fabric so you can stitch crisscrossed bars of serger thread. Once attached to the cutwork design area, the stabilizer is dissolved. Sound intriguing? It is—and it's fun, too. You could even use this technique to embellish a completed garment with simple cutwork motifs.

Get Ready

	Serger	Sewing Machine
Fabric	Washable	—
Needle	Appropriate for fabric and thread	Embroidery
Needle thread	All-purpose or rayon	Embroidery cotton or rayon
Bobbin thread	—	Embroidery cotton or rayon
UL thread	Decorative	—
LL thread	All-purpose or rayon	—
Notions	Water-soluble marking pen, water-soluble stabilizer, appliqué or embroidery scissors, tear-away stabilizer (optional), two press cloths	

Get Set

	Serger	Sewing Machine
Presser foot	Standard	Embroidery
Stitch	Flatlock or narrow rolled edge	Satin
Stitch length	Appropriate for thread	24 spi (0.5 mm)
Stitch width	Appropriate for thread	Narrow; slightly wider for the sewing machine stitching

Serge and Sew

1. Preshrink your fabric. Draw the cutwork shapes on the fabric pattern piece, using the water-soluble marking pen. Trace the shapes onto the water-soluble stabilizer, leaving at least 1 inch (2.5 cm) of space around each shape.

2. Cut out each stabilizer shape with 1-inch (2.5-cm)-wide margins. Draw a grid of straight lines inside each stabilizer shape. The more lines you draw, the more stable the finished piece.

3. Fold one of the stabilizer shapes and serge along the lines, using the desired thread and tested stitch. Don't cut the folded edge, but don't worry if you nick it now and then. Repeat for all of the horizontal and vertical lines.

4. Open out and flatten—but don't iron—the completed shape. Pin it right side up on the right side of the garment. At the sewing machine, satin stitch the shape to the garment along the traced outline of

the shape. See **Diagram 2** on the opposite page. Trim away the 1-inch (2.5-cm)-wide stabilizer margins close to the stitching.

5. On the wrong side, trim away the garment fabric between the rolled-edge stitching lines. If desired for added stability, place a piece of tear-away stabilizer on the underside of the work. On the right side, satin stitch over the original satin stitching, using a slightly wider stitch. Tear away any stabilizer.

6. Place the garment in cool water to dissolve the stabilizer. Air dry or iron dry between two press cloths.

Sharp Notion

For a little glitz, place interfacing-backed lamé on top of the fabric and behind the stitched stabilizer shape in Step 4. Then complete the remaining steps, cutting away only the garment fabric, completing the satin stitching, and removing the stabilizer.

LAYERED CUTWORK

You might recognize this as a form of reverse appliqué—an age-old embellishment technique. Geometric shapes are stitched onto layered fabrics, then material is cut away to reveal fabrics in different areas of the design.

It's easy to do this technique on the sewing machine, and the designs can be simple or more complex. If you use a print fabric on top, you can stitch the layers together following the design lines on the print. Don't be afraid to mix fabric types and colors.

Consider lamé, lightweight lace, tulle, or other sheer fabric for one of your layers, and keep in mind the suitability of the weight and drape of the layers for the garment style. Go for variety because you'll cut away one or more layers within each stitched shape.

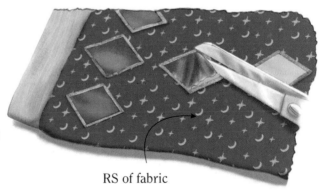

RS of fabric

Diagram 3

Get Ready	First Pass	Second Pass
Fabrics	Three or four fabrics, prints or solids	
Needle	Appropriate for fabric and thread	Appropriate for fabric and thread
Thread	Appropriate for fabric and needle	Appropriate for fabric and needle
Notions	Water-soluble marking pen, water-soluble stabilizer, machine embroidery hoop, appliqué or embroidery scissors	

Get Set

	First Pass	Second Pass
Presser foot	Darning	Appliqué or open-toe embroidery
Stitch	Zigzag	Satin
Stitch length	15 spi (1.5 mm)	12 spi (2 mm)
Stitch width	Narrow	Wide*
Needle tension	Slightly looser	—
Feed dogs	Disengaged or covered	Engaged

Make the stitching wide enough to cover the previous stitching.

Sew

1. Stack the fabrics, right sides up. Depending on the desired look for the finished garment, place the base fabric on top, or at the bottom, of the layers. Mark the top layer with the desired geometric shapes or draw the shapes on a piece of water-soluble stabilizer and place this on top of the layered fabrics.

2. Place the layers in an embroidery hoop and free-motion zigzag stitch around the design motifs. Change to the Second Press settings and stitch again. Cut away one or more layers within each motif to expose the underlying fabrics as desired. See **Diagram 3** on page 125.

SUCCESSFUL STRATEGIES FOR AVOIDING SKIPPED STITCHES

Stay straight. Make sure that the needle is sharp, free of burrs, and isn't bent. To check if it's straight, hold the flat side of the needle shank on a hard, flat surface at eye level. Make sure the needle lies parallel to the surface and isn't bent.

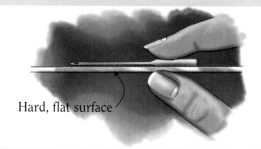

Hard, flat surface

Keep clean. If you have stitched over basting tape or other gummy surfaces, clean the needle with a cotton ball and alcohol.

Play matchmaker. Use the right needle and presser foot for the fabric and stitch that you're using.

Do it right. Make sure the machine is threaded correctly and the needle is inserted properly.

Tame dust bunnies. Check for, and remove, lint in the tension discs and in the bobbin case and bobbin-case area.

Stay tense. Adjust the pressure on the presser foot if needed (if your machine has adjustable pressure knobs) and set the tension for a balanced stitch.

Pretreat. Toss washable fabrics into the washer and dryer to remove sizing that can cause the needle to stick.

Shop wisely. Use high-quality thread.

Switch plates. Change the needle plate to the straight stitch plate for knits and lightweight fabrics (for straight stitching only).

Get help. If all else fails, have the machine serviced. Skipped stitches can be caused by faulty timing in the stitching mechanisms or a damaged hook in the bobbin mechanism. These are mechanical problems that require the attention of a trained machine technician.

Drawn Thread Work

Exposed lengthwise threads in a strip of even-weave fabric are drawn together into lacy columns by using free-motion embroidery on your sewing machine. The result is a band of trim that's ready to insert in your garment. It's the perfect edge accent for a linen pocket or cuff, or you can position it just above the bottom edge of a full skirt.

Like many of the decorative machine techniques in this book, drawn thread work has its roots in traditional needlework, but it's faster and surprisingly easy.

Get Ready

Fabric	Even-weave with a heavier lengthwise yarn (medium to heavyweight linens and cottons)
Needle	Embroidery, size 70/10 or 80/12
Thread	Machine embroidery cotton or rayon embroidery, metallic, or rayon
Notions	Embroidery scissors, tweezers, machine embroidery hoop, seam ripper

Get Set

	First Pass	Second Pass
Presser foot	All-purpose	Darning
Stitch	Straight	Zigzag
Stitch length	10 spi (2.5 mm)	0
Stitch width	0	Medium
Needle tension	Balanced	Lower by one or two settings for smoother stitches
Feed dogs	Engaged	Disengaged or covered

Sew

1. Begin with a strip of even-weave fabric several inches longer than the desired length of trim and wide enough to fit in the embroidery hoop. Cut the strip across the fabric width on the crosswise grain. The strip's lighter, crosswise threads will be pulled out of the fabric, and the lacy columns in the finished strip will be perpendicular to the crosswise grain. Mark the desired finished trim width in the center of the strip. Include a seam allowance outside both ends of the desired finished width. Create a "line" by pulling out a crosswise thread along the entire length of the fabric at each mark.

2. Staystitch just outside both lines. Remove the horizontal threads between the staystitching rows to expose the lengthwise threads. See the diagram below. After you've removed several threads, it's easier to pull out the remaining threads with tweezers. After removing the threads, place the strip in the embroidery hoop so it's taut.

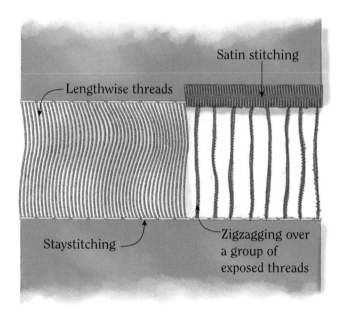

Satin stitching

Lengthwise threads

Staystitching

Zigzagging over a group of exposed threads

3. Adjust the machine for the Second Pass, and place the hoop under the darning foot. Draw the bobbin thread to the surface and lower the presser foot.

4. Beginning at one end of the open area, hold onto the thread tails and zigzag from the top to the bottom edge over several exposed, lengthwise fabric threads. Use a seam ripper or other pointed tool to help separate the threads and push them toward the needle, if necessary. Run the machine at a moderate to fast speed while you move the hoop slowly toward you to cover the threads.

5. When you reach the bottom of the "grouping" of exposed threads, move the hoop horizontally to make a few stitches on, and parallel to, the staystitching. To start the next "bar," move the hoop toward you and zigzag over the next bundle of threads. (You'll be stitching "backward," from the

bottom to the top of the next group of threads. Do not worry if you miss a thread now and then.)

6. Repeat Steps 4 and 5 until you have created stitched thread bundles along the length of the fabric strip. Remove the hoop and rehoop the strip as needed. Carefully clip any stray threads that were not caught in a vertical bar.

7. Free-motion satin stitch over the upper and lower edges of the drawn thread work to encase the raw edge and cover the staystitching. For more stitch control, you can substitute a standard satin stitch and an embroidery foot. You can also cord the satin stitch for a more pronounced edge above and below the lace you create.

8. Cut the excess fabric away from each side of the completed strip, leaving a seam allowance on each side.

Sharp Notion

For a cut-on serged casing, follow Step 4 on page 130. If necessary, trim the casing turn-under so it measures the width of the elastic from the fold line to the raw edge plus one seam allowance width. Quarter-mark the raw edge of the casing allowance, then complete Steps 7 through 11.

With a minor variation you can use this technique to attach swimwear elastic to bathing suit leg openings. Follow the steps for the cut-on serged casing, but don't trim the casing turn-under allowance to match the elastic width. Instead, position the inner edge of the elastic at the casing fold line, and allow the serger to cut away the excess allowance to the right of the elastic as you stitch. Use woolly nylon in the needle and loopers for wearing comfort against your skin. Fold the elastic to the interior of the garment and topstitch with a twin needle.

Elastic

Instructions for sewing machine elastic insertion procedures are easy to find. But serger techniques are less known, even though they give better results. Of particular note is the stretch piping, which is shown on surplice (top) of the bodysuit featured in this illustration.

Elastic application on the serger eliminates the aggravation often associated with threading the elastic through the casing, not to mention the bunched fabric and twisted elastic that typically results from most machine applications.

ELASTIC CASING

This is the best serge casing method. The secret, using elastic thread in the bobbin at the final step, eliminates the popped stitches that are common in elasticized casings. While the technique is mostly used in knit garments, it also works with woven fabrics. (If you don't have a serger, substitute a zigzag stitch. See Step 7 on page 130.) For this technique, you need a separate waistband casing.

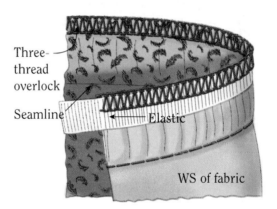

Three-thread overlock

Seamline

Elastic

WS of fabric

Diagram 1

Get Ready	Serger	Sewing Machine
Needle	Appropriate for fabric and thread	Single or twin
Needle thread	All-purpose serger	All-purpose
Bobbin thread	—	Elastic*
UL thread	All-purpose serger	—
LL thread	All-purpose serger	—
Notions	Elastic in width specified on pattern, marking pen	

Get Set	Serger	Sewing Machine
Presser foot	Standard	All-purpose
Stitch	Three-thread overlock	Straight
Stitch length	5 mm	8 spi (3.5 mm)
Stitch width	Medium	0

*Wind by hand to avoid stretching.

Serge and Sew

1. Cut the waistband twice the width of the elastic, plus one waistline seam allowance. Cut it long enough to fit easily over your hips, then add 1¼ inches (3 cm) for two seam allowances. If you're using woven fabric for a fitted garment, the top edge of the assembled skirt or pants should be the same measurement as the waistband length. For stretch fabrics, you can decrease the waistband length a bit—1 to 2 inches (2.5 to 5 cm)—and ease in the upper edge of the garment to match the band length.

2. Pin the waistband ends together and slip the waistband over your hips to make sure that it easily fits on your body.

3. Cut the elastic at least 2 inches (5 cm) to as much as 5 inches (13 cm) shorter than your waistline measurement (the stretchier the elastic, the shorter you can make it).

4. At the sewing machine, sew the elastic into a circle, overlapping the ends and stitching with a wide zigzag or a tri-motion zigzag stitch. Using one of these, rather than a straight stitch, will give your waistband added strength.

5. Sew the waistband into a circle and press the seam allowances open.

6. With right sides together, sew one edge of the waistband to the garment's waist. Trim the seam allowances to ¼ inch (6 mm), and press them toward the waistband.

7. Pin-mark the waistband into quarters. Repeat with the elastic.

8. Place the elastic on the wrong side of the waistband so that one lengthwise edge is even with the raw edge of the waistband and the pins match. The elastic is smaller than the waistband, so only pin them together at each quarter mark.

9. With the elastic facing up, serge it to the waistband along the unattached edge. See **Diagram 1** on page 129. Stretch the elastic to fit the band and remove each pin as it approaches the presser foot's toe. Take care not to cut the elastic with the knives. (If possible, disengage the cutting action.) If you don't own a serger, use a long, wide zigzag stitch instead.

10. Turn the elastic to the inside of the garment and pin it to the garment.

11. With the garment right side up, use your sewing machine to stitch in the ditch through all layers, stretching the elastic as needed.

SUCCESSFUL STRATEGIES FOR ELASTIC INSERTION

Stop short. Stitching through most elastic reduces its ability to recover shape. Cut the elastic a bit shorter than the desired finished size to help it last longer, but don't cut it so short that it's a struggle to pull on the garment; that will weaken it, too. You should be able to cut most elastic shorter by as much as 2 to 3 inches (5 to 8 cm).

Go for less. When serging elastic, use a two- or three-thread stitch. The extra needle in a four-thread stitch weakens the elastic even more.

Stitch long. Use a long, wide stitch to serge or sew elastic in place. The fewer needle holes, the better. Short stitches also prevent the elastic from relaxing—one more reason it loses its stretch. (Remember, you stretched it while you attached it.)

Nick not. Take care not to nick the elastic with the serger cutting knife. Only transparent elastic can stand up to this kind of attack without weakening.

Stretch twice. To "set" transparent elastic to its finished length, hand-stretch it twice before sewing. This makes it grow to its permanent length.

LINGERIE ELASTIC

The most comfortable elastic applications for lingerie rely on serged two thread flatlocking. Woolly nylon is the thread of choice because it's compatible with stretchy lingerie fabric, soft against the skin, and long-wearing. For the easiest application, use the special elastic foot and flat construction. Leave one seam open. This will be completed after you have applied the elastic.

Get Ready

Needle	Stretch needle for knits, if available, universal for wovens
Thread	Woolly nylon
Notion	Narrow elastic of your choice

Get Set

Presser foot	Elastic
Stitch	Two- or three-thread flatlock*
Stitch length	Long
Stitch width	Medium
Upper knife	Disengaged, if possible

Two-thread flatlocking is the least bulky and lies the flattest.

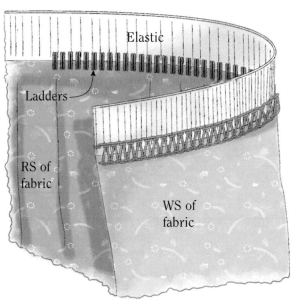

Diagram 2

Serge

1. Cut away the seam/casing allowance on knits. For woven lingerie fabric, overlock the cut edge and turn the seam allowance to the inside. Press. Cut the elastic 3 inches (8 cm) longer than required to fit your waistline.

2. On the right side of the garment place the right-hand edge of the elastic even with the raw edge (knits) or fabric fold (wovens). Extend the elastic about 3 inches (8 cm) beyond the start of the fabric. With the elastic side up, serge on the right-hand edge of the elastic. Be careful not to cut the elastic with the serger knives. The stitching may not cover the entire width of the elastic.

3. Open the elastic to expose the "ladders." See **Diagram 2.** For loops on the outside, position the elastic on the underside and stitch from the elastic side.

Sharp Notion

Clear elastic is a great seam stabilizer in stretchy sweater knits and seams that are on the bias. Catch the elastic in the stitching while you sew, but don't stretch it. The resulting seam is stable, yet has the necessary give to flex when stressed. Elastic stabilizer prevents the seam from growing over time, too.

NEVER-TWIST STRAPS

Smooth, twist-free elastic isn't an impossible goal! Once you've tried this simple serger technique you'll continue to use it every time you make swimwear and other knit clothing. This slick method will result in a smooth strap with the elastic caught in the seam stitching. Imagine—a strap that can never twist and tur once it's inside the fabric. You'll have smooth, comfy straps in no time at all.

Get Ready

Needle	Ball point or universal, size 65/9 to 80/12
Thread	Woolly nylon
Notions	Cotton/spandex braid elastic in width specified on pattern, safety pin

Get Set

Presser foot	Standard
Stitch	Three- or four-thread overlock
Stitch length	Medium
Stitch width	Medium
Upper knife	Disengaged, if possible

Serge

1. Cut the fabric for the strap twice the width of the elastic, plus ½ inch (1.25 cm). Make sure to cut it so the length of the strap is parallel to the direction of the greatest fabric stretch and 3 to 4 inches (8 to 10 cm) longer than the strap pattern piece length.

2. Fold the strap in half lengthwise with right sides together and raw edges even. Pin the elastic in place on top and even with the raw edge. Serge all the layers together along the raw lengthwise edge, being careful not to cut the elastic. See **Diagram 3.** Don't stretch the fabric or the elastic. Leave an elastic tail at one end.

3. Securely attach the safety pin to the elastic tail and thread it back through the tube to turn it right side out.

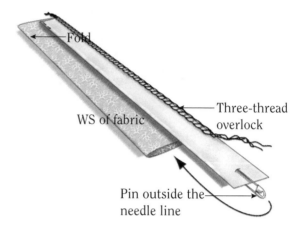

Fold

WS of fabric

Three-thread overlock

Pin outside the needle line

Diagram 3

Workroom Secret

When stitching ridged, mesh elastic in place, try using the buttonhole foot. The tunnels on the bottom fit nicely over the ridges for a smooth ride. Examine the other feet in your collection for bottom tunnels that might accommodate the ridges. Possibilities include the invisible zipper foot, piping foot, and pintuck foot.

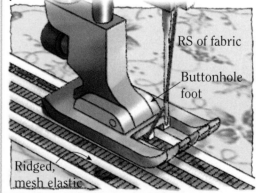

RS of fabric

Buttonhole foot

Ridged, mesh elastic

STRETCH PIPING

Garments that stretch need piping that also has "give," so overlocking part of the width of clear elastic creates the ideal trim. You can use clear elastic as the foundation for piping for bodysuits, lingerie, dancewear, swimwear, and other garments made with knit fabric. You stitch along one edge of the elastic and use the remaining elastic for the seam allowance that is caught in the garment, just like any other fabric-covered piping.

Get Ready

Needle	All-purpose or woolly nylon
UL thread	Decorative or woolly nylon*
LL thread	All-purpose or woolly nylon
Notions	Clear elastic, ⅜ inch (1 cm) wide or wider; elastic cord (optional)

Get Set

Presser foot	Standard†
Stitch	Three-thread overlock
Stitch length	Short
Stitch width	Narrow

Try the heavier woolly nylon version for superior coverage, or use two strands of regular woolly nylon.

†*For thicker piping use a beading or cording presser foot.*

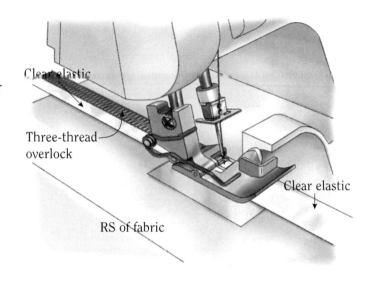

Clear elastic

Three-thread overlock

Clear elastic

RS of fabric

Diagram 4

Serge

1. Arrange the elastic under the presser foot and serge, allowing the knives to barely cut off the edge of the elastic. The stitching doesn't cover the entire width of the elastic. See **Diagram 4.** Stretch the elastic slightly as you stitch, holding it firmly behind and in front of the foot. For fatter stretch piping, use a cording foot and, as you serge, feed elastic cord through the foot on top of the clear elastic. You may need to widen the stitch a bit to accommodate the cord.

2. Insert the completed piping between the seams of a knit garment where desired, as you would normal piping. The unstitched portion of the elastic is inserted into the seam allowance.

Make It Easy

Getting elastic started under the presser foot often causes a stitch jam. To prevent this, attach the elastic flat, leaving one seam unstitched to join after attaching the elastic. Cut the elastic 2 to 3 inches (5 to 8 cm) longer than required. Serge over the extra "tail" before inserting the fabric under the presser foot and the elastic. Next, take a few stitches to anchor the elastic, then serge it in place.

Embroidery by Machine

Often some of the least explored features of a sewing machine, the built-in utility and embroidery stitches offer unusual design possibilities. Even with utility stitches, there's an untapped wealth of creativity in a "plain Jane" zigzag sewing machine.

You do not need one of the new embroidery machines to try the ideas included here. (Lucky you, if you do own one!) Go a step further and combine decorative machine embroidery with decorative serging for even more excitement.

SUCCESSFUL STRATEGIES FOR MACHINE EMBROIDERY

Channel it. Attach an embroidery or satin stitch foot. The channel on the bottom rides over the wider, thicker ridge of stitches to prevent stitch hang-ups, tunneling, and puckering.

Lighten up. Use a two-ply, 50- or 60-weight silk-finish cotton in the bobbin. It will not pile up, even when using the finest stitch length for very close satin stitching, because the thread is lightweight. Special bobbin threads are also available for this purpose. See pages 8–11.

Choose wisely. Cotton, rayon, or metallic embroidery thread are all good choices for the needle. They are finer and more lustrous, so the stitches are far prettier and less coarse than those obtained with an all-purpose thread. (The secret to really beautiful decorative stitching is in the thread.)

Stop split ends. Use an embroidery needle for cotton or rayon thread or a Metalfil/Metallica needle for metallic threads to avoid thread shredding.

Get help. A thread lubricant, such as Sewers Aid, prevents slit and frayed decorative threads, particularly rayon and metallic versions.

Hang loose. Loosen the needle tension by about two numbers for any type of decorative stitch that is made with satin stitches. This keeps the upper thread from pulling the bobbin thread to the surface of your work as you stitch.

Break rules. Test the stitch at the owner's manual-recommended length and width, but don't be afraid to adjust both to create the look you want with the thread you're using.

Firm up. Stabilizers eliminate puckers and tunneling—the two chief challenges to embroidered perfection. A stabilizer is of great benefit with any stitch that contains satin-stitched elements.

DECORATIVE SEAMLINES AND EDGES

Delicate, decorative edges replace bulky allowances on hems, collars, and cuffs when you edgestitch. Since the excess fabric allowance is trimmed away after the edge is stitched, use a fabric that frays minimally. The benefit of this sewing machine seam finish is the elimination of standard trimming, grading, and understitching. You can use a similar technique to sew over structural seams in garments, too.

Get Ready

Needle	Embroidery or Metalfil/Metallica in size appropriate for fabric and thread
Needle thread	Embroidery
Bobbin thread	Size 50 or 60 cotton
Notions	¾-inch (2-cm)-wide strip of lightweight fusible web (optional), tear-away or water-soluble stabilizer, appliqué or embroidery scissors

Get Set

Presser foot	Satin stitch or embroidery
Stitch	Decorative satin-stitch-based (scallops, half circles, or triangles, for example)
Stitch length	50 spi (0.5 mm)
Stitch width	Variable
Needle tension	Looser

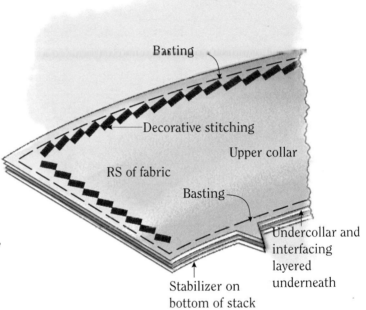

Diagram 1

Sew

1. For clarity, these instructions are for a collar, although this technique is also suitable for hems, cuffs, and pocket edges. The method varies slightly for a two-piece cuff or a neckband. To minimize fraying along the trimmed edges, you may want to fuse the seam allowances of the layers together with ¾-inch (2-cm)-wide strips of lightweight fusible web.

2. Stack the fabric pieces and stabilizer as follows, from bottom to top: stabilizer; under collar, wrong side up; interfacing, if required; and upper collar, right side up. Baste together on the seamlines.

3. Adjust the decorative stitch on a scrap of similarly layered fabrics for a close, even stitch with no hint of the bobbin threads on top. Use a stabilizer underneath the layers.

4. Decorative stitch the layers so that the stitching just covers the basting on the collar or sits just inside the basting. See **Diagram 1.** Carefully remove the stabilizer and basting, if it shows.

5. Trim away the seam allowance as close to the outer edge of the stitches as possible without cutting the stitches.

EMBROIDERING CURVES AND CORNERS

Straight-line decorative stitching is very easy, but how many garments are constructed with only straight lines? It's when you're faced with curved seams that you can use a few "secrets" to make the pattern repeat end at a corner and maintain a constant stitch width while navigating curves. When you tackle decorative stitching while turning corners and curves using a satin stitch pattern, there are some successful sewing machine stitching strategies that you can employ.

Get Ready

Needle   Appropriate for fabric, thread, and stitch

Thread   Appropriate for fabric and stitch

Notions   Water-soluble or disappearing-ink marking pen, or pencil (for open and closed curves); sharp embroidery or appliqué scissors; stabilizer

Get Set

Presser foot   Foot and settings appropriate for your fabric, thread, and stitch

Sew

1. Stitch a test sample of your pattern on stabilizer-backed fabric. You'll need this to determine repeats in areas of the seamline that aren't straight.

2. Examine the seamline that you're going to stitch. Note wherever there's a curve or corner that you'll need to navigate. Mark these according to the instructions on this and the opposite page.

3. Start stitching your seamline at a corner, if possible. Stitch corners and curves following the specific directions below and on the opposite page.

Open Curve

1. Divide the curved area into short sections, each one the width of the pattern repeat, and mark the divisions for each section with tiny dots.

2. Sew the first pattern repeat at the start of the curve, in the first section, and end with the needle down. (Use the single pattern stitch function on computerized machines.)

3. Raise the presser foot, and shift the fabric so the dot marking the start of the next short section is directly in front of the needle. See **Diagram 2.**

4. Lower the foot and stitch to the next repeat, continuing in this fashion to complete the stitching.

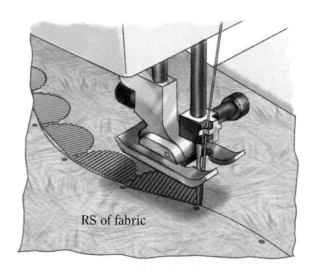

RS of fabric

Diagram 2

Closed Curve

1. Apply a strip of stabilizer to the back of a narrow scrap of your fabric. Make sure that the fabric scrap is wide enough for your stitch pattern and long enough for several repeats.

2. Stitch a test pattern on the stabilized fabric scrap. Clip into the fabric, up to the stitching at the end of each repeat.

3. Use the clipped strip to mark guiding dots on the closed curve of the garment. See **Diagram 3.** If you end up without a complete pattern, adjust the design shape or adjust the stitch so that it will fit perfectly.

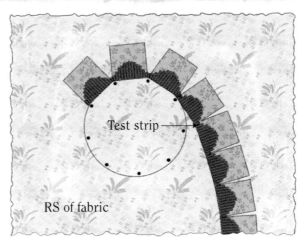

Diagram 3

Corner

1. It's easiest to start the stitch pattern at a corner and stitch away from it in both directions. Or, you can stitch across a corner to round it off. If this isn't possible, you can still arrange your stitching so that a pattern repeat falls nicely at each corner.

2. To calculate the position of the stitch pattern at corners, start with a test. Cut a narrow scrap of fabric that's a bit wider than the stitch pattern and that will hold at least six full pattern repeats. Back the fabric scrap with stabilizer. Stitch at least six full pattern repeats on the stabilizer-backed fabric scrap. Trim off the excess fabric close to the stitching on one side.

3. Place the test sample on the garment and mark the six pattern repeats. See **Diagram 4.** Decoratively stitch toward the corner, stopping at the first mark you encounter. See **Diagram 5.**

4. If your stitch pattern lines up, continue stitching. If not, adjust the stitching feed by gently pushing the fabric into the needle or holding the fabric slightly taut in front of the needle as you stitch, until the pattern is aligned. There will be a slight variation among the last six motifs, but it won't be noticeable.

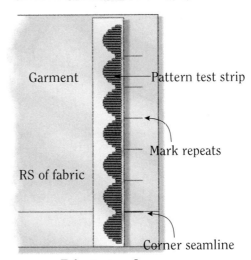

Diagram 4

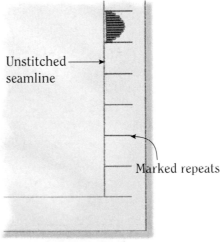

Diagram 5

FANCY STITCHING

It's possible to make some truly unusual effects with decorative stitches, either alone or in combination with other machine embroidery stitches, including serging. Stitch combinations can create some interesting trims to add to other garments. And a little fancy stitching has substantial impact when used to highlight a seam or the edge of a garment.

If you're not experimental by nature, search fashion magazines and catalogs for decorative stitching ideas that you can duplicate. While you may not be able to copy them exactly, they will definitely spark your creativity and help you push your machine to new limits. Look at decorative detailing and ask yourself, "How did they do that? How can I do it with the equipment that I have?" Then don't be afraid to experiment, knowing that some of your ideas won't pan out and that you may stumble on an exciting stitch variation by accident.

The ideal time to experiment is when you have only a few minutes to sew. Another idea is to flip your test strips over. Occasionally, the back side of one of your samples will have a really interesting stitch due to thread and tension combinations.

After you create the samples, store them in a box or book for future reference. With each sample note the tension adjustments, along with the stitch widths and lengths, for ease of use in the future.

As you work, you'll discover that there are times when you can improvise when stitching. For example, if you don't have a free-motion darning presser foot, you can use a spring needle. Another option is a darning spring, which attaches to your needle. However, the free motion darning foot is the best option because it provides protection for your fingers during free-motion stitching—a good idea for the novice or young stitcher.

Here are a few ideas to get you started.

Use a decorative or utility stitch to replace straight topstitching or to attach flat lace and trims.

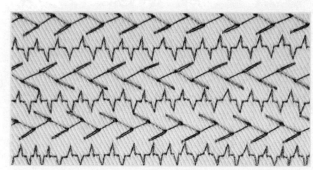

Combine stitches in an all-over pattern on a base fabric. Do the stitching on stabilizer-backed fabric squares and rectangles large enough to accommodate the pattern piece, rather than embroidering it later.

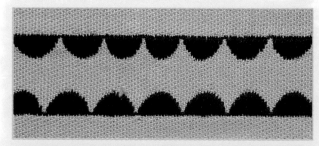

Align or offset side-by-side rows of stitches. Or sew side-by-side rows from opposite directions. (Use the mirror image function on a computerized machine for smoother stitching.)

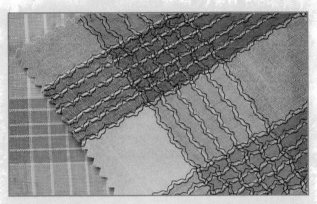

Use a twin needle to "echo" a stitch. You can also combine decorative stitches with alternating rows of pintucks or frame the pintucks with decorative stitching. Enhance prints and plaids by outlining design lines with straight or satin stitching. Twin-needle stitch along plaid and check lines with a contrasting color or outline select floral motifs in a print, for example.

Frame a seamline with the same stitch on each side, or stitch over the seamline to disguise it. Here, the fabric was stitched wrong sides together. The seam allowances are on the outside of the garment and are embellished with stitching to hide the seamline. Note that automatic and utility stitches are combined with serging.

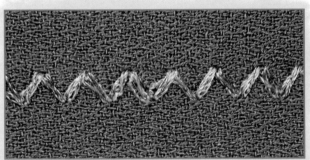

Blend two threads in a larger needle. This has a different effect than stitching with variegated thread. (See "Thread Blending" on page 12.)

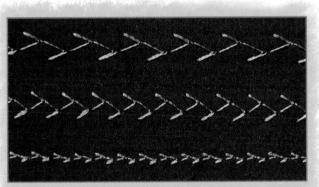

Change the character of each stitch by varying stitch width and stitch length.

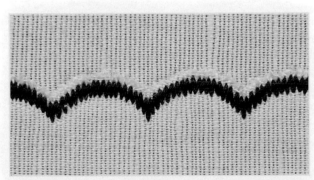

Try satin stitch variations, such as the scallop stitch, for decorative stitch seaming.

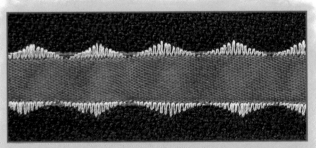

Decorative stitch in a contrasting color to attach flat braid or ribbon. (Pull the trim taut while stitching to prevent puckers, and use a stabilizer.) Try stitching bias tape this way, too.

FANCY STITCHING (CONTINUED)

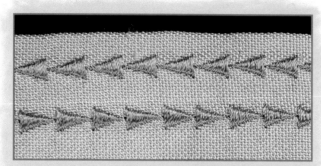

Combine rows of decorative stitches on front bands and garment edges. Or stitch parallel rows on a strip of fabric to use as an applied band of trim.

Overstitch wide flatlocking. Make interesting braid trims by stitching multiple parallel rows.

Scallop a decoratively serged or rolled edge with a picot, blindstitch, or mirror-image blindstitch.

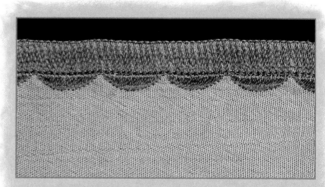

Enhance serged edges, seams, or tucks with decorative stitching alongside the serging.

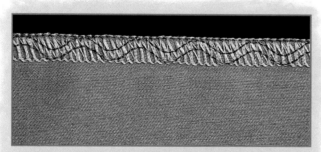

Finish an edge with a decorative satin-length, three-thread overlock. Using an embroidery foot, overstitch with a favorite decorative or utility stitch in a matching or contrasting color.

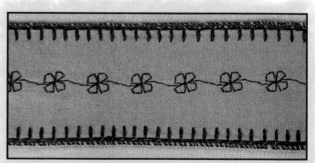

Make your own heirloom trims. Roll-edge finish narrow strips of fabric and add one or more pattern stitches through the center.

Entredeux

This delicate-looking yet very strong machine-made trim is used between other trim and fabric strips to add stability to the resulting heirloom fabric. A series of small reinforced holes creates a ladderlike appearance in the trim. Available in several widths and styles, the most versatile entredeux has a seam allowance on each side of the "ladder," which you can trim away or use, depending on the application method.

ENTREDEUX INSERTION

There are a number of ways to insert entredeux between other strips of fabric, puffing, or flat trim. (See page 184 for instructions for making puffing.) Each of these techniques requires at least two steps. The most common technique is called "rolling and whipping" in imitation of the hand method it mimics. It is possible to do this on the sewing machine, and the directions follow.

For even more creative options, you can imitate the technique on a serger. To do this, join the strips together with a narrow rolled-edge seam.

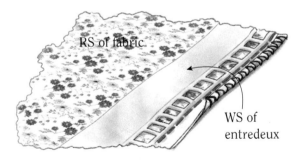

RS of fabric

WS of entredeux

Diagram 1

Get Ready

Needle	Embroidery, size 60/8, 65/9, or 70/10
Thread	Cotton machine embroidery thread or lightweight cotton-covered polyester
Notions	Spray starch, ready-made entredeux or imitation entredeux insertion

Get Set

	First Pass	Second Pass	Third Pass
Presser foot	Edgestitch, open-toe embroidery, or all-purpose	Open-toe embroidery or all-purpose	Open-toe embroidery or all-purpose
Stitch	Straight	Zigzag	Zigzag
Stitch length	12 spi (2 mm)	20 spi (1 mm)	8 to 12 spi (3.5 to 2 mm)
Stitch width	—	Narrow	Narrow

Sew

1. For general guidance on techniques and supplies, see "Heirloom Sewing" on page 155. Starch the wrong side of the entredeux and the wrong side of the fabric strip to which it's being attached, and press from the right side. Don't starch puffing strips if you're using these.

2. If necessary, trim the entredeux seam allowance to match the ¼-inch (6-mm)-wide seam allowance width on the fabric strip. Position the entredeux face down on the fabric strip with the lengthwise raw edges even. Sew them together, stitching right next to the right "ladder" of the entredeux (essentially, in the ditch of the entredeux). When attaching imitation entredeux (see the opposite page), stitch in the row of holes closest to the seam allowance edge. Trim the seam to ⅛ inch (3 mm).

3. Adjust the machine for the Second Pass so the zigzag stitch goes from the straight stitching over the edge of the seam allowance, drawing it into a tiny roll. See **Diagram 1** on page 141. If it does not roll, increase the needle thread tension gradually. Press the seam allowance toward the fabric strip. When sewing entredeux to puffing, take care to press only in the seam allowance so you don't crush or flatten the gathers that are part of the puffing strips.

4. Adjust your machine for the Third Pass, and place your seamed entredeux face up on the machine bed. Sew along the ladder of the entredeux that's closest to the seam, zigzagging in and out of the entredeux holes. Adjust the stitch width as needed to accommodate the entredeux hole spacing and the width of the ladder. The stitch should barely catch the fabric beyond the entredeux. When doing this step with entredeux and puffing, it's usually easier to control the placement of the rolled seam by stitching from the wrong side.

Sharp Notion

To join entredeux to flat lace, trim the seam allowance from the entredeux right along the ladder leg. Butt the entredeux next to the lace's heading edge and zigzag together, working on top of a piece of stabilizer.

Sharp Notion

On the serger, use a medium-width, balanced three-thread overlock stitch to sew entredeux to fabric strips. Position the entredeux so that the needle enters alongside the ladder legs (or in the outer row of holes in imitation entredeux) and stitch, trimming away the excess seam allowance. Press the serged seam away from the entredeux. Adjust the sewing machine for a zigzag stitch and stitch in and out of the entredeux holes on the right side, as directed for the machine application (Step 4), to keep the seam flat underneath.

IMITATION ENTREDEUX

Ready-made entredeux is most widely available in white, but it's nice to know you can make imitation entredeux on the sewing machine using other fabrics and colors. The wing needle and a simple tri-motion zigzag stitch are all you need to create your own entredeux on organdy. Newer machines equipped with more stitch patterns often have an entredeux stitch (or several variations) that you can use instead. The Venetian stitch is particularly good for this technique.

Get Ready

Fabric	1¼-inch (3-cm)-wide, straight-grain strips of cotton organdy
Needle	Wing, size 100/16*
Thread	Fine (#60) machine embroidery cotton or rayon
Notions	Machine embroidery hoop, tear-away or water-soluble liquid stabilizer (all optional)

Get Set

Presser foot	Open-toe embroidery
Stitch	Tri-motion zigzag
Stitch length	22 spi (0.75 mm)†
Stitch width	Narrow

For finer holes, use a denim, size 110/18 needle.
†*For larger holes, set your machine at 15 spi (1.5 mm) and a narrow (2 mm) stitch width.*

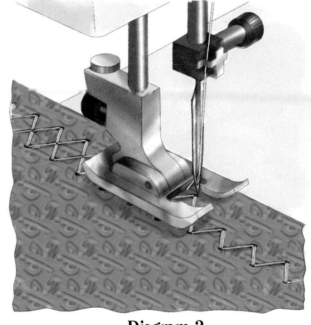

Diagram 2

Sew

1. For general guidance on techniques and supplies, see "Heirloom Sewing" on page 155. Layer two strips of organdy for each piece of finished entredeux. Sew them together along one lengthwise edge using a ⅝-inch (1.5-cm) seam allowance. If puckering is a problem in your fabric, particularly when working with lightweight fabrics, mount the fabric strip in a machine embroidery hoop, use a tear-away stabilizer underneath, or coat the fabric with water-soluble liquid stabilizer and allow to dry thoroughly before proceeding.

2. At the end of the strip, stop stitching with the needle in the left-hand needle hole. Raise the presser foot and turn the fabric strip in a counter-clockwise direction for 180 degrees. Stitch, making sure that the needle repierces the original center needle holes. (If available, use the + or - balance button to keep the stitching aligned.) The resulting strip will have three sets of holes with narrow bars of fabric between the holes in the center row. See **Diagram 2.**

3. Trim away the excess organdy ¼ inch (6 mm) from each side of the completed stitching. Insert the entredeux (join it to other heirloom-stitched fabric strips), following the directions for "Entredeux Insertion" on page 141.

Eyelets

Even if you lack an eyelet setting on your sewing machine or a special eyelet-making accessory, you can create this versatile stitch. The eyelet is a valuable addition because it has decorative and functional uses. Try clusters with other decorative stitches or thread ribbon through offset rows.

Get Ready

Needle	Appropriate for fabric and thread
Thread	Appropriate for fabric
Notions	Sharp-pointed awl (or a leather punch), to punch a hole; machine embroidery hoop

Get Set

Presser foot	Darning or open-toe embroidery
Stitch	Satin stitch
Stitch length	Almost 0
Stitch width	Narrow to wide (2 to 5 mm)

Sew

1. Use the awl to punch a hole of the desired size in the fabric at the desired location. Load the work in a machine embroidery hoop.

2. Stitch slowly, making sure that the needle goes over the cut edge on each left-hand swing. Take several stitches, then stop with the needle in the fabric.

3. Raise the presser foot and pivot the fabric slightly. Repeating the procedure described in Step 2, take the same number of stitches. Continue stitching and pivoting in the same manner until you reach the starting point. Stitch around the eyelet a second time, if desired. See the diagrams at right.

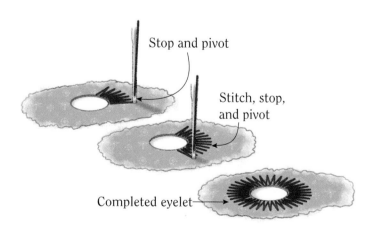

Stop and pivot

Stitch, stop, and pivot

Completed eyelet

Fagoting

Fagoting creates decorative open areas. Horizontal threads are drawn from parts of a woven fabric, then the remaining threads are stitched into bunches. There are several ways to imitate this work so that you can work on a wider range of fabric types. On the silk blouse at right, fagoting is a decorative touch for the hem and the bodice.

CURVED FAGOTING

Most ready-to-wear examples of this heirloom technique show up as a straight line or two along a placket front, sleeve, or pocket edge. But it's possible to join curved seams or edges with fagoting for an unexpected approach. Of course you can use this sewing machine method to join straight edges, too.

Get Ready

Needle	Appropriate for fabric and thread
Thread	Cotton embroidery*
Notion	Stabilizer

Get Set

Presser foot	Open-toe embroidery
Stitch	Tri-motion zigzag or fagoting
Stitch length	6 to 12 spi (4 to 2 mm)
Stitch width	Stitches catch the folded fabric edges
Needle tension	Loosen†

*This is for light- to medium-weight fabrics. Use topstitching or decorative thread for medium- to heavy-weight fabrics.
†The bobbin thread shouldn't show on the surface.

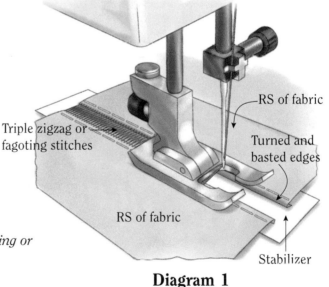

Triple zigzag or fagoting stitches

RS of fabric

Turned and basted edges

RS of fabric

Stabilizer

Diagram 1

Sew

1. Trim the seam allowances to ¼ inch (6 mm) and zigzag or overlock the raw edges. Turn under and press ⁵⁄₁₆ inch (8 mm) along each finished seam edge.

2. Baste one folded edge to a strip of stabilizer. Baste the remaining turned edge to the stabilizer ⅛ inch (3 mm) away.

3. Center the work under the open-toe embroidery foot and stitch, just catching the folded edges with each swing of the needle. See **Diagram 1.** Remove the basting (if it shows) and the stabilizer.

FLATLOCK FAGOTING

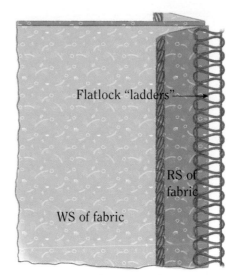

Here's another fun way to use the flatlock stitch on your serger. Flatlock fagoting is a nice embellishment to use when designing and making your own heirloom fabric, as discussed on page 155. The trick to flatlock fagoting lies in learning how to guide the fabric under the foot so that the needle just barely catches the folded edges that you wish to join. Fabric thickness affects your stitching strategy, so you'll need to test the position of the stitching on fabric scraps first.

Diagram 2

Get Ready	Serger	Sewing Machine
Needle	Appropriate for fabric and thread	All-purpose or embroidery
Needle thread	Topstitching or decorative	Embroidery
Bobbin thread	—	Embroidery
UL thread	Transparent	—
LL thread	Transparent	—

Get Set	Serger	Sewing Machine
Presser foot	Standard or blind hem	Embroidery
Stitch	Two- or three-thread flatlock	Straight or decorative
Stitch length	Varies*	Varies*
Stitch width	Widest	Widest

The longer the stitch, the more open the finished work.

Serge and Sew

1. Finish each seam allowance with a balanced three-thread overlock stitch. Turn under and press the seam allowance.

2. Place the fabric right sides together with folded edges even. Place pins parallel to the edge out of the way of the presser foot.

3. Adjust the fabric under the foot so the needle just catches both folded edges. Use a blind hem foot, if available, to ensure perfectly even flatlock stitching. Stitch so that the stitches hang off the edges. See **Diagram 2.**

> ## Sharp Notion
> An heirloom effect is easy to achieve using ⅛-inch (3-mm)-wide ribbon. To make it look as if you stitched ribbon into the seam, just weave ribbon in and out of the fagoting after the "seam" is opened.

4. Open and pull apart the layers. Edgestitch or decorative stitch along each folded edge of the completed fagoting. Trim the excess seam allowance close to the stitches on the underside.

STRAIGHT FAGOTING

Using a tailor tacking (also called fringe) foot is the simplest way to add a straight row of delicate openwork between two fabric layers. On your sewing machine thread loops form over a bar on the foot, then the completed stitching is anchored with another row of stitching. For curved seams and attaching trim, refer to "Curved Fagoting" on page 145.

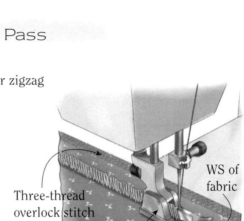

Instead of a plain-Jane straight stitch, try one of your decorative embroidery stitches to anchor the First Pass stitching.

Get Ready

Needle	Appropriate for fabric and thread
Thread	Cotton embroidery*

Get Set

	First Pass	Second Pass
Presser foot	Fringe or tailor tacking	Embroidery
Stitch	Fagoting or zigzag	Decorative or zigzag
Stitch length	24 spi (0.5 mm)	As desired
Stitch width	Narrow	As desired
Tension	Loosen†	Balanced

Use this for light- to medium-weight fabrics. For medium- to heavy-weight fabrics, use topstitching or decorative thread.
†Loosen needle tension so the bobbin thread doesn't show.

Sew

1. Serge finish or zigzag each seam allowance edge before stitching the seam, unless you plan to use a dense decorative stitch along the fagoting edges.

2. Draw the needle thread through the opening and behind the fringe foot. Place the fabric, right sides together, under the presser foot. Stitch with the foot positioned so the center of the zigzag stitches is on the seamline, which is probably ⅝ inch (1.5 cm) from the raw or finished edges. See **Diagram 3.** (If the fringe foot's bar is centered in the foot, position the bar on the seamline. If it isn't centered, adjust to a right-needle position.)

3. Pull the seam apart, and press the seam allowances toward the fabric. See **Diagram 4.**

Diagram 3

WS of fabric

Three-thread overlock stitch

Fringe foot

WS of fabric

RS of fabric

Diagram 4

4. Adjust the machine for the Second Pass, and decorative stitch close to the fabric fold on each side of the fagoting. If you use a dense stitch, trim the seam allowances close to the decorative stitching.

Free-Motion Machine Stitching

Contrary to their appearance, free-motion techniques are relatively easy to execute with only a little practice. You control stitch placement rather than letting the feed dogs move the fabric. Even if your sewing machine makes only a simple zigzag stitch, you can achieve truly beautiful results. Gauntlet-style cuffs, like those shown at right, are an ideal "canvas" for free-motion embroidery or another technique that uses free-motion stitching, like Battenberg lace, cutwork, drawn thread work, and needle lace.

Get Ready

Needle	Machine embroidery or Metalfil/Metallica
Thread	Cotton, rayon, or metallic embroidery
Notions	Extra bobbin case (if yours is a front-loading style), extra bobbins, water-soluble stabilizer (optional), machine embroidery hoop, appliqué or embroidery scissors

Get Set

Presser foot	Darning or open-toe darning*
Stitch	Straight, zigzag, or decorative, depending on the technique
Stitch length	Usually 0
Stitch width	Varies
Feed dogs	Disengaged, covered, or 0 stitch length
Tension	Varies†

You can use a spring needle and eliminate the presser foot.
†*The needle tension is loosened for straight, zigzag, and satin stitching, but not necessarily for whip stitching.*

Make It Easy
To prevent fabric from slipping in the wooden hoop or to protect delicate fabrics, wrap the hoop's inner ring with narrow twill tape. Glue one end of the tape to the frame, then wrap it, overlapping the tape by half its width as you work around the ring. Glue the remaining end.

Sew

1. Adjust the tension as directed for the free-motion stitching technique you're doing. If you must loosen the bobbin tension, turn the bobbin case screw counterclockwise in small increments. Dangle the loaded bobbin case by the thread, holding it over your other hand. It should slide slowly down the thread under its own weight for the whip stitch. For the feather stitch there should be no resistance on the bobbin thread. If your bobbin case is built in, there should be almost no tension on the thread when you pull it through the tension spring. Before adjusting the needle tension, do some test stitching.

2. Load the fabric into a hoop. If you're filling a design motif with stitching (as opposed to creating a free-form design), trace the motif onto water-soluble stabilizer and place the stabilizer on top of the background fabric. Load both layers into the embroidery hoop and adjust so that they are taut.

3. Position the fabric-loaded hoop under the needle and presser foot to begin stitching. Rotate the flywheel by hand (or use the one-stitch feature, if available on your machine) to draw the bobbin thread to the top, then lower the presser foot. Even if you work without a presser foot, you must lower the presser bar in order for the machine to stitch properly. Holding on to both threads, lower the needle into the fabric. Make a few stitches in place, and clip the threads close to the fabric.

4. Follow the directions for the free-motion technique you're using, moving the hoop smoothly to avoid breaking the thread or needle. You control the length of the stitch with the machine's speed and the motion and direction of the hoop. Begin to move the hoop slowly while you run the machine at a moderate to fast speed. Move the hoop in tight circles to fill in design motifs, working the large areas first. Move the hoop back and forth for more linear effects—outlining, for example. See the diagram below.

Stabilizer on top of RS of fabric

SUCCESSFUL STRATEGIES FOR FREE-MOTION WORK

Sew fast. Move the hoop slowly and stitch at a moderate to fast speed for short stitches.

Sew slow. Move the hoop quickly while stitching at a normal speed for longer stitches and less thread buildup.

Go easy. Avoid jerky movements that bend or break the needle, or snag the thread.

Go with the flow. It isn't usually necessary to pivot your work when free-motion stitching since you're free to move the hoop from side to side or toward or away from you. That means you don't have to start and stop stitching to turn the work in the direction you wish to stitch.

Take a rest. For long stints at the machine, push your machine away from the table edge so that you can rest your arms on the table.

Fringe

Long, swingy fringe adds elegance to a tunic or a dramatic wool or rayon challis shawl. Cut from fabric that curls, it's a playful touch for a sweatshirt.

Included on the following pages are several ways to make fringe and fringe trim. For some methods, you need a tailor tacking (also called fringe) foot. This is one of the rarely used (but often standard) feet included with many sewing machines.

DECORATIVE FRINGE

The decorative "head" on this fringe makes it pretty enough to topstitch it to a garment rather than burying it in a seam. Made with a fringe fork, this serge-and-sew technique is suitable for any yarn, narrow ribbon, or rolled edge serger chain. The selected fringe material is wrapped around the fork, then secured along one lengthwise edge by stitching the "wraps" to Seams Great. The finishing touch is overlocking, then decorative stitching, along the Seams Great.

Get Ready	Sewing Machine	Serger	Sewing Machine
Needle	Appropriate for needle and thread	Appropriate for needle and thread	Appropriate for needle and thread
Needle thread	Decorative or all-purpose	Decorative	Decorative or all-purpose
Bobbin thread	Decorative or all-purpose	—	Decorative or all-purpose
UL thread	—	Pearl cotton; pearl rayon, or shiny, heavy rayon	—
LL thread	—	All-purpose or fusible	—
Notions	Yarn, thread, or other fringe material; fringe fork; 1-inch (2.5-cm)-wide tricot or Seams Great; tear-away stabilizer; seam sealant*		

Get Set

	Sewing Machine	Serger	Sewing Machine
Presser foot	Standard†	Standard	Embroidery or open-toe embroidery
Stitch	Straight	Three- or four-thread overlock Short	Decorative
Stitch length	8 spi (3.5 mm)	Wide	As desired
Stitch width	—		As desired

If desired, serge yards and yards of rolled-edge chain to use for the fringe. See page 154 for instructions on making a fringe fork.

†*You can substitute a no-snag (also called net) presser foot, if available.*

Sew, Serge, and Sew

1. Hold the fringe fork with the open end away from you and wrap the fringe material around the legs, keeping loops as close together as possible. Don't cut the remaining fringe material from the wrapped fork. Place the excess in your lap.

2. Cut a piece of Seams Great the desired length of the finished fringe. Machine baste it, lengthwise, to the center of a 1½-inch (4-cm)-wide strip of tear-away stabilizer.

3. Center one leg of the fringe fork lengthwise on the Seams Great/stabilizer strip. From the open ends of the fork, baste about ⅜ inch (1 cm) from the leg toward the looped end of the fork. See **Diagram 1.** Pull the fork toward you, so that the loops at the end are no longer on the fork. Wrap more fringe material on the looped end of the fork. Don't cut the fringe material. Continue basting the loops to the Seams Great/stabilizer strip until the fringe is the desired length. Remove the fork. Tear away the stabilizer.

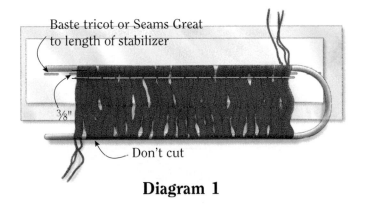

Baste tricot or Seams Great to length of stabilizer

⅜"

Don't cut

Diagram 1

4. Fold the Seams Great back on itself along the basting so that the edge extends away from the fringe, past the edge of the fringe. See **Diagram 2.**

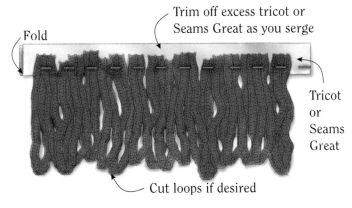

Fold

Trim off excess tricot or Seams Great as you serge

Tricot or Seams Great

Cut loops if desired

Diagram 2

5. Serge the top edge of the stitched fringe, trimming away the excess Seams Great as you stitch. See the illustration on page 150.

6. Decorative machine stitch through the center of the serging or, for a wider head, below the serging. Remove the machine basting if it shows.

7. If desired, treat the loop ends of the serger chain with seam sealant, and let them dry before cutting them.

8. Position the completed fringe on the garment or project. Pin (or fuse, if you used fusible thread in the lower looper), and machine stitch in place.

FRINGED EDGING AND INSERTION

For subtler fringe that's finer than decorative fringe, use a tailor tacking presser foot on your sewing machine. (You may know this foot by another name, such as fringe, net, or marking.) Looped needle-thread fringe, which is stitched right to the fabric pattern piece or a fabric strip, can be used to finish an edge—a pocket or hem, for example—or to make fringe to insert in a seam. Heavier thread, such as topstitching, makes heavier fringe. Try blending two threads and using a sewing machine needle with a larger eye for multicolor results.

Whatever name you know it by, the tailor tacking foot is identified by a central bar over which thread loops form.

Get Ready

	First Pass	Second Pass
Needle	Embroidery or topstitching*	Embroidery or topstitching*
Thread	Embroidery cotton or rayon, topstitching, or buttonhole twist	Embroidery cotton or rayon, topstitching, or buttonhole twist

Get Set

	First Pass	Second Pass
Presser foot	Tailor tacking†	Embroidery
Stitch	Satin	Decorative
Stitch length	Almost 0	As desired
Stitch width	Narrow	As desired
Needle tension	Loosen	Balanced

*Select a size that's appropriate for your thread.
†Also known as a fringe or marking foot. See the photo above.

Sew

1. Don't finish the edge to which you plan to apply the fringe. Instead, chalk-mark the entire length along the intended finished edge of the garment piece (like the hemline on a skirt, for example) so that you'll have a guide to follow as you stitch.

2. With the machine set up for the First Pass, stitch along the marked line. Use a longer stitch length with thicker thread or more than one thread in the needle.

Workroom Secret

The no-snag or net foot has closed, turned-up toes. If it is not available for your machine, tape across the toes of your open-toe embroidery or appliqué foot. This prevents the toes from catching the fringe yarns as you stitch.

3. Turn the allowance to the inside, along the finished edge marked in Step 1, and press.

4. Set up the sewing machine for the desired decora-tive stitch and Second Pass. This will be used to secure the allowance. Stitch along the top edge of the fringe to secure it. If you prefer, you can top-stitch with just a simple row of straight stitching.

SINGLE-ROW FRINGE

A single row of fringe is most suitable if you want to use heavy threads and yarns that won't fit through the eye of a sewing machine needle. For a lush, loopy texture, try making full, elaborate fringe directly on a base fabric. You can also create fringe as a separate strip to apply to a fabric surface or insert in a seam. This technique uses decorative yarns, threads, or ribbons.

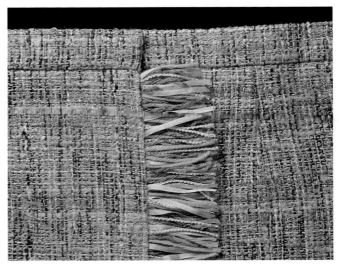

All you need is a straight-stitch sewing machine and a fringe fork to make single-row fringe.

Get Ready

Needle	Jeans or topstitching, size 90/14 (or larger for heavy yarns)
Thread	All-purpose*
Notions	Fringe fork; tear-away stabilizer; trim, such as cord, embroidery floss, fabric strips, narrow braid, ribbon, or yarn†

Get Set

Presser foot	Appliqué or open-toe embroidery
Stitch	Zigzag or straight
Stitch length	8 spi (3.5 mm)
Stitch width	Narrow (for zigzag)

You can use transparent thread in the needle.
†*See page 154 for instructions on making a fringe fork.*

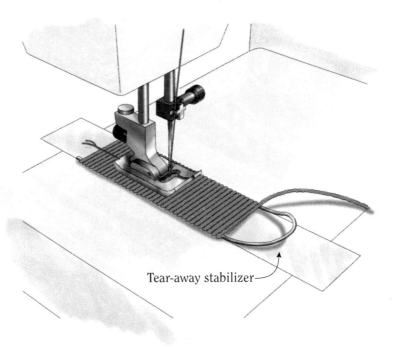

Tear-away stabilizer

Diagram 3

Sew

1. Hold the fringe fork with the open end away from you. Wrap the trim around it, keeping the loops as close together as possible. Take care not to wrap so tightly that you distort the fork's width. Don't cut the trim.

2. Position the fork on top of a strip of tear-away stabilizer cut the same width as the fork. Place the trim in a cup or in your lap. Stitch through the center of the wrapped yarns, adding stabilizer strips underneath as needed. See **Diagram 3** on page 153. (For wider finished fringe, stitch close to one of the fork legs using the zipper foot.)

3. As you stitch, draw the frame toward you so the stitched loops slide off the legs. Continue wrapping the legs as needed. It isn't necessary to remove the work from the machine. When your fringe is the desired length, cut the trim and pull out the fork. Leave the stabilizer in place.

4. Position the fringe on the garment as desired. Topstitch the fringe to the garment, stitching on top of the previous stitching. Cut the fringe loops if desired. Remove the stabilizer.

Sharp Notion

You can turn and press the hem allowance to the inside of the garment before stitching the fringe, then sew ⅛ to ¼ inch (3 to 6 mm) from the folded edge through both layers. (The gap leaves room for your favorite decorative stitch to hold the fringe firmly in place. See page 152.) This variation allows the fringe to lie against the garment rather than along the edge.

Workroom Secret

You can make your own fringe fork. Cut the lower, horizontal bar off a wire coat hanger at the curved ends. Reshape the upper portion of the hanger so the sides are vertical and the desired distance apart. Tape the ends with masking tape, and poke them into a short length of a cardboard tube (the kind that's wrapped around the horizontal bar on some hangers). This will prevent the prongs from spreading.

How wide should you space the "legs" of the fork? That depends on how long or high you want the fringe to be and how you plan to stitch it in place. If you plan to stitch through the center of the fringe, space the legs twice the desired fringe height plus ¼ inch (6 mm). If you plan to stitch along one side, just add ¼ inch (6 mm) to the desired length.

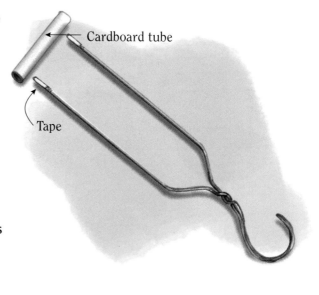

Cardboard tube

Tape

Heirloom Sewing

Typically, heirloom sewing is created by stitching together strips of plain and embellished fabrics and delicate trims. With computerized machines, it's really easy to design your own trims for this work, but even some of the simplest zigzag machines can be used. Combining sewing machine and serger techniques offers the most design versatility for this kind of work, and projects that would normally take weeks of hand sewing turn into weekend wonders.

GUIDELINES FOR EXQUISITE STITCHING

Heirloom sewing involves using your sewing machine or serger to create a piece of lacelike fabric. It's best to plan your fabric first, working from the center out, to determine the desired arrangement of lace, entredeux, embroidery, and fabric strips. Then assemble the components to create an oversize square or rectangle of heirloom fabric from which to cut the pattern piece.

Get Ready

Fabric	100 percent cotton
Needle	Suitable for fabric and thread
Thread	Machine embroidery cotton or rayon

Get Set

Settings	Refer to the specific technique

Sew

1. Prewash all fabrics and trims before you begin.

2. Plan your combination of techniques and create a fabric rectangle from which to cut your pattern pieces. Refer to "Entredeux" on page 141, "Fagoting" on page 145, "Hemstitching" on page

Heirloom sewing combines delicate lace insertion, embroidered trims, fagoting, entredeux, hemstitching, lace-to-lace seams, narrow rolled-edge seams, puffing strips, and tiny pintucks. The straps on this nightgown feature lace-to-lace seams. Horizontal pintucking adds interest to the wide band below the decorative stitching. A potpourri of heirloom techniques graces the front: lace insertion, hemstitching, flatlocking with lace, and twin-needle serpentine stitching. See Step 2 for help finding instructions for these techniques.

159, "Lace Insertion" on page 162, "Lace-to-Lace Heirloom Sewing" on page 164, "Rolled Edges and Hems" on page 185, and "Puffing" on page 184 for inspiration and step-by-step instructions.

3. Cut the fabric strips for your techniques along the crosswise grain to reduce puckering. For joining seam allowances and hem allowances, allow an additional ¼ inch (6 mm) at each edge, as appropriate.

4. Before stitching, apply spray starch to the wrong side of all fabric strips and laces (except those for puffing). Press from the right side.

5. The traditional fabrics used for these techniques are delicate, so insert a new needle in your sewing machine or serger even if you have used the current one very little.

6. Set your machine and stitch your fabric as instructed for the technique you selected. Do not sew over the pins when doing this fine work.

7. Join each set of fabric and lace strips with entredeux for added durability and visual interest.

8. For hems and edge finishes, use a rolled hem, which can be stitched on either a sewing machine or a serger.

Sharp Notion

White organdy and fine Swiss cotton batiste are generally the fabrics of choice, but feel free to experiment on other lightweight fabric (and in other colors), including handkerchief linen, cotton lawn, cotton voile, and high-quality cotton/poly blends. Heirloom sewing can form the basis of luxurious lingerie and delicate blouses when made with sensuous silks and silklike fabrics.

SUCCESSFUL STRATEGIES FOR COMBINING STITCHES

Chain a reaction. Chainstitch through a ribbon using a decorative thread in a looper of your serger. Stitch with the ribbon face down so the chain-stitching appears on the right side.

Have a pipe dream. Substitute flatlocked piping (see page 49) for rolled-edge pintucks.

Create handlooms. Make your own trims using decorative pattern stitches on a single or double layer of organdy or starch-stiffened batiste. What you create can replace ready-made "handlooms," the embroidered insertion strips you often see in heirloom garments. Combine stitch patterns on a computerized machine to design a special pattern and consider using one or more pastel colors of rayon embroidery thread to add subtle hints of color. Finish the trim with rolled edges, or use the rolled-edge stitch to join the trim to other lace, fabric, or trim.

Sew it "wrong." When using the rolled-edge stitch to join edges, stitch the pieces with the wrong sides together so the rolled edge becomes an integral part of the design.

"Lock" it up. Add rows of decorative flatlocking to fabric strips that are positioned between lace and entredeux strips. Flatlocked diamonds, woven flatlocked ladders, and ladders without weaving are all possibilities. See page 48.

Nip and tuck. Make pintucked strips using the narrow rolled-edge stitch to sew over fabric that is folded with wrong sides together. Use the width of the presser foot to space the tucks and use uneven numbers for the best balance: experiment with three or five pintucks to a strip. You can also pull a thread to mark the fold line location for each tuck in the strip.

Hems

Gone are the days when the only acceptable garment hem meant hours of tedious hand stitching. Garment designers tailor their hem and edge finish choices to the fabric, and so can you.

The decorative flatlocked hem is shown in this illustration, but this section also includes instructions for a flatlocked blind hem and a shirttail hem. The rolled-edge hem, another suitable hemming option, is covered in a separate entry in this book.

FLATLOCKED BLIND HEM

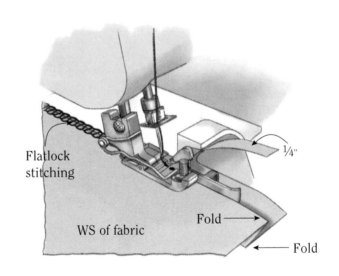

This one-step method finishes the raw edge while securing the hem! Akin to blind hemming on a sewing machine, the serger version is easiest to do with a special presser foot guiding the fold.

The standard stitch for serger blind hemming is a balanced three-thread overlock, but flatlocking is an interesting alternative. It's great on knits, and with transparent thread the "ladders" virtually disappear into the fabric. For a decorative option on knits and medium- to heavy-weight textured wovens, you can weave ribbon through the ladders.

Flatlock stitching

¼"

WS of fabric

Fold

Fold

Get Ready

Needle	Size 75/11
Needle thread	All-purpose, cotton embroidery, or transparent
UL thread	All-purpose serger
LL thread	All-purpose serger

Get Set

Presser foot	Blind hem or standard
Stitch	Two- or three-thread flatlock
Stitch length	3 to 4 mm
Stitch width	2 mm
Needle tension	0
UL tension	Minimal
LL tension	Tight

Serge

1. With the wrong side up, press the hem allowance to the wrong side of the garment.

2. Fold the hem back to the right side of the garment so that ¼ inch (6 mm) of the fabric's raw edge extends past the second fold.

3. Position the fabric under the foot, and adjust it. To stitch effectively, the serger needle should just catch the edge of the fabric fold.

4. Adjust the blind hem foot so that the adjustable guide rides along the fold.

5. Serge, catching the folded edge with the needle stitching and allowing the knives to trim away some of the extended raw edge. See the diagram on page 157.

6. Open the hem so the stitching is flat. Press lightly on the wrong side.

Sharp Notion

Attach a bottom band without making one! The mock blind hem is an appropriate finish for knits, especially on sweatshirts and other active wear. What a great solution if you can't find ribbing to match your fabric. Replace the flatlocked blind hem with a three-thread overlock at a 2 mm stitch length. Prepare the hem as described in Steps 1 and 2 of "Flatlocked Blind Hem" on page 157. Place the fabric under the blind hem foot and stitch through all layers, barely trimming the folded edge. A seamline appears on the front, as if you had attached a separate band to the edge.

Workroom Secret

One of the easiest ways to make a flat shirttail hem is to use your serger...and you don't need the differential feed feature!

First trim the hem allowance to ¼ inch (6 mm). With the garment right side up and using a medium length and width three-thread overlock stitch, serge along the edge. Tighten the needle tension slightly when stitching along a curved area to ease the curve.

Return to a normal needle tension along the straight sections. Turn the serged edge to the inside and press. Machine straight stitch ⅛ inch (3 mm) from the raw edge. Use a twin needle on knits to imitate a cover-stitched hem. See the diagram.

This technique is also great to use when you don't have quite enough fabric for a standard 1-inch (2.5-cm) hem.

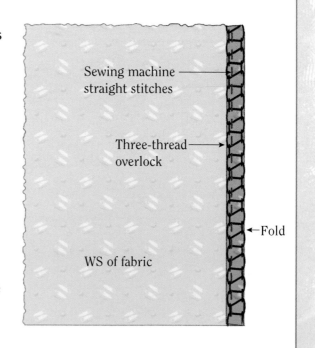

Sewing machine straight stitches

Three-thread overlock

←Fold

WS of fabric

Hemstitching

Most often used in heirloom sewing projects, hemstitching makes an airy, lacelike pattern of stitched holes. It can be a delicate accent, or a bold statement when stitched in a grid, as shown at right. You can imitate it on the machine with crisp fabric, a wing needle, and straight, functional, or decorative stitches.

"BLIND" HEMSTITCHING

Interlocking rows of blindstitches result in a unique version of hemstitching. The sewing machine instructions that follow are for a single wing needle, but you can also use a double wing. Experiment with a different thread color in each needle for added design interest.

Get Ready

Fabric	Crisp wovens: batiste, handkerchief linen, organdy, or organza
Needle	Wing or universal, size 100/16*
Thread	Rayon or cotton embroidery
Notions	Spray starch; iron-on, tear-away or water-soluble liquid stabilizer

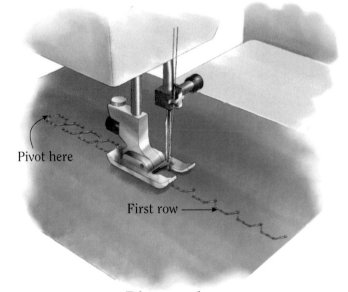

Pivot here

First row

Get Set

Presser foot	Open-toe embroidery
Stitch	Blindstitch
Stitch length	20 spi (1 mm)
Stitch width	Medium

Diagram 1

*On very fine fabrics use a 90/14 universal. If a wing needle puckers the fabric, try a 120/20 universal.

Sew

1. For general guidance on techniques and supplies, see "Heirloom Sewing" on page 155. Starch and press the fabric. Back it with a stabilizer.

2. Stitch the first row, stopping when the needle just pierces but doesn't complete the stitch on the last left swing. Turn the flywheel just enough to raise the needle out of the fabric. Raise the foot and rotate the fabric counterclockwise 180 degrees.

3. Position the needle so it pierces the last hole again and continue stitching, making sure that each left swing of the wing needle enters the holes of the previous row of stitching. See **Diagram 1.**

MOCK HEMSTITCHING

Unlike true hemstitching, the needle hole here isn't obvious since you don't use a wing needle. You can do this stitch on any fabric, knits, silks, and silk-like fabrics included, since the stitches don't rely on pronounced holes in the fabric to create the look of hemstitching. You'll use your sewing machine to draw the flatlocked stitches into delicate thread bundles on the fabric surface.

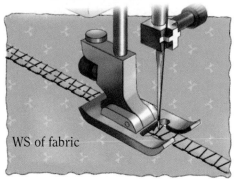

WS of fabric

Diagram 2

Get Ready

	Serger	Sewing Machine
Needle	Appropriate for fabric and thread	Appropriate for fabric and thread
Needle thread	All-purpose, rayon, or cotton embroidery	Matching all-purpose
Bobbin thread	—	Transparent thread
Looper threads	All-purpose	—

Get Set

	Serger	Sewing Machine
Presser foot	All-purpose	Embroidery
Stitch	Two-or three-thread flatlock	Straight or tri-motion straight stitch
Stitch length	1.5 to 2 mm	8 to 12 spi (3.5 to 2 mm)
Stitch width	As desired	—

Serge and Sew

1. Draw hemstitch positioning lines on the wrong side of the fabric.

2. Fold along the first line with the right sides together and flatlock with the loops hanging halfway off the fold. Open out the flatlocking.

3. Place the fabric right side down on the sewing machine. Topstitch through the center of the flat-locking loops. See **Diagram 2.** The transparent bobbin thread will catch the flatlock ladder stitches into thread bundles on the fabric right side. Test first. If bundles are not apparent, loosen the upper tension or tighten the bobbin tension slightly for a more pronounced effect.

Workroom Secret

True hemstitching is more pronounced when done on the bias or the crosswise grain of the fabric. When sewing along the lengthwise grain, loosen the needle-thread tension slightly and pull out a thread or two of the fabric along the stitching line before sewing to enhance the openwork effect of the stitching.

Increased needle-thread tension defines the hemstitched holes. Test all settings on a scrap of the same fabric you'll use for your project.

SINGLE-NEEDLE HEMSTITCHING

Not everyone has the luxury of owning a sewing machine with preprogrammed hemstitches. This is a great excuse to buy a new machine, but if your old model has a few good years left in it, you can still try hemstitching. All you really need is a zigzag or decorative stitch and a standard or wing needle.

Get Ready

Fabric	Crisp wovens: batiste, handkerchief linen, organdy, or organza
Needle	Wing or universal, size 100/16*
Thread	Rayon or cotton embroidery
Notions	Spray starch; iron-on, tear-away or water-soluble liquid stabilizer

Get Set

Presser foot	Open-toe embroidery†
Stitch	Zigzag or decorative
Stitch length	12 to 20 spi (2 to 1 mm) or to suit stitch
Stitch width	Narrow or to suit stitch

*On very fine fabrics use a 90/14 universal. If a wing needle puckers the fabric, try a 120/20 universal.

†Use a five-groove pintuck foot for side-by-side rows of decorative stitching.

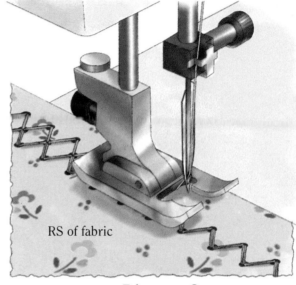

RS of fabric

Diagram 3

Sew

1. For general guidance on techniques and supplies, see "Heirloom Sewing" on page 155. Starch and press the fabric. Back it with a stabilizer.

2. Adjust your machine for a zigzag stitch or choose a decorative stitch that requires the needle to enter the same hole more than once (star, honeycomb, picot, Parisian, or Venetian stitches, for example). Stitch the first row. Clip the threads close to the fabric surface.

3. Stitch another row alongside the first, positioning the first row of stitching to the left of the needle. Stitch so the left swing of the needle repierces the first stitch of the previous row of stitching. See **Diagram 3**. Remove the stabilizer.

STRATEGIES FOR SUCCESSFUL HEMSTITCHING

Take it easy. Stitch slowly to define and control the stitches. Set the machine at half speed, if possible.

Stop tugging. Try not to push or pull the work through the machine. This avoids problems with matching stitches in multiple rows.

Reflect on it. Experiment with the mirror-image function, if available, to combine rows of the same stitch done from one side of the needle and then the other.

Double up. Use two layers of fabric whenever possible. Trim away the layer underneath close to the stitching, if desired.

Lace Insertion

Strips of lace are one of the most distinctive elements of heir-loom sewing. While these can be joined lace-to-lace (see page 164), you can also insert the strips between pieces of other fabric. Then the fabric/lace can be joined to fabric strips that feature other heirloom techniques, like entredeux, puffing, and hem-stitching. Cut your pattern pieces from the resulting "fabric" to create the look of traditional French hand sewing.

DECORATIVE LACE INSERTION

There's an easy way to make "peekaboo" lace on your sewing machine. Sew the lace to the fabric surface and then trim away the fabric that's underneath. You can make an entire garment section this way, or add a single row of lace to the garment interior. Before trying this you may want to review "Heirloom Sewing" on page 155.

Get Ready

Needle	Embroidery, size 70/10
Thread	Cotton machine embroidery or lightweight cotton-covered polyester
Notions	Spray starch; fabric strip; flat lace insertion; chalk; embroidery scissors

Get Set

Presser foot	All-purpose, open-toe embroidery, edgestitch, or blind hem
Stitch	Zigzag or straight
Stitch length	15 spi (1.5 mm)
Stitch width	Narrow

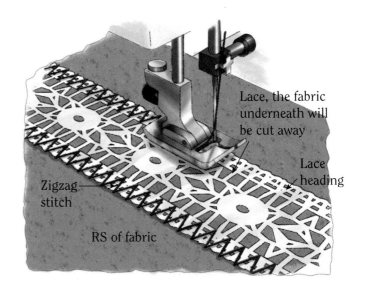

Diagram 1

Sew

1. Starch both the fabric strip and lace on their wrong sides and press from their right sides. Pull a length-wise thread in the fabric to mark the desired position of one lace heading. Pin the lace, right side up, on top of the right side of the fabric strip along the pulled thread line.

2. Zigzag along both edges of the lace. If you prefer, you can straight stitch here and use your edgestitching or adjustable blind hem foot to ensure even stitching. See **Diagram 1** on the opposite page.

3. The goal in this step is to "fold back" the fabric that's behind the lace. Place the stitched lace/fabric on your work surface so that the fabric is wrong side up. On the wrong side, carefully cut the fabric only between the two rows of stitching. You now

have two fabric "allowances." Press the fabric allowances away from the lace.

4. On the right side, zigzag again along each edge through all layers. If desired, you can replace the zigzag stitch with a more decorative stitch, to change the appearance of your work.

5. Trim close to the zigzag stitching that's on the fabric wrong side.

FLATLOCKED LACE INSERTION

This versatile serger technique offers two options for lace insertion. To imitate piping along the lace edge, use a narrow rolled edge. Or use the flatlock stitch to enhance the lace edges with decorative looper threads.

Get Ready

Needle	Appropriate for fabric and thread
Needle thread	All-purpose serger
UL thread	All-purpose, rayon embroidery, or topstitching
LL thread	All-purpose serger
Notions	Flat lace insertion, spray starch

Get Set

Presser foot	All-purpose, heirloom/lace, or tape guide*
Stitch	Two- or three-thread flatlock*
Stitch length	Appropriate for thread in UL
Stitch width	Narrow

For a "piped" look, use a rolled-edge stitch and rolled-edge presser foot.

Serge

1. For general guidance on techniques and supplies, see "Heirloom Sewing" on page 155. Cut two fabric strips, making them both the desired finished width plus ½ inch (1.25 cm) for seam allowances. These strips will be attached to each side of the lace. Apply

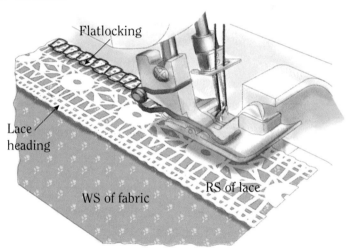

Diagram 2

spray starch to the wrong side of the fabric strips and lace. Press from the right side.

2. Place the lace, right side up, on top of the wrong side of one fabric strip with the edge of the lace heading even with the fabric's raw edge. Serge slowly and carefully over the lace heading edge. The stitches should cover the heading but not eat into the lace pattern. See **Diagram 2**.

3. Open the fabric layers so the looper threads float on the surface along the lace. Join the second fabric strip to the other side of the lace in the same manner.

Lace-to-Lace Heirloom Sewing

Join fabric strips featuring a variety of "heirloom" stitches to create delicate lengths of fabric from which to cut pattern pieces. You may want to review the information featured in "Heirloom Sewing" on page 155 before trying lace-to-lace sewing. Entredeux (see page 141) is often used between two lace strips, but you can also join lace strips to each other.

Get Ready

Needle	Embroidery, size 60/8, 65/9, or 70/10
Thread	Cotton embroidery
Notions	Spray starch, flat lace insertion, tear-away stabilizer

Get Set

Presser foot	Open-toe embroidery, all-purpose, edgestitch, or adjustable blind hem
Stitch	Zigzag
Stitch length	15 spi (1.5 mm)
Stitch width	Narrow

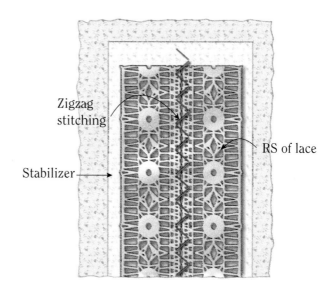

Sew

1. For general guidance on techniques and supplies see "Heirloom Sewing" on page 155. Apply spray starch to the wrong side of the two pieces of lace insertion and press on the right side.

2. Place the lace, right side up, on top of a strip of stabilizer with the headings butted, not overlapping. When joining side-by-side rows of the same lace, match the position of the lace motifs that are across from one another. Begin stitching on the stabilizer.

3. Zigzag the headings together. The stabilizer will prevent the stitches from pinching the lace headings together. See the diagram above. Carefully remove the stabilizer, tearing gently so that you don't damage the delicate lace.

Lettuce Hems and Edges

A flirty edge that's suitable for the edge of stretchy knits and bias-cut woven fabrics, the lettuce leaf finish is fast and easy. It looks great as a hem on a knit dress, as well as an edge finish on a short sleeve, a ribbed collar and cuffs, or a single-layer soft-knit sash.

The finish works best on stretchy knits, including interlock knits and T-shirt ribbing, as well as on single knits that curl to the right side when stretched crosswise.

ROLLED LETTUCE EDGE

This fluted, lettucelike edge is often featured as a hem for ready-to-wear knit garments, but you can also use it to create design interest and add color by serging over a folded edge—on rib knit cuffs, collars, and socks, for example. The technique is similar to "Zigzag Lettuce Edging" on page 166. However, you have the option of stretching the fabric as it's being stitched or waiting until after it's serged.

Get Ready

Needle	Appropriate for fabric and thread
Thread	All-purpose or decorative*
Notions	Appliqué or embroidery scissors

Get Set

Presser foot	Standard or rolled edge
Stitch	Rolled edge
Stitch length	Short
Stitch width	Narrow
Differential feed	Use a minus setting, if available

Use a contrasting, decorative thread in the upper looper, if desired.

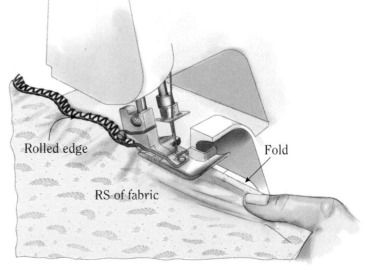

Rolled edge

Fold

RS of fabric

Diagram 1

Serge

1. Trim the hem allowance to ½ inch (1.25 cm) and press it under.

2. Serge along the fold, making sure the knife doesn't cut the fold. Stretch the fabric as you serge or serge first, then stretch it. See **Diagram 1** on page 165. A differential feed can create ample rippling along the edge without any fabric stretching.

3. Trim the excess hem allowance close to the stitching on the inside of the garment.

SUCCESSFUL STRATEGIES FOR LEAFY LETTUCE

Lighten up. Use a fabric that's lightweight.

Sew directionally. Stitch and stretch on the crossgrain of knits or the true bias of wovens.

Tighten up. Increase the pressure on the presser foot.

Get shorty. Shorten the stitch length.

ZIGZAG LETTUCE EDGING

Closely spaced satin stitching, most commonly used for appliqué and other decorative stitching, makes lettuce edging a cinch on the sewing machine. Because of the way the closely spaced stitch forms over a folded edge, stretchy fabrics, including bias-cut edges, ripple while you stitch. The result is a fluted edge that looks very similar to—you guessed it—the edge of a lettuce leaf. You can obtain an edge that's even more fluted by stretching the fabric after it's stitched.

Get Ready

Needle	Appropriate for fabric and thread
Thread	All-purpose or cotton embroidery
Notions	Appliqué or embroidery scissors

Get Set

Presser foot	All-purpose
Stitch	Satin
Stitch length	20 spi (1 mm)
Stitch width	Medium

Sew

1. Trim the hem allowance to ½ inch (1.25 cm) and press it under.

2. Satin stitch along the fold, making sure the needle catches fabric on the left swing and goes over the edge on the right swing. The fabric will ripple automatically. For more rippling, stretch the edge after stitching it. See **Diagram 2.**

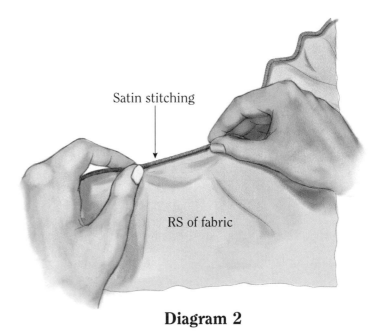

Satin stitching

RS of fabric

Diagram 2

3. Trim the excess hem allowance close to the stitching on the inside of the garment.

Needle Lace

Several sewing groups were treated to a sneak preview of needle lace before this book was printed. All were fascinated and surprised by the simplicity of the technique. Thanks to the availability of stabilizers, you can easily sew a piece of open, lacy fabric for a collar, inset, or overlay. Several methods are featured in this section, including a trim that's created on a serger.

NEEDLE LACE FABRIC

Lace fabric is a creative use for thread leftovers, since it takes a lot to make this airy confection. You will build up a rhythmic pattern while stitching, so it's best to complete the lace in one sitting rather than stopping and starting.

Create a piece of lace to appliqué to a collar using free-motion stitching on a stabilizer and decorative threads in the bobbin.[†]

Get Ready

Needle	Metalfil or Metallica, size 80/12
Needle thread	Cotton embroidery
Bobbin thread	Matching embroidery*
Notions	Two or more bobbins for each thread; water- or heat-soluble stabilizer; machine embroidery hoop (optional)[†]

Get Set

	First Pass	Second Pass
Presser foot	All-purpose or straight	Darning
Throat plate	Straight stitch, if available	Straight stitch, if available
Stitch	Straight	Straight
Stitch length	8 spi (3.5 mm)	8 spi (3.5 mm)
Bobbin tension	Looser for thicker threads	Looser for thicker threads
Needle tension	Loosen by 1 to 1½ settings	Loosen by 1 to 1½ settings
Feed dogs	Engaged	Disengaged or covered

*You may want to substitute assorted colors and types of decorative threads, including ribbon floss and metallic embroidery.

[†]Choose the one that will work best with your selected threads. Water-soluble stabilizers are best for heat-sensitive, flat lamé, or tinsel metallic threads.

Sew

1. Fill your bobbins with decorative thread. For thicker threads, bypass the bobbin-winding tension post. Instead, pinch the thread between your thumb and forefinger to provide the tension, and wind slowly. Keep the thread from piling up on one side of the bobbin.

2. Cut a piece of stabilizer 2 to 3 inches (5 to 8 cm) larger than the desired finished size. If the area is bigger than a sheet of stabilizer, overlap and zigzag a second piece to the edge of the first.

3. Set up the machine and test the technique on a scrap of stabilizer. If it puckers, adjust the tension, switch to a straight stitch foot and throat plate, and add a second layer of stabilizer. With a water-soluble stabilizer, place the layers between two press cloths and lightly press them together. If necessary, put the work in an embroidery hoop. If you cannot adjust the bobbin tension for thicker decorative threads, try bypassing the tension spring.

4. Cover the stabilizer with stitches, sewing in long, continuous lines. Turn corners with wide curves rather than by pivoting. Stitch until the thread on the bobbin runs out. Cut the thread close to the stabilizer. Continue with another bobbin of thread. Work until the spaces between the lines are from ⅛ to ½ inch (3 mm to 1.25 cm) apart.

5. Change your thread and machine settings as indicated for the Second Pass. Stitch in loops and swirls to fill in the stitching as desired. The photo on page 167 shows the finished effect.

6. Remove the stabilizer. Press your lace with a steam iron set on low. Use a press cloth. Cut and handle the "fabric" like a lightweight lace when constructing the garment.

Sharp Notion

For zigzag needle lace, sew overlapping rows of wide, medium-length zigzag stitches onto the stabilizer. Stitch vertical rows, then cross these with horizontal and diagonal rows, leaving spaces for an open mesh look.

NEEDLE LACE INSERTIONS

Often a garment "asks" for a small, lace insert. A shell, for example, looks great with a lacy teardrop shape at center front.

Rather than appliquéing a piece of needle lace to the garment, you can sew the lace into the fabric piece. That way, you eliminate the hassle of attaching the work to the fabric. Try cutting your shape from paper and experimenting with its position on your garment before you make the lace.

Freehand zigzagging over stitched bars

Satin stitching around outside edges

Get Ready

Needle	Embroidery, Metalfil, or Metallica, to suit fabric and thread
Needle thread	Cotton embroidery*
Bobbin thread	Transparent or all-purpose, to match the needle thread
Notions	Machine embroidery hoop, water soluble stabilizer, lightweight fusible interfacing (optional), chalk pencil, appliqué or embroidery scissors

Get Set

	First Pass	Second Pass	Third Pass
Presser foot	Darning	Darning	Embroidery
Stitch	Straight	Straight	Satin
Stitch length	0	0	24 spi (0.5 mm)
Stitch width	—	2.5 mm	Medium to wide
Feed dogs	Disengaged or covered	Disengaged or covered	Engaged

You can make needle lace with decorative threads, including metallic threads.

Sew

1. Plan the shape and location of your motif. It's usually best done in small areas of a design. For larger motifs you can keep moving and repositioning the hoop as you work.

2. If desired, apply lightweight fusible interfacing to the wrong side of knits or lightweight fabrics to support the extra weight of the decorative work.

3. Mark the desired design shapes on the right side of the fabric. With a layer of stabilizer on the bottom, load the fabric into the hoop and place it under the darning foot. You can try this technique without the stabilizer as long as the fabric is taut in the hoop.

4. Draw the bobbin thread to the top of the fabric at the drawn line and take a few straight stitches to anchor the thread. Trim the thread tails. Make reinforcing stitches by straight stitching around the design lines of each motif. Do this two or three times if you're not using a stabilizer or if the design shape is irregular. The rows of stitching can be on top of one another or close together. They don't have to be perfect because they're covered up later.

5. Remove the hoop from the machine and, working on one motif at a time, carefully cut away the fabric

in the area that you're filling with lace. Don't cut the stabilizer. If it's easier, remove the work from the hoop. Put it back in the hoop and insert it under the presser foot.

6. Anchor the threads. Create a web of stabilizing bars by straight stitching on the stabilizer, across the opening, to the opposite fabric edge. Make two or three stitches in place, then sew along the edge to a new location, and stitch back across to another location on the opposite side of the opening. Stitch so that there are always two lines of stitching parallel and close together. See **Diagram 1.** Be sure the outermost points of designs with uneven edges are connected with a line of stitches. Sew at a moderate and even pace. Cover the entire open area in this manner. If a

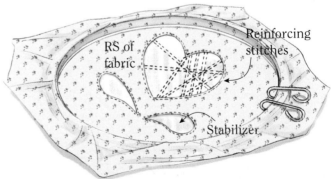

Diagram 1

thread breaks or wraps around the needle in the middle of your motif, clip the threads close to the work, then go back to a cut edge, draw the bobbin thread to the top, anchor the stitches as explained in Step 4, and continue.

7. Change to the Second Pass settings and sew across the "web," allowing the stitching to catch and draw together two of the lines of stitching. It isn't necessary to return to a fabric edge with every "line" of stitching. Try stitching in circles as well as back and forth. For areas of heavier stitching, change to the widest stitch width on your machine.

8. Stitch back to the cut edge of the shape and change to the Third Pass settings. Satin stitch around the edges, making sure that the right swing of the needle goes over the cut edge to capture and cover it. If you are comfortable with free-motion stitching, you can free-motion satin stitch instead, but you may need to sew over the first satin stitching with a slightly wider stitch to completely cover the edges.

9. Tear away the stabilizer. If necessary, spritz or dip in cold water to remove any additional residue caught in the stitching. If you used metallic thread and want to press your work, use only the low setting.

SERGER LACE

Overlapped rows of serging create a lacy edge. The technique calls for stitching directly on the garment, but you can make piping by stitching the folded edge of a 1¼-inch (3 cm)-wide bias fabric strip. Try rayon embroidery, metallic, and variegated threads to make really interesting serger lace.

Get Ready

Needle	Appropriate for fabric and thread
Needle thread	All-purpose or lightweight decorative*
UL thread	Decorative
LL thread	Decorative

Get Set

Presser foot	Standard
Stitch	Balanced three-thread overlock
Stitch length	As desired
Stitch width	Medium
Upper knife	Disengaged, if possible

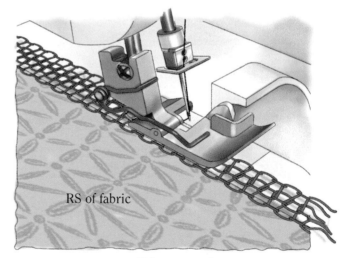

RS of fabric

Diagram 2

Use matching all-purpose thread in the needle with heavier thread in the loopers.

Serge

1. Position the garment edge under the needle so that it will just catch the fabric and the stitches will hang off the edge. Serge.

2. Serge a second row over the loose edge of the previous row of serging. Add as many additional rows as desired. See **Diagram 2.**

THREE-DIMENSIONAL NEEDLE LACE

It's fun to make three-dimensional needle lace appliqués on your sewing machine. For example, stitch metallic and rayon embroidery threads into needle lace leaves, then hand-tack them across the shoulder of a suede jacket. Or combine a few loose petals into flat appliquéd floral designs. You can also make a pretty corsage to pin to the lapel of a jacket.

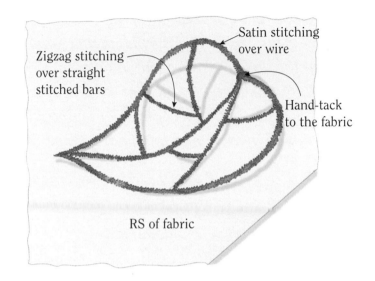

Zigzag stitching over straight stitched bars

Satin stitching over wire

Hand-tack to the fabric

RS of fabric

Diagram 3

Get Ready

Needle	Embroidery, Metalfil, or Metallica
Needle thread	Cotton embroidery*
Bobbin thread	Transparent, all purpose, or to match the needle thread
Notions	Machine embroidery hoop; water-soluble stabilizer; lightweight fusible interfacing (optional); appliqué or embroidery scissors; 32-gauge wire (optional)

Get Set

	First Pass	Second Pass	Third Pass
Presser foot	Darning	Darning	Open-toe embroidery
Stitch	Straight	Straight	Satin
Stitch length	0	0	24 spi (0.5 mm)
Stitch width	—	2.5 mm	Medium
Feed dogs	Disengaged or covered	Disengaged or covered	Engaged

You can make needle lace with decorative threads, including metallic threads.

Sew

1. Follow the first two passes above and Steps 1 through 7 of "Needle Lace Insertions" on page 168, using a scrap as the base fabric.

2. Remove the work from the hoop and cut out the shape as close to the stitches as you can get without cutting into them.

3. Set your sewing machine to the Third Pass settings. In this step you'll finish the outer edges of the three-dimensional needle lace shapes so that they won't fray and they can stand out from the fabric surface. Baste the needle lace to a piece of water-soluble stabilizer and place it in the hoop. Engage the feed dogs and attach an open-toe embroidery foot. (If you wish to make it easy to shape the needle lace pieces into realistic positions, catch 32-gauge wire along the edge with a narrow zigzag stitch.) Satin stitch over the outer edges of the work to catch and hide the raw edges (and the wire if you used it). Remove the stabilizer. See **Diagram 3.**

Picot Trim

Picot loops are usually found in embroidery or along the edge of a ribbon or trim. With these instructions you can create your own picot piping to insert in a seam or trim a hem. You'll love the picots that you can make using the built-in scallop stitch on your sewing machine. Try it for an edging on a collar, or accent the pocket on a blouse. It's also fun creating picot piping with a decorative thread in the upper looper of your serger.

OVERLOCK PICOT PIPING

This softly looped picot trim is ideal for enhancing the edges and seams of a garment that you're making. It's created by serging on a strip of fabric with a decorative thread, using a three-thread overlock stitch, then inserting the stitched fabric strip into a seam. You sew it into the seam in the same manner that you attach piping. Overlock picot piping trim is rather delicate, so it's best to use it only where the loops won't easily get caught during normal wear. Ideal locations include places like interior band edges and at the outer edges of a collar or the lower edge of a yoke.

To further stabilize the completed trim, zigzag over the serger needle stitching with "invisible" transparent thread.

Get Ready	Serger	Sewing Machine
Fabric	1½-inch (4-cm)-wide bias-cut strip of the desired length for your seam	
Needle thread	Transparent	Transparent
Bobbin thread	—	All-purpose
UL thread	Crochet cotton; heavy pearl cotton; pearl rayon ribbon floss; or soft, fine yarn	—
LL thread	Transparent	—

Get Set

	Serger	Sewing Machine
Stitch	Three-thread overlock	Zigzag
Stitch length	Longest possible	12 spi (2 mm)
Stitch width	Widest possible	Narrow
Tension	0	Balanced
Upper knife	Disengaged, if possible	—

Serge and Sew

1. Test the serger stitch and adjust for more closely spaced loops, if desired. To adjust the tension, you may want to leave the decorative thread out of the tension discs and perhaps one or more of the thread guides.

2. Fold the fabric strip in half lengthwise, wrong sides together, with raw edges even. Press.

3. Place the strip on the serger so that the needle stitches close to the fold with the thread loops falling off the edge. Don't trim the edge as you stitch.

4. At the sewing machine, zigzag over the serger needle stitching, catching every loop with transparent thread. See the photo on the opposite page.

5. With right sides together and raw edges even, pin the piping to the garment. Put contrasting thread in the bobbin and use a needle thread that matches your fabric. From the piping side, machine baste along the edge of the picot stitches on the fabric. Add the remaining layer of fabric, pin, and stitch just inside the row of contrasting basting stitches.

Workroom Secret

If you have a Husqvarna sewing machine, you can use the manufacturer's braiding guide to stitch cord to a fabric surface. This metal attachment, which extends over the top of the presser foot and guides the cord into the best position, will make it easier for you to create the Scallop-Stitch Picots featured on page 174. But if you don't have this attachment or you lack the presser feet specified in the instructions, you can use your fingers to guide the cord under an all-purpose presser foot. To do this, simply hold the cord up (in front of the foot) between your thumb and forefinger, as shown in the diagram. With the cord in this position, sew as directed.

SCALLOP-STITCH PICOTS

This technique is a very creative way to use the satin scallop stitch that is built into many sewing machines. You stitch on a water-soluble stabilizer and the stitching looks like hand crocheting when the stabilizer is removed. The finished edge of a tuck, collar, cuff, or hem are all perfect candidates for this lacy edge treatment. You can also create multirow scallops for a wider edging.

Get Ready

Needle	Appropriate for fabric and thread
Thread	Machine embroidery
Notions	Buttonhole twist, #5 pearl cotton, or other cord to match thread color; water-soluble stabilizer

Get Set

Presser foot	Braiding, cording, or rolled hemmer
Stitch	Scallop
Stitch length	24 spi (0.5 mm)
Stitch width	Wide
Needle tension	Loosen slightly

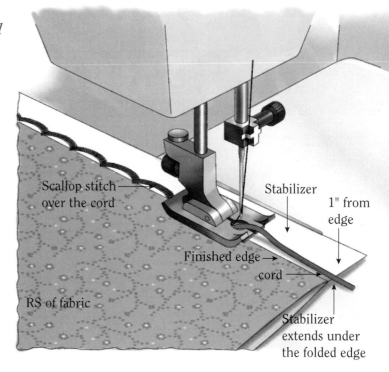

Scallop stitch over the cord

Stabilizer

1" from edge

Finished edge

cord

RS of fabric

Stabilizer extends under the folded edge

Sew

1. Thread the cord under the presser foot with 2 to 3 inches (5 to 8 cm) extending behind the foot.

2. Place a 1½-inch (4-cm)-wide strip of water-soluble stabilizer under the garment's finished edge. Extend the stabilizer at least 1 inch (2.5 cm) to the right of the finished edge.

3. Scallop stitch, guiding the work so that the point of each scallop catches the finished fabric edge and corded scallops form on the stabilizer. See the diagram above. Remove the stabilizer.

Sharp Notion

It's easy to make picot piping using the directions for scallop-stitch picots. This is done by stitching scallops to the folded edge of a 1¼-inch (3-cm)-wide strip of lightweight fabric.

Pintucks

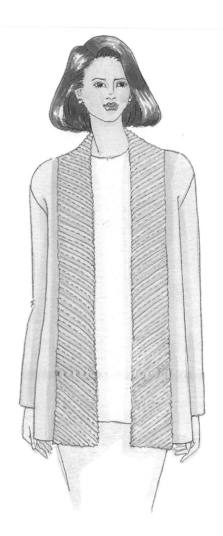

Play with pintucks to create a decorative surface. Tuck a sleeve band, add texture around the bottom of a full skirt, or fill a sweatshirt yoke with crisscrossed rows. Combine varying tuck widths, stitch decorative line designs borrowed from books of quilting patterns to create a medallion effect, or crosshatch rows of pintucks for even more variety. To create pintucks, you'll need twin needles, available in a variety of sizes and styles, including stretch, denim, embroidery, and Metalfil. The distance between the points determines the size of the tuck. Pintuck feet are also available in a number of sizes, to match the needles. Use the table below as a guide when choosing a needle size (and width) and pintuck foot.

Expert's Guide to Pintuck Feet

Tuck	No. of Grooves	Needle Spacing*	Needle Size*	Typical Uses
Fine	Nine-groove	1.6 mm	70/10, 80/12	Batiste, organdy, and similar weights; baby clothes, heirloom sewing projects, sheer blouses
Medium-fine	Seven-groove	2 and 2.5 mm	75/11, 80/12	Most medium to heavyweight fabrics
Medium	Five-groove	3 mm	75/11, 90/14	Denim, fleece, knit terry, sweatshirt fabric, synthetic suede, woolens
Jumbo	Three-groove	4 mm	70/10, 80/12, 90/14	Same as for medium size tucks or even heavier fabrics (with large needle sizes)

*6 and 8 mm 100/16 twin needles are also available for machines with wider stitch capabilities.

CORDED PINTUCKS

A special pintuck presser foot, used in tandem with a twin needle, makes quick and accurate work of row after row of tiny tucks on the sewing machine. The pronounced effect of cording is optional and not recommended for fine fabrics requiring the nine-groove foot.

Get Ready

Needle	Twin*
Needle thread	All-purpose or decorative
Bobbin thread	Woolly nylon or all-purpose
Notions	Fine white cord such as #5 or #8 pearl cotton, buttonhole twist, gimp, or topstitching thread; drinking straw (optional); tailor's chalk or water-soluble marking pen; quilting guide (optional)

Get Set

Presser foot	Pintuck†
Stitch	Straight
Stitch length	12 spi (2 mm)
Needle tension	Increase slightly‡

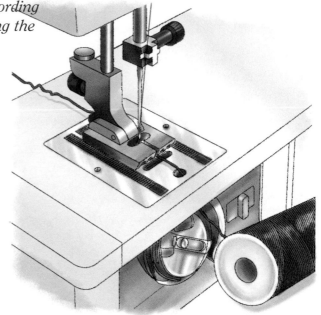

Diagram 1

* *Select the type and size appropriate for the fabric, thread, and pintuck presser foot that you're using.*

†*See "Expert's Guide to Pintuck Feet" on page 175.*

‡*Tighter tension helps raise the tucks. The tighter the tension and the thinner the fabric, the more raised the tucks will be.*

Sew

1. Feed the cord through the cording hole in your needle plate. See **Diagram 1.** If your machine doesn't have a cording hole, guide the cord through a short length of drinking straw taped to the needle plate in front of the needle. See **Diagram 2.** Draw the cord to the back of the pintuck foot. Hold the cord and thread tails as you begin to stitch. The cord will continue to feed as you stitch.

2. Mark the position for the first tuck in the center of the area to be tucked. Stitch with the line centered between the needles. Turn the fabric 180 degrees.

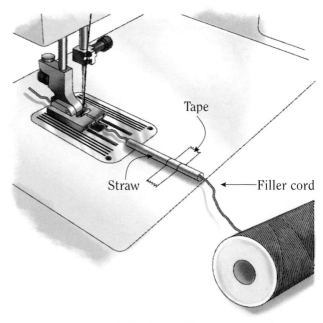

Diagram 2

3. Place the completed tuck under one of the grooves in the foot and stitch the next tuck. Turn the fabric 180 degrees and stitch the next one. Continue in this manner until you have completed all the tucks.

You can use every groove for closely spaced tucks or skip one or more (depending on the number of grooves in the foot) for wider spaces between the tucks. You can also use the edge of the presser foot for spacing, or you can attach a quilting guide. If you wish to do machine embroidery between tucks, be sure to leave adequate space for the desired stitch pattern and width.

ROLLED-EDGE PINTUCKS

The narrow rolled-edge stitch is perfect for adding tiny pintucks to an heirloom sewing project. Using a pastel rayon embroidery thread in the upper looper of your serger adds a hint of color and sheen. March these tiny tucks around a hemline or down the front of a blouse, alternating them with other heirloom techniques. See "Heirloom Sewing" on page 155 for even more appeal.

Get Ready

Needle	Appropriate for fabric and thread
Needle thread	All-purpose serger
UL thread	Decorative*
LL thread	All-purpose or woolly nylon

Get Set

Presser foot	Standard or rolled edge
Stitch	Rolled edge
Stitch length	Short†
Stitch width	Narrow†
Upper knife	Disengaged, if possible

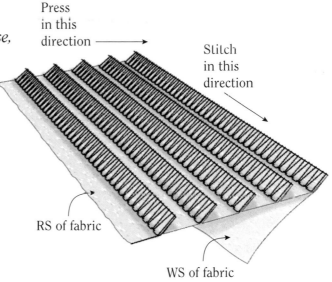

Press in this direction →

Stitch in this direction

RS of fabric

WS of fabric

Diagram 3

You can use rayon, cotton, or metallic embroidery thread; acrylic thread; silk buttonhole twist; woolly nylon; or topstitching thread.

†*Adjust the serger for a narrow rolled edge and test on fabric scraps. Fine-tune the stitch length and width for the thread and the desired appearance. Serger pintucks are generally stitched at a short, satin-stitch length for maximum thread coverage of the fabric underneath.*

Serge

1. Fold the fabric wrong sides together along the tuck placement line, and press.

2. Serge over the fabric fold, taking care not to cut the fold with the serger knives.

3. Position the next tuck a presser foot's width away from the first, and stitch. Take care to stitch all the tucks from the same edge and press all the tucks in the same direction, with the upper looper thread showing. See **Diagram 3.**

Piping

At some point in their careers, many designers explore using piping to accent edges and seamlines on their creations, and many of today's classic garments don't seem complete without it. To add this ready-to-wear detailing to your garments, you can go the traditional route of inserting fabric-wrapped cord between two layers of fabric, but there are other creative variations—even a few that you can do on the serger.

DECORATIVE SERGER PIPING

Heavy decorative threads add drama and dimension to ordinary piping. The serger procedure is simple: Roll-edge stitch over a fabric fold that's filled with cords. The key element is heavy thread in the upper looper (ribbon floss or Pearl Crown Rayon, for example).

Get Ready

Needle	Appropriate for fabric and thread
Needle thread	All-purpose
UL thread	Decorative*
LL thread	All-purpose
Notions	#8 pearl cotton or other filler; 1¼-inch (3-cm)-wide tricot or Seams Great†

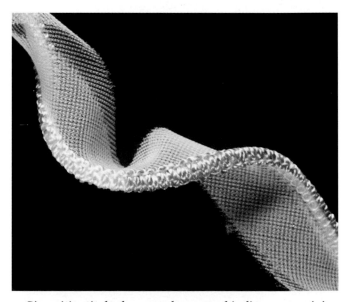

Get Set

Presser foot	Standard or rolled edge
Stitch	Rolled edge
Stitch length	Short‡
Stitch width	Narrow‡
Differential feed	+ or 2, to prevent curling
Upper knife	Disengaged, if possible

Since it's stitched on a nylon seam binding, your piping will have a tendency to curl. You can control this by adjusting your differential feed.

*Try Pearl Crown Rayon, fine metallic, or acrylic yarn or thread; pearl cotton; ribbon floss; or woolly nylon.
†You can substitute straight- or bias-cut organza strips.
‡Test and adjust to achieve a satin finish that completely covers the tricot seam binding and filler without piercing the filler.

Serge

1. Cut three or four strands of filler to the required length.

2. Serge over the strands for 2 inches (5 cm). Don't remove them from the machine.

3. Stretch the tricot until it curls. Place it on the bed of the serger so it curls away from the feed dogs.

4. Lift the presser foot and wrap the tricot around the bare filler with the fold toward the needle and the raw edges even and to the left of the needle. Lower the foot. Holding the tricot and the filler taut behind the presser foot, stitch over the filler and tricot. Don't stitch into the filler. See **Diagram 1**.

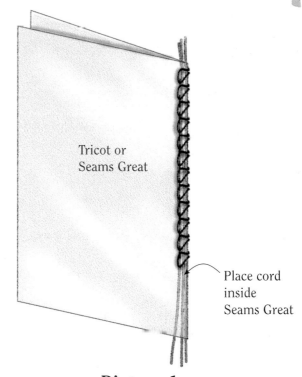

Tricot or Seams Great

Place cord inside Seams Great

Diagram 1

MOCK PIPING

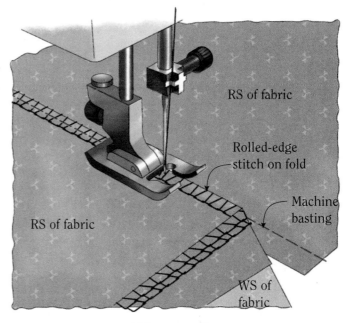

Hassle-free piping is as close as the rolled-edge setting on your serger. Traditionally, piping is stitched into a seam by sandwiching it between the two layers of fabric. But you can forget about cutting bias-strips and hand basting. Just make mock piping by serging along the folded seamline of one garment piece, and topstitching it to its companion piece.

RS of fabric

Rolled-edge stitch on fold

Machine basting

RS of fabric

WS of fabric

Diagram 2

Get Ready	Serger	Sewing Machine
Needle	Appropriate for fabric and thread	Appropriate for fabric and thread
Needle thread	All-purpose serger	Transparent
UL thread	Decorative	—
LL thread	All-purpose serger	—
Bobbin thread	—	All-purpose

Get Set

	Serger	Sewing Machine
Presser foot	Standard	Zipper or open-toe embroidery
Stitch	Rolled edge	Straight
Stitch length	Short	12 spi (2 mm)
Stitch width	Narrow	—

Serge and Sew

1. Along the seamline, turn under the seam allowance on one of the two fabric pattern pieces that will be joined. Don't sew the pieces together.

2. With the right side up, roll-edge serge over the folded edge. Do not cut the fold.

3. Machine baste a guideline along the seamline of the remaining garment piece. With both garment pieces right side up, place the serged edge on top of the basted guideline on the second garment piece. At the sewing machine topstitch the two layers together close to the serged edge. See **Diagram 2** on page 179.

MULTICOLOR PIPING

Whether fashionable or classic, this piping, made at your sewing machine, can suit your garment. For a tweed jacket, pick out piping fabric in two of the dominant colors. Or use three or more fabrics to accent and strengthen selected seamlines on a solid-color sundress.

If you want to make piping from a single fabric but need to join shorter strips to create a longer length, refer to Step 3 of these instructions. If you plan to apply piping to a curved edge, use bias-cut strips.

Get Ready

Fabric	Bias-cut or straight-grain strips
Needle	Appropriate for fabric and thread
Thread	All-purpose
Notions	Acrylic yarn, polyester cable, or twisted cotton for filler cord

Get Set

Presser foot	Piping, Pearls 'N Piping, or zipper
Stitch	Straight
Stitch length	8 spi (3.5 mm)

This piping is a perfect match for the garment fabric, but it's actually made from several different fabrics that are pieced together to create the multicolor effect when finally assembled.

Sew

1. To determine the width that you will need to cut the fabric strips for the piping, wrap a scrap of the fabric around the filler cord and pin the edges together close to the cord. Now pull the cord out of the fabric scrap. Measure the width from the fold to the pins, and double this number. Add 1¼ inches (3 cm), for two seam allowances. For ruched piping, make the width three times the diameter of the filler cord, plus two seam allowances. See page 183.

2. The length of your fabric strip is usually the length of the seamline on your tissue pattern. Fabric strips for ruched piping are two to three times the finished length, plus 6 inches (15 cm).

3. Seam short lengths of assorted fabrics together to make a fabric strip long enough to cover the filler. To join two fabric strips, place a short cut end of each strip, right sides togethe, at a right angle. Stitch on the diagonal from corner to corner. See **Diagram 3.** Trim the seam allowances to ¼ inch (6 mm), and press them open.

4. Wrap the fabric strip, right side out, around the filler. Secure it with a pin or two to get started.

5. Stitch down the length of the fabric as close as possible to the filler. When stitching straight-grain strips, hold the fabric taut behind and in front of the foot. When using bias strips, stretch the fabric while stitching.

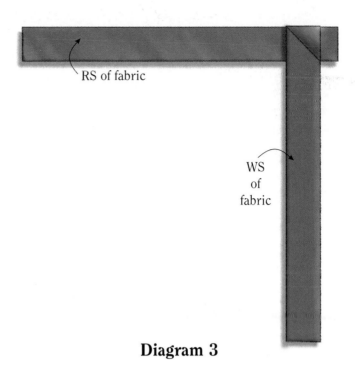

RS of fabric

WS of fabric

Diagram 3

Workroom Secret

For an adjustable seam gauge, secure a piece of ¼-inch (6.0-mm)-wide elastic around the free arm of your sewing machine. Slide it to any location on the machine's bed for an extra-wide seam allowance guide.

Workroom Secret

For very fine piping, you can experiment with presser feet to find one that's suitable for guiding the piping. Try using an invisible zipper foot, or even one of the grooves in the bottom of a pintuck foot.

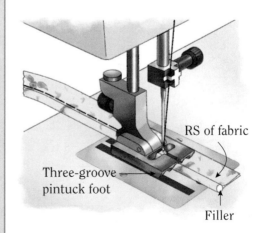

RS of fabric

Three-groove pintuck foot

Filler

PINTUCK PIPING

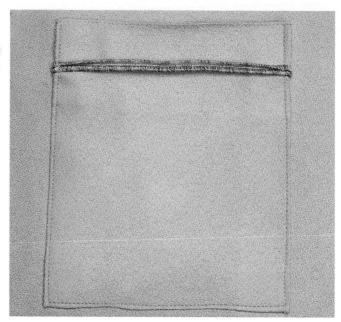

Here's yet another decorative option for the versatile rolled-edge stitch. Side-by-side pintucks on a fabric strip make an interesting and more decorative piping trim. You can even widen the stitch width for the second pintuck for another version of this serged piping trim.

For a striped effect, use a contrasting thread in the upper looper for each pintuck.

Variegated metallic thread in the upper looper results in a flexible, subtle piping.

Get Ready

	Sewing Machine	Serger
Fabric	2¼-inch (5.6-cm)-wide fabric strips (bias-cut for curved seams)	
Needle	Appropriate for fabric and thread	Appropriate for fabric and thread
Needle thread	All-purpose	All-purpose
Bobbin thread	All-purpose	—
UL thread	—	Decorative
LL thread	—	All-purpose

Get Set

	Sewing Machine	Serger
Presser foot	All-purpose	Standard or rolled edge
Stitch	Straight	Rolled edge
Stitch length	6 spi (4 mm)	Short (1 to 2 mm)
Stitch width	—	Narrow
Upper knife	—	Disengaged, if possible

Sew and Serge

1. Machine baste ¼ inch (6 mm) from one long edge of one strip. Fold the strip with wrong sides together and one long edge at the basted line. Press lightly.

2. Serge over the folded edge.

3. To make a second line of stitching, refold the fabric strip so the needle stitching for both tucks meet

when serged. See the photo above. The resulting seam allowance should be ⅝ inch (1.5 cm) wide from the stitching line closest to the raw edges of the finished piping. Trim if necessary.

4. Place the piping right side up on the garment and turn the pintuck closest to the raw edges toward the other pintuck. Using a zipper foot, stitch as close to the needle stitching as possible.

MARCHING TO A DIFFERENT PIPING

You can create unique detailing by varying the "cord" that you insert into the seam when you're at the sewing machine. The examples on this page are a launching point for your imagination.

Since piping is such a straightforward procedure, you will find that all of the ideas shown on this page are simple variations on the instructions for "Multicolor Piping" on page 180. The results, however, are so dramatic that others will assume that you spent a considerable amount of time making and inserting the piping.

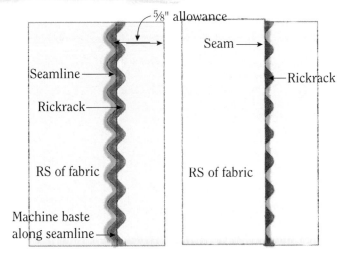

Attach rickrack piping just as you would soutache to create a delicate scallop along the seam.

For double piping, stack and stitch together two separate lengths of piping, using a contrasting bobbin thread. Align the contrasting thread with the garment seamline.

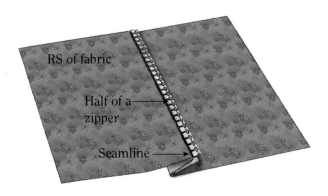

Although not functional, a zipper makes fun piping. Buy an extra-long separating zipper, then stitch one half into each seam using a zipper or piping presser foot.

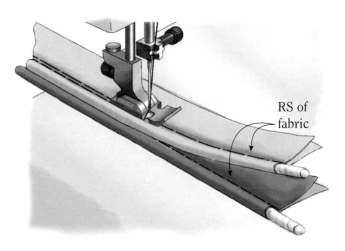

Stitch soutache to the center of a seamline with contrasting bobbin thread. Sew exactly on top of the first stitching when joining the piped layer to the matching garment piece.

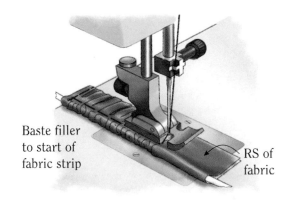

Ruched piping is best with a thick filler. Use a zipper foot. As you baste, stop every 6 inches (15 cm) and pull the filler to gather the fabric.

Puffing

Gathered strips of puffing add a soft dimension between trims and lace in heirloom sewing. Consider combining puffing with fabric strips featuring entredeux, lace insertion, and hemstitching.

The serger's differential feed makes all the difference because you can adjust the gathers for more or less fullness even after completing the stitching. It's a real time-saver, and the gathers are more uniformly spaced than with any sewing machine method.

Get Ready

Needle	70/10
Thread	All-purpose serger or rayon embroidery

Get Set

Presser foot	Standard
Stitch	Three-thread overlock
Stitch length	Medium
Stitch width	No wider than ¼ inch (6 mm)
Differential feed	+ or 2, if available*

If differential feed is not available, serge over a fine cord using a cording foot. Pull the cord to gather.

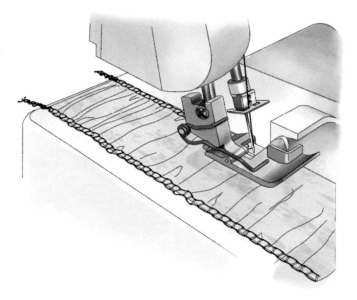

Serge

1. For general techniques see "Heirloom Sewing" on page 155. Cut fabric strips the desired width plus ½ inch (1.25 cm), and two to three times the required finished length.

2. Serge along each long edge of the puffing strip. Small pleats will form as you serge. See the diagram above.

3. Working on a padded pressing surface, adjust the fullness by sliding the tiny tucks along the needle thread. For more closely spaced gathers, draw up the needle thread as you would the bobbin thread in sewing machine stitching. Remember, the needle thread is always the shortest thread in the chain of serger stitches. Arrange the gathers so they are perpendicular to the long edges of the strip. Steam and allow to dry thoroughly.

4. Attach the puffing strips to flat fabric strips with conventional straight-stitch seams or with a narrow, medium-length, balanced three-thread overlock seam.

Rolled Edges and Hems

Some sewers think they need a serger to make a rolled edge. Not true! In addition to some unique uses for the serger rolled hem, this section includes techniques for the sewing machine. See "Designer Rolled Hem" on page 188 and "Fine Edge Finish" on page 189.

Hemming long expanses of fabric on a serger is a breeze. And when you serge a rolled hem with decorative threads, you can create a delightful collection of decorative finishes, from the appearance of a densely covered piped edge to a fine picot.

AUTHENTIC ROLLED HEM

The rolled-edge serger stitch is one of the most attractive ways to finish an edge, and it has so many applications. The short, narrow stitch wraps the fabric edge into a tight roll that, with decorative thread in the upper looper, has the appearance of fine piping.

Get Ready

Needle	65/9 or 75/11*
Needle thread	All-purpose or transparent
UL thread	All-purpose or decorative
LL thread	All-purpose or decorative

*You may need a larger needle size for heavier fabrics.

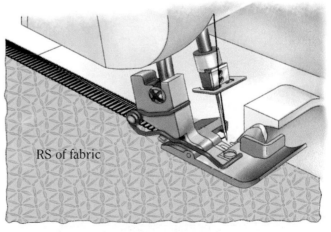

RS of fabric

Diagram 1

Get Set

Presser foot	Standard or rolled edge
Stitch	Two- or three-thread rolled edge*
Stitch length	Short†
Stitch width	2 mm or narrower
Needle tension	Tighten
LL tension	Tighten for a three-thread rolled-edge stitch
Differential feed	-.7 to -.85

*Use only the right needle on a three/four model unless the owner's manual says otherwise.

†For a softer, more delicate edge on sheer fabrics, use a longer stitch length.

Serge

1. Trim the hem allowance if necessary, leaving only a ¼-inch (6-mm)-wide allowance. Trim the seam allowances within the hem allowance to remove excess bulk.

2. With the fabric right side up, serge along the edge, allowing the knives to trim away ⅛ inch (3 mm). See **Diagram 1** on page 185. (If you're making a rolled edge on tricot, place the fabric right side down, as tricot always rolls to the right side. If you try to roll the edge with the fabric right side up, you and your serger are in for a fight!)

SUCCESSFUL STRATEGIES FOR ROLLED-EDGE STITCHING

Do the wash. Prewash washable fabrics to remove sizing. The fabric will be softer and will roll more easily.

Cover up. For the best edge coverage, use woolly nylon thread in the upper looper. Loosen the upper tension so this soft thread fluffs out and covers the fabric edge when you use a short stitch length. Be sure to use woolly nylon or transparent nylon or polyester in the lower looper for the best roll. With other decorative upper looper threads, remember that thinner threads require a shorter stitch length for the best coverage, but thicker threads need a longer length so the loops have space to lie next to each other without clumping.

Fold it and roll it. Before you give up entirely on a stubborn fabric, turn under a ½-inch (1.25-cm)-wide hem first, then do the serger rolled-edge finish over the fold without cutting it. Use appliqué scissors to trim away the excess hem allowance on the underside.

Banish whiskers. Get rid of pesky cut threads that poke out at the edge by widening the serger stitch slightly. If that doesn't work, place a narrow strip of water-soluble stabilizer on top of the fabric edge, then serge through both of the layers. Spritz away, or carefully tear away the water-soluble stabilizer from the rolled edge.

Hold that edge. If the serger rolled edge pulls away from the fabric edge, leaving a new raw edge behind —sometimes a problem on straight-cut edges on sheer or loosely woven fabrics—try lengthening the stitch so the needle perforations aren't so closely spaced. Other remedies include widening the stitch a bit or loosening the lower looper tension a little. If all else fails, settle on a different edge finish. Note: Fabrics with prominent crosswise ribs are unlikely candidates for the rolled-edge finish. The ribbing thread is difficult to force into a roll, and even if you conquer the rolling, the finished edge pulls away easily.

CHAINING ON AND ON

A serger chain made with the rolled-edge setting is tremendously versatile. By stitching without fabric you'll end up with a cord that can be braided or couched, or that can have a more functional use on your garment. As you play with the rolled-edge stitch, you'll discover that switching just one thread or setting can dramatically affect the results.

Get Ready

Needle	Appropriate for fabric and thread
Thread	All-purpose serger, decorative, or transparent*

Get Set

Presser foot	Rolled edge
Stitch	Rolled edge
Stitch length	Short
Stitch width	Narrow

*If you want the needle thread to almost disappear, use a transparent thread. For a firm, tight chain, use woolly nylon or transparent thread in the lower looper.

Serge

1. Thread the serger with the desired thread combination and test your stitch settings. To prevent stitch jamming, use a slightly longer stitch when adjusting the rolled edge for heavier decorative threads.

2. Lower the presser foot and hold onto the threads behind the foot as you begin to serge. Stitch, making as much serger chain as you wish.

3. Some decorative threads may catch when you first start stitching. To chain with ease, tuck a 2-inch (5-cm) square of fabric under the foot and begin to serge. Trim away the square and discard.

4. If you have a bit of extra time, you can put it to good use when making serger chain. Rather than stopping when you have enough chain for your project, keep on serging. Wrap the extra chain on cardboard and store for future use.

Combine lengths of chain to make tassels or fringe. You can customize by matching the thread colors to your fabric.

SUCCESSFUL STRATEGIES FOR MAKING SERGER CHAIN

Think long. To prevent stitch jamming, use a slightly longer stitch when adjusting the rolled edge for heavier decorative threads.

Roll on. For the strongest chain, stitch at the narrow rolled-edge setting.

Play hide 'n seek. The upper looper thread will be the most obvious and the needle thread the least obvious. (If you want the needle thread to almost disappear, use a transparent thread.)

DESIGNER ROLLED HEM

Sometimes called a Calvin Klein hem, it's used for fine- to medium-weight cottons, rayons, and silks. This rolled hem, made at the sewing machine, works on straight grain or bias edges and can be used to hem scarves, sleeves, and skirts. It's a nice alternative when you don't have a serger.

Get Ready

Thread	All-purpose to match the project
Notions	Appliqué or embroidery scissors

Get Set

Presser foot	Edgestitch or blind hem with adjustable center guide*
Stitch	Straight
Stitch length	8 to 12 spi (3.5 to 2 mm)
Needle position	Left

*If you don't have an edgestitch or adjustable blind hem foot, use a zigzag presser foot and adjust your needle to the right so that you can stitch closer to the folded edge.

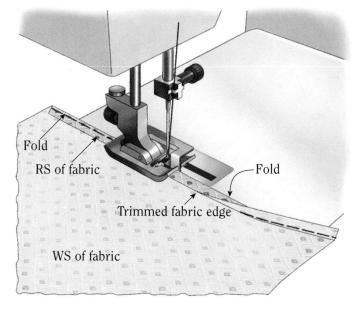

Diagram 2

Sew

1. Trim the hem allowance to ⅝ inch (1.5 cm).

2. Turn under ⅜ inch (1 cm) and press. Stitch with the folded edge along the center guide in the foot.

3. Trim as close to the stitching as possible.

4. Turn under the stitched, trimmed edge again and edgestitch. See **Diagram 2**. Press.

Sharp Notion

On the sheerest of fabrics, chiffon for example, try a floating hem. It's called a floating hem because there's so little hem allowance at the edge. It works best and is most durable on a bias edge. Press the hem allowance to the wrong side. Open the hem and straight stitch at 12 spi (2 mm) on the crease. Turn up the hem and edgestitch (with the blind hem or edgestitching foot) ⅛ inch (3 mm) from the fold. Trim away the hem allowance next to the stitching.

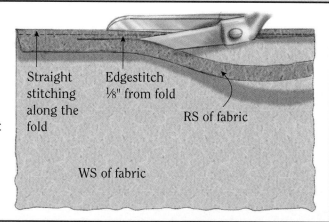

FINE EDGE FINISH

If you don't have a serger, you can emulate a rolled edge on the sewing machine with this technique. It's an appropriate single-layer finish on fine or lightweight fabrics. Try the technique on a single-layer handkerchief linen blouse collar or a sheer gauze skirt, for starters. This finish is best on straight-grain or almost straight-grain edges.

Get Ready

Needle	Sharp, size 60/8 to 70/10
Thread	Embroidery cotton, rayon, or all-purpose polyester*
Notions	Pearl cotton #12 (optional)

Get Set

Presser Foot	Buttonhole
Stitch	Zigzag
Stitch length	24 to 50 spi (0.5 mm)—almost 0
Stitch width	Medium (3 mm)
Needle position	Left, if possible
Needle tension	Loosen one to two settings

*Finer thread for finer fabrics is the general rule here.

Sew

1. Test-stitch with the fabric right side up and right side down. Some fabrics may roll under, and some may roll to the right side.

2. Position the fabric so that the raw edge is under the right-hand tunnel on the bottom of the foot.

3. Sew, making sure that the stitches grab and roll the edge. See **Diagram 3.** If the edge tends to flute a little or if you prefer a more stable edge, place a single strand of fine pearl cotton under the left tunnel on the bottom of the foot. Slightly pull on it while stitching to prevent stretching. You may need to practice a little to avoid catching the cord in the stitching. It should lie under the stitching.

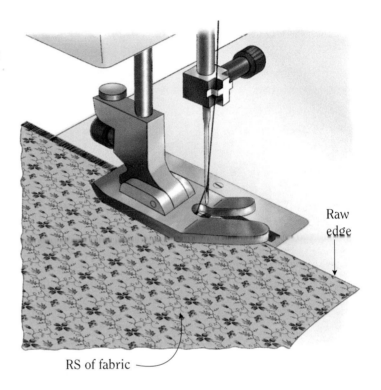

Raw edge

RS of fabric

Diagram 3

Sharp Notion

If you want a more decorative, flat, single-layer edge finish, try wider satin stitching with machine embroidery thread. To keep the edge from curling under, use an overcasting or Satinedge presser foot. Both of these feet have a pin, like a serger stitch finger, over which the stitch forms. The pin keeps the stitching taut so it won't draw up, causing tunneling and puckering. If neither one of these feet is available, use your embroidery foot and stitch with the fabric on top of a layer of water-soluble stabilizer.

GETTING THE MOST FROM YOUR ROLLED-HEM PRESSER FOOT

The roll (also called shell) hemmer and flat hemmer presser feet make it possible to do a rolled hem on the sewing machine. Available in several sizes, these specialty feet feature a scroll in front, on the top of the foot, through which you feed the fabric. When it comes out the other end, the fabric edge has been rolled or turned twice and stitched in place in one step—a little magic!

Roll (shell) hemmers have a round groove on the bottom to accommodate the fabric roll as it forms. When you use the shell stitch (or a mirror-image blindstitch) with this foot, the resulting edge has a soft, scalloped effect. The 2 mm roll hemmer makes a rolled hem approximately $\frac{1}{16}$ inch wide on fine fabrics and tricot knits. A 4 mm version may also be available for your machine.

The flat hemmers have a flat groove, so the resulting hem is flat. They are generally available in 2 to 6 mm widths and make flat edgestitched hems in widths from $\frac{1}{16}$ to $\frac{1}{4}$ inch (2 to 6 mm). The width of the bottom groove multiplied by two is the required hem allowance width for the foot you are using.

When purchasing a hemmer, note that some have a round hole for straight stitching and some have a wider hole, enabling you to use them with zigzagging. With the wider hole you can adjust the needle position to stitch as close to the edge as desired.

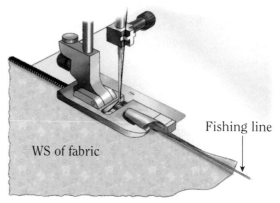

Capture fishing line in the rolled edge of a bias ruffle to make it stand up and ruffle. Use the 2 mm roll (shell) hemmer foot and a short, wide zigzag stitch.

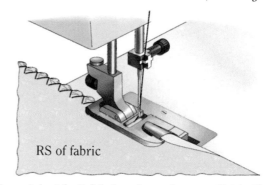

Tame tricot knit fabric using a 2 mm roll (shell) foot with a wide, medium-length zigzag stitch. Sew with the fabric right side up since tricot rolls to the right side when pulled. Don't pull on the tricot while hemming.

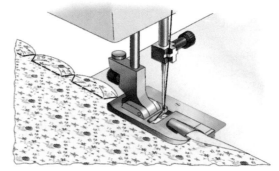

For a true shell edge on tricot knit, use the 2 mm roll (shell) hemmer with a short, wide shell stitch (or mirror-image blindstitch). Tighten the needle tension and use polyester or transparent thread in the needle to make deep shells. Again, sew with tricot right side up.

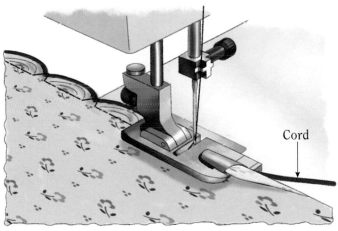

Define the shell edge on your tricot knit garment with cord. Make the edge with the shell stitch (or mirror-image blindstitch), laying cord alongside the fabric fold. As the zigzag stitch swings to the right, it will catch the cord and pull it in next to the rolled edge.

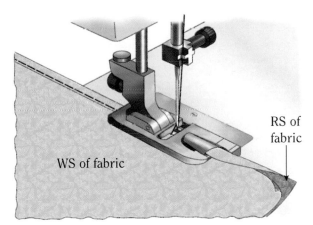

Make a mock French seam on a wedding dress or sheer blouse. Position the fabric pieces right sides together with the top layer ⅛ inch (3 mm) from the raw edge of the other fabric piece. Feed both layers through the scroll and press the resulting narrow seam to one side.

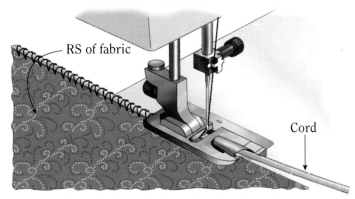

Attach a length of cord to the edge of any type of fabric. Insert cord into the scroll on the presser foot, place it on the fabric right side, then sew over it with a narrow, medium-length zigzag stitch.

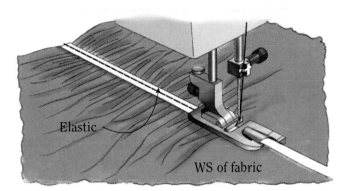

Sew ⅛-inch (3-mm)-wide elastic to the fabric wrong side, guiding it through the scroll and under the groove of a 3 mm roll (shell) hemmer. Adjust the needle position, if necessary, so that the stitching is in the center of the elastic.

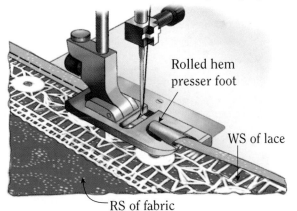

Attach lace by catching it in the stitching while making a rolled hem. The lace doesn't feed through the scroll in the presser foot. Fold the lace down over the rolled edge. With the fabric right side up, zigzag through all layers, catching the hem on the garment on the left swing and the lace on the right swing of the needle.

Sharp Notion

If you're sewing fine fabrics or lace, a rolled edge may be the best seam for your garment. Whether stitched on your sewing machine or your serger, a fine edge will show through from the wrong side of sheers and lace. The thread may also be visible, so take care choosing one that is attractive.

SUCCESSFUL STRATEGIES FOR THE ROLLED HEM

Perfect your technique. Always take the time to practice on an actual fabric scrap before stitching on the garment. This way you'll refine your tension so it's perfectly set before you sew your fabric pattern pieces.

Choose wisely. Thicker fabrics require a wider hem, so you'll need one of the wider presser feet to accommodate the extra fabric. For example, medium-weight denim requires the 6 mm hemmer foot. Check the bottom groove in the foot for the finished hem width.

Feed the foot. Make sure the fold of the fabric stays next to the inside right edge of the hemmer. If you see that the raw edge is running out of the scroll, move the fabric to the right so more fabric can feed into it.

Pick a stitch. When using a roll (shell) hemmer, use a zigzag, blindstitch, or overlock stitch. It's also a good idea to start sewing with a left needle swing into the fabric.

Let your fingers do the work. Hold the fabric slightly taut and off the bed of the machine with your thumb and middle finger. Use your forefinger to coax the raw edge into a curl before it goes into the scroll. Guide the bulk of the fabric with your left hand.

Keep scrolling. Make sure the fabric fills the scroll on the machine's presser foot. If it looks like too much fabric is rolling into the scroll, move the fabric to the left.

Roll along. If the edge stops rolling into the scroll, stop and use your fingers to preroll the edge for a few inches in front of the foot.

Adjust positions. If the foot has a wide needle hole and you can adjust needle positions on your machine, move the needle left or right so the stitching is very close to the folded edge.

Seam sheers and lace. A fine edge will show through from the wrong side. Try woolly nylon thread for good coverage and comfort against the skin, especially when sewing with lace.

Stiffen up. If stubborn fabric won't stay in the scroll, apply a bit of spray starch to the edge of the problem fabric. Spray the starch into the cap of the can and use a small brush to apply it in a controlled manner.

Take it slow. Sew at a slow, even speed for a smooth roll.

Parallel park. Keep the folded fabric edge parallel to the presser foot at the needle. This will keep your machine rolled hem straight.

Go lightly. On sheer fabrics, lengthen the stitch a little bit and also try using cotton or rayon embroidery thread for a soft edge. Heavier, stronger needle and bobbin threads may cut fine fabric fibers. This can result in a stiff rolled edge, which is undesirable on soft fabrics where the edge should seem weightless.

Make your own. Create ribbon by finishing both edges of a fabric strip with the rolled-edge stitch. Include wire in the stitching, for inexpensive, French wire-edged ribbon. Or, you can use two layers of two different fabrics, wrong sides together, for reversible ribbon.

Go fish. Encase fishing line for very ruffled edge—great for bridal and evening wear.

Stitch fine work. Attach lace or entredeux to fabric strips for heirloom sewing (see page 155). Use a contrasting thread to make it look like fine ribbon.

Rouleau

Little round fabric tubes, called rouleau, are used for a number of decorative and functional purposes—including spaghetti straps, button loops, and Chinese ball buttons. With seam allowances left inside the tubing, the completed rouleau is firm and round. You can also enhance tubes by encasing cord or yarn.

Stitching and turning these bias-cut tubes is often enough to send even the least faint-hearted sewer into fits of hysteria. Use the methods described in this section to avoid frustration.

CORDED ROULEAU

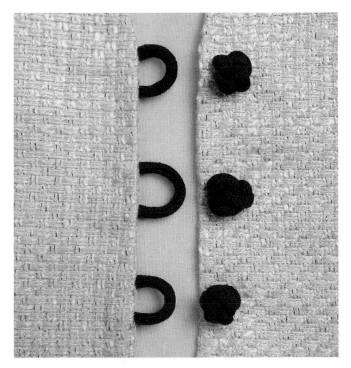

Sometimes hollow rouleau, as described in "No More Tears Rouleau" on page 196, just isn't substantial enough. Decorative closures such as Chinese ball buttons and frogs, button loops, and couched rouleau all look better with cord-filled tubes. Making it on your sewing machine is easier than you think. Using double the required cord length is the secret to turning and filling the tube.

Get Ready

Needle	Appropriate for fabric and thread
Thread	All-purpose or transparent
Notions	Seam sealant (optional), preshrunk cotton cord or acrylic yarn

Get Set

Presser foot	Zipper
Stitch	Straight
Stitch length	12 spi (2 mm)

Rouleau has many functional and decorative applications, including button loops and Chinese ball buttons. To prevent a button loop from popping off the button, fill the rouleau with elastic, using the instructions for "Corded Rouleau."

Sew

1. Cut a true bias strip twice the desired finished width plus two seam allowances. (Usually, the finer the fabric, the narrower the strip.)

2. Cut a piece of preshrunk cotton cord or acrylic yarn twice the length of the strip, plus 6 inches (15 cm).

3. Place the cord lengthwise on the right side of the strip, with an inch of cord extending at one end of the strip. Anchor the opposite end of the cord by sewing it to the fabric strip.

4. Fold the strip right sides together and sew down its length, close to the cord, stretching the strip as you stitch. See **Diagram 1A.** Trim the seam allowances to ⅛ inch (3 mm). If the fabric ravels, treat it with seam sealant.

5. Turn the tube right side out, working the fabric back over the exposed cord. See **Diagram 1B.** Trim away the excess cord.

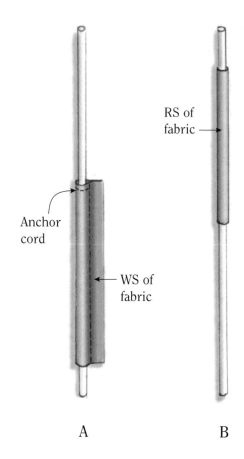

RS of fabric →

Anchor cord

← WS of fabric

A   B

Diagram 1

SUCCESSFUL STRATEGIES FOR DECORATIVE ROULEAU

Hide the seam. When attaching rouleau to the garment surface, keep the seamline against the garment.

Sew invisibly. Use transparent thread and the blindstitch to catch just an edge of the rouleau.

Hand sew. Use a short slipstitch to sew the rouleau in place. Take care not to draw the stitches too tightly.

Link up. Connect finished rouleau strips with fagoting for a custom trim.

Sew a pot 'o gold. Use multicolor bias strips for rainbow rouleau.

Try flat-"wear." To couch, machine stitch the rouleau in place on your garment. This will flatten the rouleau.

Twist and sew. Braid three lengths of rouleau to make decorative trim, a belt, or a strap for your garment.

Add beads. Knot them in place at random intervals on narrow rouleau trim. Then use your "beaded" rouleau as trim by couching it to your garment fabric.

Get wired. Thread craft wire into rouleau for easy shaping.

DAINTY ROULEAU

These instructions describe the process for making rouleau at your sewing machine from fine material like China silk or other lightweight silky fabric. As you probably suspect, the trickiest part is turning the thin, ⅛-inch (3-mm)-wide rouleau. A doubled length of topstitching thread is the key, and making the beginning and end of the tube wider also helps.

Get Ready

Fabric	1¾-inch (4.5-cm)-wide bias cut strip
Needle	Appropriate for fabric and thread
Thread	All-purpose or transparent
Notions	Tapestry or double-eyed needle, seam sealant

Get Set

Presser foot	¼ inch or all-purpose
Stitch	Straight
Stitch length	12 spi (2 mm)

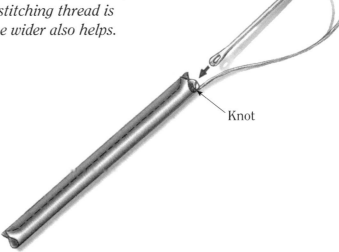

Diagram 2

Knot

Sew

1. Thread the needle with a doubled length of topstitching thread. Machine stitch over the thread to the center of one end of the fabric strip. Fold the fabric in half lengthwise with right sides together.

2. Stretching as you sew, stitch ¼ inch (6 mm) from the fold for several stitches, then taper to ⅛ inch (3 mm) from the fold. End by stitching back out to ¼ inch (6 mm) from the fold. Trim the seam allowances close to the stitching. Treat the cut edges with seam sealant.

3. Insert the needle through the tube without catching it in the fabric, and pull the needle through to turn it. See **Diagram 2.** Cut away the thread.

4. Dampen the tube, stretch, and pin it to a padded surface to dry. If the fabric isn't washable, steam it, roll it in your hands, restretch and pin it, then steam it again. Continue until all the fabric's stretch is eliminated.

Make It Easy

For successful rouleau, fabric preparation is important. No matter which technique or application you plan to use, cut your fabric strip on the true bias. Begin by cutting the strip twice the desired finished width plus two seam allowances.

You may have to join fabric strips to obtain the length desired for your rouleau. You can sew the fabric strips together the same way that you join fabric strips for bias binding or piping. (See page 181.)

Achieve an angled seamline by placing the ends of each strip at a 45 degree angle to one another. In other words, the short side of one strip is aligned with the end of the long side of the second strip. Now sew diagonally across the ends and trim the seam allowances to ¼ inch (6 mm).

NO MORE TEARS ROULEAU

Save time and avoid frustration by using rotary-cutting equipment to carefully cut true-bias rouleau strips and a serger to stitch them. Turn them quickly with rolled-edge chain laid inside the fabric tube while you stitch. This is the easiest way ever to make and turn even the skinniest spaghetti straps.

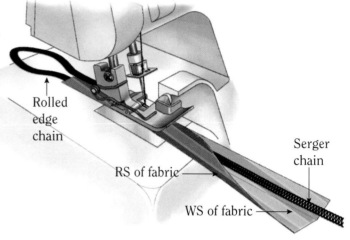

Diagram 3

Get Ready

Needle	Appropriate for fabric and thread
Thread	All-purpose or woolly nylon*

Get Set

Presser foot	Standard
Stitch	Three-thread rolled edge†
Stitch length	1.5 to 2 mm
Width	Narrow

Use a colorful decorative thread in the upper looper when stitching on sheer fabrics for an interesting decorative serging "shadow."

†*You can use a three-thread overlock stitch for wider tubes.*

Serge

1. Cut a true bias strip twice the desired finished width plus two seam allowances. (Usually, the finer the fabric, the narrower the strip.)

2. Serge a rolled-edge chain 8 inches (20 cm) longer than the rouleau fabric strip and leave it attached to the machine. Loop the chain to the front of the serger and center it on the right side of the fabric strip.

3. Fold the fabric, wrong side out, around the chain. Serge the lengthwise edges together, gently stretching the fabric strip in front and holding on to it behind the foot. As you stitch, keep the chain in the fold so you don't catch it in the stitching. See **Diagram 3.**

4. After serging, remove the strip from the machine. Pull on the serger chain to turn the tube.

Workroom Secret

You can also make "No More Tears Rouleau" at your sewing machine by substituting a length of cotton piping cord that's 4 to 6 inches (10 to 15 cm) longer than the fabric strip for the serger chain. Center the cord down the length of the right side of the fabric strip. Let the cord extend about 1 inch (2.5 cm) beyond one end of the fabric strip. At the opposite end, anchor the cord to the fabric by sewing across it. Fold the fabric strip in half lengthwise with right sides together. The cord will be inside the unsewn "tube." Sew the length of the fabric strip using a straight stitch and a zipper foot. Take care not to catch the cord in the stitching. Sew close to the cord, stretching the strip as you sew. Trim the seam allowances and apply a seam sealant. Pull on the cord to turn the tube right side out. Cut away the cord at the stitched end.

Sashiko

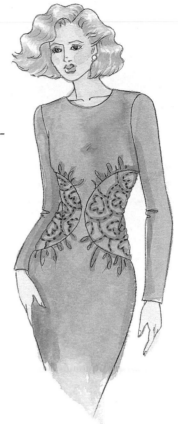

With its allover stylized motifs, this form of quilting is a beautiful accent for a yoke, cuff, or even a sleeve. To imitate the hand stitching on your sewing machine, use thick thread and loosen your bobbin thread tension.

Get Ready

Fabric	Medium-weight, even-weave or twill garment fabric; preshrunk cotton flannel or very thin cotton batting
Needle	Jeans or topstitching, size 90/14 or 100/16; or universal, size 120/20
Needle thread	Heavy, white, decorative*
Bobbin thread	All-purpose or fine†
Notions	Fine-point permanent marking pen; water-soluble stabilizer; machine embroidery hoop (optional)

Get Set

Presser foot	Embroidery, appliqué, or walking
Stitch	Straight
Stitch length	6 spi (4.5 mm)
Needle tension	Tighten slightly
Bobbin tension	Loosen slightly

Try 30-weight, multi-ply rayon, six-ply metallic, topstitching, or cordonnet.

†*Use black or navy. Bobbinfil is a nice choice for a fine thread.*

Sew

1. Cut the garment pieces from both the fabric and the flannel (or thin batting). Layer the pieces with the garment fabric right side up and on top.

2. Trace your selected design onto water-soluble stabilizer with the marking pen. Position the stabilizer on the garment piece and pin it in place.

3. Adjust the tensions so that the bobbin thread comes slightly to the surface to separate the stitches.

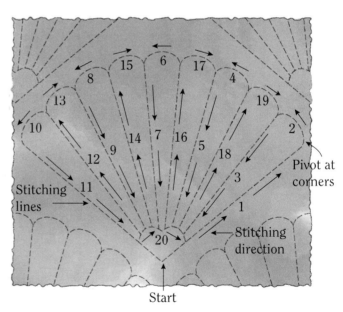

4. Insert the fabric, batting, and stabilizer into an embroidery hoop, if desired. Stitch along the marked lines on the stabilizer. Don't backstitch along any of your design lines. Pull the top thread to the underside and tie off securely. Remove the stabilizer.

5. Plan your stitching for the design so that you can do as much as possible in continuous lines. See the diagram above.

Scalloped Edges

You don't need a built-in scallop stitch on your sewing machine to create this feminine edge finish. There are a number of ways to create scalloped edges. The versatile blindstitch, in combination with serging, draws an edge into scallops in a jiffy. And, if your serger has a movable stitch finger, you can scallop an edge.

CORDED SCALLOPS

Large scallops look great along the front edge of a shawl-collar jacket, and tiny scallops are the perfect accent for a dainty handkerchief hem on a skirt or collar edge. To achieve this finish, you need little more than a combination of straight and satin stitching on your sewing machine.

Get Ready

Needle	Appropriate for fabric and thread
Thread	Embroidery cotton or rayon
Notions	Sharp chalk or lead pencil; water-soluble marking pen; appliqué or embroidery scissors; pearl cotton #5 or #8 to match the thread

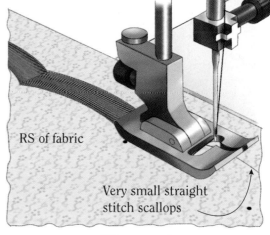

RS of fabric

Very small straight stitch scallops

Diagram 1

Get Set

	First Pass	Second Pass	Third Pass
Presser foot	All-purpose	Open-toe embroidery	Braiding, cording, or embroidery
Stitch	Straight stitch scallop stitch* (if available) or straight stitch	Satin	Zigzag
Stitch length	As desired	Almost 0	15 spi (1.5 mm)
Stitch width	As desired	Medium or wider	Medium
Needle tension	Balanced	Loosen slightly	Balanced
Needle position	Centered	Left, if available	Centered

This is a special stitch that makes a scalloped design with straight stitches. It's not available on all machines.

Sew

1. If your machine has a built-in or preprogrammed straight stitch scallop stitch, adjust for the desired scallop size and sew ⅜ inch (1 cm) from the raw edge. This marks the scallops on the fabric. If you don't have a straight stitch scallop stitch, use the chalk or lead pencil to mark the desired scallops at least ⅜ inch (1 cm) from the edge. Straight stitch along the marked line.

2. With the machine set for the Second Pass, adjust the satin stitch width as desired. Mark the new stitch width above the inner point of each scallop by placing a dot on the fabric using the water-soluble marking pen. See **Diagram 1** on the opposite page.

3. Satin stitch, following the stitched line made in Step 1. Guide the work so that the stitching line rides under the inner edge of the right toe. See **Diagram 1** on the opposite page.

4. Satin stitch to the first inner point, ending with the needle in the fabric at the dot. Pivot the work so the stitched line is along the inner edge of the foot, and continue satin stitching to the next point. The stitching is not tapered; the angle appears because of the angle of the pivot that you make.

5. Trim as close to the outer edge of the scalloped stitching as possible without cutting the stitches.

6. Adjust the machine settings for the Third Pass and hand guide the pearl cotton into the presser foot. Zigzag over the scalloped edge and the pearl cotton, holding the pearl cotton straight and guiding the curved edges to the cord.

Sharp Notion

For flat trim, cut a strip of the desired width plus two ½-inch (1.25-cm)-wide seam allowances. Turn under and press a seam allowance on each long edge, and stitch as directed above for the First Pass. Add decorative stitching down the center of the scalloped strip.

Workshop Secret

If you don't have a cording or braiding presser foot, there's still a way that you can set up your machine so that the cord is automatically guided into position for stitching. The only catch is that your machine must have a thin wire bar just above the needle. You use this wire bar to guide the cord. First thread the cord under the wire, and then position it under the presser foot, preferably a zigzag foot. Your stitching will now be relatively hands-free. All you really need to do is hold the cord with two fingers of your right hand. To maintain stability and avoid strain, it's best to do this with your right hand resting on the table. This will also keep the cord straight and level.

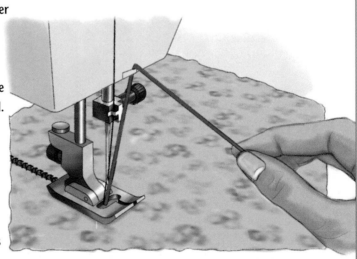

LOCK AND ROLL SCALLOPED EDGE

If you love to push your serger to its creative limits, try this innovative technique for a scalloped rolled edge. (However, keep in mind that your serger must have a retractable stitch finger lever on the outside of the machine so that you can easily reach it while serging. This way you can alternate between the basic overlock stitch and the narrow rolled-edge stitch.) Give yourself some extra time when you first try out this technique because it takes a little practice to develop a stitching rhythm. Test this technique on single-layer scraps and over a folded edge to determine what works best on your fabric.

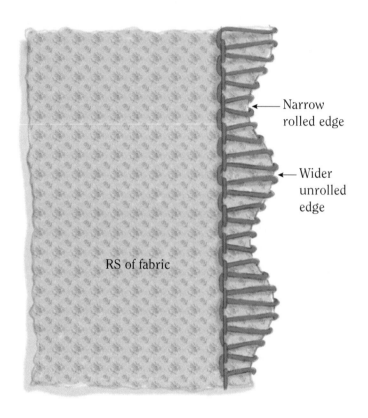

Narrow rolled edge

Wider unrolled edge

RS of fabric

Diagram 2

Get Ready

Needle	Appropriate for fabric and thread
Needle thread	All-purpose serger
UL thread	Decorative
LL thread	All-purpose serger

Get Set

Presser foot	Standard
Stitch	Three-thread rolled edge
Stitch length	1 to 2.5 mm
Stitch width	Narrow to wide

Serge

1. Serge for several stitches. Stop.

2. Adjust the stitch finger for a wide, unrolled edge, and sew a few stitches. Return the serger to the narrow setting. See **Diagram 2.** Repeat Steps 1 and 2 for the length of your edge. As you make the scallops, count the stitches to identify the scalloping combination you like the best. Use more stitches when stitching at the wider width, fewer for the narrow one, to create the most pronounced scallops.

Sharp Notion

A built-in scallop stitch can be corded. This will give the finished edge added durability. To add cord, just follow the instructions for "Corded Scallops" on page 198.

SHELL-STITCHED SCALLOPS

The shell stitch, which is actually the mirror image of the blindstitch, creates a self-fabric scallop when worked over an edge. You can make this edging, even if your sewing machine doesn't have a shell stitch. Instead, use the blindstitch and sew with the fabric to the right of the needle. The effect is very feminine, which makes the technique a pretty edge finish on a hem, sleeve, or neckline on knits and lightweight silkies.

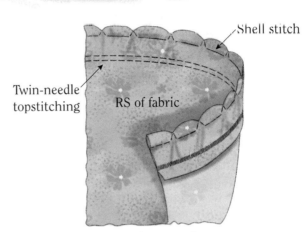

Twin-needle topstitching

Shell stitch

RS of fabric

Diagram 3

Get Ready

	First Pass	Second Pass
Needle	Appropriate for fabric and thread	Twin (stretch or universal)*
Thread	All-purpose or embroidery	All-purpose or embroidery†

Get Set

	First Pass	Second Pass
Presser foot	Blind hem or shell	All-purpose
Stitch	Blindstitch or shell	Straight*
Stitch length	12 to 15 spi (2 to 1.5 mm)	8 spi (3.5 mm)
Stitch width	Medium (4 mm) or wider	—
Needle tension	Tighten slightly	—

*You can substitute a single needle and tiny zigzag stitch for the twin-needle and straight stitching.
†You can also use transparent thread in the needle.

Sew

1. Turn under and press the hem or seam allowance.

2. Arrange the work under the presser foot so the zigzag part of the stitching goes over the folded edge and the straight stitches are on the garment. If the zigzag stitches do not pull the edge in to form a scallop, tighten the needle tension slightly.

3. Set up the machine for the Second Pass. (See "Threading for Twin-Needle Stitching" on page 16.) Stitch ¼ to ½ inch (6 mm to 1.25 cm) from the fold. See **Diagram 3.** Trim any excess seam or hem allowance close to the zigzag stitches.

Sharp Notion

To make your own scalloped insertion, cut a 1¾-inch (4.5-cm)-wide strip of knit or bias woven. Fold it in half, wrong sides together, and press. Stitch over the edge as described in Step 2 of "Shell-Stitched Scallops," and trim the excess ⅝ inch (1.5 cm) from the straight stitches. Insert the strip between two seam allowances as you would piping.

TOP-NOTCH SCALLOPED EDGE

This procedure is very similar to the one that you have probably used to make scallops at the sewing machine. You still need to use the blindstitch or shell stitch at your sewing machine, but for this technique it's worked over a rolled edge done on the serger. This works best on lingerie and other lightweight fabrics.

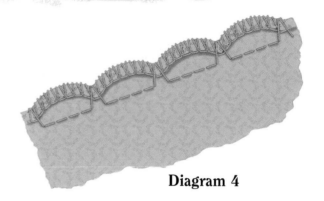

Diagram 4

Get Ready

	Serger	Sewing Machine
Needle	Appropriate for fabric and thread	Appropriate for fabric and thread
Needle thread	All-purpose	Transparent
Bobbin thread	—	Transparent
UL thread	Decorative	—
LL thread	Decorative	—

Get Set

	Serger	Sewing Machine
Presser foot	Standard	Piping
Stitch	Two- or three-thread rolled edge	Blindstitch or shell
Stitch length	Short, to cover fabric	8 spi (3.5 mm)
Stitch width	Narrow	Medium to wide
Needle tension	Balanced	Tighter

Serge and Sew

1. Adjust the serger stitch to achieve good edge coverage. Serge the raw or folded fabric edge.

2. Adjust the sewing machine as directed above. Try transparent thread in the needle and bobbin to accentuate the scallops and make the machine stitching invisible. Tighten the needle tension slightly, if necessary.

3. Stitch so that the zigzags catch the serged edge and cause it to scallop. See **Diagram 4.** If using the blindstitch, position the bulk of the garment to the right of the needle. The rolled edge should ride easily under the tunnel in the bottom of the piping foot.

Make It Easy

If it's possible to do so on your machine, make Step 3 easier by setting the machine for a mirror-image blindstitch. Then you can sew with the bulk of the fabric or garment to the left.

Shirring

Shirring imitates smocking but has built-in "give." It's commonly used for yokes or pockets, dress bodices, sleeves, or vests. The easiest methods involve zigzag or flatlock stitching over elastic, then drawing up the fullness manually. Other methods require elastic thread in the bobbin to draw up the fullness while stitching.

Shirring works best on light- and medium-weight fabrics, but you can use it on heavier material, even though the fabric won't gather as tightly.

FLATLOCK SHIRRING

A skirt yoke or jacket peplum are suitable places to shirr with this serger method. Thread rows of flatlocking with elastic thread or narrow transparent elastic. Allow extra fabric, about one and a half to two times the actual pattern piece width, for the fullness. After stitching, cut the desired pattern shape from the resulting fabric.

Get Ready

Needle	Appropriate for fabric and thread
Thread	Woolly nylon
Notions	Elastic thread, tapestry needle

Get Set

Presser foot	Standard*
Stitch	Two- or three-thread flatlock
Stitch length	Medium
Stitch width	Medium
Upper knife	Disengaged, if possible

It's handy to use the presser foot as a spacer so you don't have to premark rows, but the spacing can be as desired.

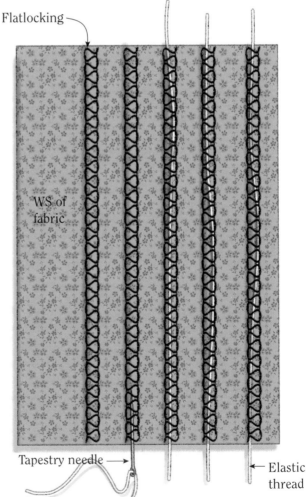

Flatlocking

WS of fabric

Tapestry needle →

← Elastic thread

Diagram 1

Serge

1. When finished, shirring creates "give" in one direction—along the stitching lines—so decide if you want these to be vertical or horizontal on your fabric pattern piece. To shirr part of a garment, create the effect on a rectangle of the garment fabric and then cut out the pattern piece from that fabric. Mark stitching lines ½ to 1½ inches (1.25 to 4 cm) apart on the fabric wrong side, or use the presser foot width as a guide.

2. To begin shirring, fold the fabric right sides together and flatlock over the fold, being careful not to cut the fabric with the knives. Open and flatten the fabric, then fold and flatlock each successive row in the same manner.

3. Thread a length of elastic thread onto the tapestry needle and under the loops of each row of flatlocking, allowing 3 inches (8 cm) of extra elastic at each end. See **Diagram 1** on page 203.

4. Hold the elastic thread ends together at both ends of the fabric and stretch them to draw up the fabric fullness. Adjust the gathers.

5. To anchor the elastic thread ends, catch them in a seam or stitch across each one several times, making sure the needle pierces the thread.

Make It Easy

For entire garment sections, shirr the fabric first, then cut out the pattern pieces. Cut a rectangle of fabric for each piece of fabric that you plan to shirr for your garment, rather than trying to shirr the entire fabric. Depending on the technique you plan to use, cut the rectangle one and a half to three times the desired finished width. It's best to test your fabric with the selected shirring technique to determine just how much "shrinkage" occurs, then cut the rectangles accordingly.

LINEAR SHIRRING

Also known as zigzag shirring, this is one of the simplest ways to incorporate flexible fullness into fabric before cutting out garment pieces. It's an easy technique because you're machine stitching parallel rows on a flat piece of fabric. You'll find that it works on most lightweight and drapable medium-weight fabrics. This should be your method of choice if you want a linear shirring pattern.

Get Ready

Needle	Appropriate for fabric and thread
Thread	All-purpose
Notions	Water-soluble marker (optional); quilting guide (optional); round cord elastic

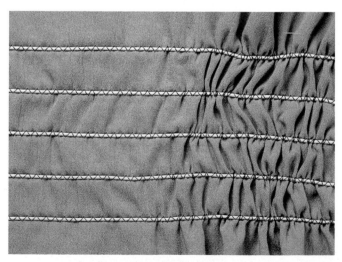

Requiring little more than a zigzag stitch, this shirring technique is achieved when rows of elastic cord are couched to the fabric, then drawn up.

Get Set

Presser foot	All-purpose, cording, or braiding
Stitch	Zigzag
Stitch length	10 spi (2.5 mm)
Stitch width	Medium*

The stitch must clear the width of the cord.

Sew

1. When finished, shirring creates "give" in one direction—along the stitching lines—so decide if you want these to be vertical or horizontal on your fabric pattern piece. To shirr part of a garment, create the effect on a fabric rectangle and then cut out the pattern piece. Mark your stitching lines on the fabric wrong side, or mark only the first line and attach a quilting guide to the presser foot. Adjust it for the desired distance between stitching rows, usually ½ to ¾ inch (1.25 to 2 cm) apart.

2. Thread the elastic through the cording or braiding foot, or place it between the toes of the all-purpose foot. Stitch over the elastic without stretching it, along the first marked line on the wrong side of the fabric. Leave a few inches of elastic extending at each end of the stitched line. Stitch the remaining rows in the same manner, following the marked lines or using the quilting guide to space the rows. See **Diagram 2.**

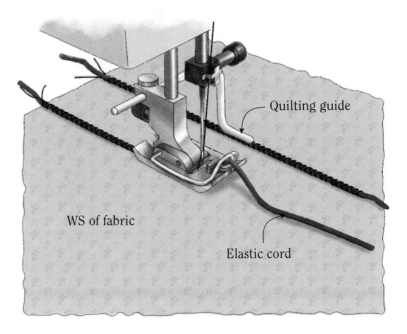

WS of fabric

Quilting guide

Elastic cord

Diagram 2

3. At one edge, straight stitch across one end of each of the stitched rows two or three times to anchor the elastic, or tie pairs of the elastic in secure knots.

4. Draw up the free elastic ends, in pairs, to shirr the fabric to the desired width. Secure the elastic ends as explained in Step 3.

SUCCESSFUL STRATEGIES FOR SHIRRED FABRIC

Go single. Cut the pattern pieces from a single layer of shirred fabric, making sure to line up the grainlines as usual.

Secure ends. Before cutting out the pattern pieces, straight stitch along the marked lines twice to secure the elastic thread ends. Cut out the pattern piece next to the outer line of stitching.

Be excessive. With patterns pinned in place, mark around the pattern pieces ⅜ inch (1 cm) from the pattern edges. This will give you 1-inch (2.5-cm)-wide seam allowances for fitting leeway.

Curves ahead. Pin the pattern pieces to relaxed fabric, except at the neckline, shoulder, and armhole edges. In these areas only, smooth out the fullness. A bubble of fabric will form in the pattern interior—the area that will stretch over your body's curves in the finished garment.

Stitch twice. Stitch the permanent seams twice, once at the seamline and again ⅛ inch (3 mm) away, in the seam allowance, to secure the elastic thread ends. Serge finish if desired and press the seam allowances to one side. You'll have a better garment, with elastic that doesn't pull out of the seams.

MOTIF SHIRRING

Shirring doesn't have to be an allover effect. By planning ahead, you can stitch only a portion of your garment with a repeating pattern of design motifs. Done at your sewing machine, this will result in a pattern of selective gathering. The stitching is done with elastic thread in the bobbin, and the fabric surface is kept taut when under the presser foot. The fabric draws in at each motif when it's released from the machine embroidery hoop. This technique works on most medium and lightweight fabrics. Choose a simple motif, like a flower or circle.

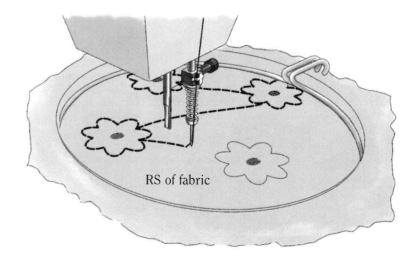

Imitating fabrics in ready-to-wear, motif shirring is worked in a machine embroidery hoop with free-motion stitching.

Get Ready

Needle	Appropriate for fabric and thread, or spring needle
Needle thread	Cotton or rayon embroidery
Bobbin thread	Elastic
Notions	Water-soluble marking pen, machine embroidery hoop, hand sewing needle

Get Set

Presser foot	Darning or none*
Stitch	Straight
Tension	Balanced
Feed dogs	Disengaged, covered, or 0 stitch length

*If you use a spring needle, stitch without a presser foot.

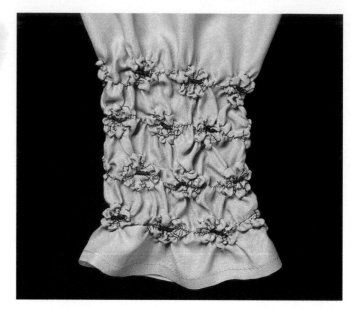

RS of fabric

Diagram 3

Sew

1. Hand-wind the elastic thread onto the bobbin. Draw a shape onto the fabric with the water-soluble marking pen. Create a grid on the fabric by repeating the traced shape both horizontally and vertically. You can align the motifs or offset each row, depending on the results that are desired.

2. If you want to add embroidered motifs to the surface in addition to the motifs used to shirr the fabric, machine embroider a single motif or satin stitch a shape in the center of each design area, if appropriate.

3. Thread the machine, using elastic thread in the bobbin. Don't bypass the tension spring. The elastic thread must be under tension so it stretches during the stitching process and relaxes when released from the embroidery hoop.

4. Load the marked fabric in the embroidery hoop, right side up and taut. Place the hoop on the bed of the machine, under the foot. Draw the bobbin thread to the top of the work and hold the threads out of the way while you work.

5. Lower the presser bar (even if there is no foot attached). Beginning at an outer edge of one motif, stitch along the drawn lines of the motif, moving the hoop at a steady speed so the resulting stitches are short and as even as possible. When you reach the starting point, take a few stitches in place to lock them, or stitch over to the next motif and continue stitching. See **Diagram 3** on the opposite page. After completing all of the motifs in the hoop, stitch in place a few times at the end of the last one. Clip the threads.

6. Remove the hoop from the machine. Thread the bobbin and needle thread ends into a hand sewing needle and draw them to the underside of the work. Tie off securely and trim ½ inch (1.25 cm) from the knot. There will be short stitches on the surface and loopy ones on the underside of the fabric.

7. Use a damp cloth to remove the marks (or wait and wash the completed piece of fabric). Remove the hoop, and voilà! The elastic draws in to create a puckered surface texture.

8. Put the fabric back in the hoop and stitch any remaining motifs in the same manner.

Sharp Notion

For even more texture, try popcorn shirring with interlocking, side-by-side rows of serpentine zigzag stitches. Practice with regular thread so you don't waste the elastic. Success relies on matching the stitch pattern in successive rows. Try other decorative stitches that you can match in this way.

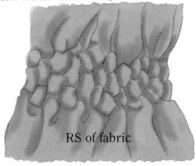

RS of fabric

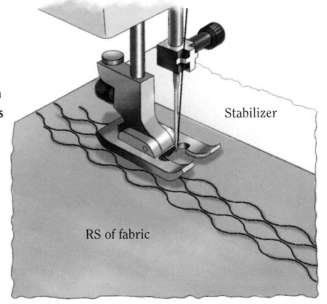

Stabilizer

RS of fabric

Silk Ribbon Work

If you can do it by hand, you can do it by machine! Undaunted by those who said it was only a hand technique, creative sewing machine buffs developed several methods for adding the dimension and beauty of silk ribbon embroidery to their work. Now you can imitate many of the hand-embroidered motifs and embellish the work with machine-couched silk ribbon.

The effect of silk ribbon work is stunning when several techniques and types of embroidered motifs are combined and positioned on a garment front. Vests, for example, are ideal "canvases" for practicing your stitches.

COUCHED SILK RIBBON

This method involves stitching with the fabric wrong side up and using silk ribbon in the bobbin. Use straight, simple zigzag, open decorative, or functional stitches on your sewing machine. (Don't use satin-stitched patterns because the stitches will jam.) Only use this technique to embellish short seams or small areas so that you don't have to worry about running out of the ribbon that's wound onto the bobbin.

Get Ready

Needle	Appropriate for fabric and thread
Needle thread	Transparent or all-purpose
Bobbin thread	2- to 4-mm-wide silk ribbon
Notions	Lightweight fusible knit or weft insertion interfacing (optional), water-soluble marking pen, large-eyed sewing needle, machine embroidery hoop (optional)

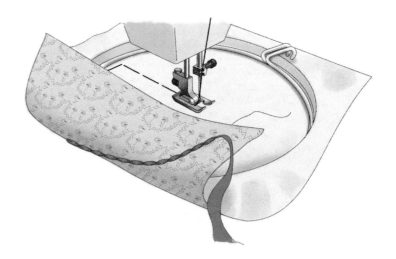

Diagram 1

Get Set

Presser foot	Open-toe embroidery
Stitch	Straight, zigzag, or open decorative
Stitch length	As desired
Stitch width	As desired
Needle tension	Loose
Bobbin tension	Loose

Sew

1. Back lightweight fabric with a lightweight fusible knit or weft insertion interfacing for support and to prevent dark ribbon ends from shadowing through to the right side.

2. Carefully hand-wind the silk ribbon onto the bobbin, keeping the ribbon smooth and flat.

3 Fill several bobbins at one time. The bobbins only hold about 2 yards (1.8 m) of ribbon, and you don't want to interrupt your sewing every time you run out of bobbin thread. Also, decorative stitches take more thread than straight ones.

4. Adjust your settings, insert the bobbin, and thread the machine. For built-in bobbin cases, bypass the tension spring and bring the ribbon up through the needle hole. The resulting stitching will have a cabled or loopy effect.

With removable, front-loading bobbin cases, loosen the tension until the ribbon flows easily through the case. For looser, loopier stitching, you can bypass the tension spring in this type of case, too.

5. Test the stitches on interfacing-backed scraps. Lengthen your stitches somewhat to accommodate the ribbon width and prevent jamming.

6. Mark the desired design on the wrong side of the garment with the water-soluble marking pen. Place the fabric in the hoop right side down and stitch slowly. If your machine has a speed adjustment dial, be sure to switch to the slower speed. Stitch slowly, following the marked design. See **Diagram 1** on the opposite page. Be sure to leave long thread and ribbon tails to begin and end the work. Check the

bobbin each time you stop and start to make sure there is enough ribbon for the next design area.

7. On the right side, thread ribbon ends into a large-eyed sewing needle and draw to the underside of the work. Tie off the ends with a dressmaker's knot or weave them under the stitches.

Make It Easy

Filmoplast Stic is a new thin, lightweight yet firm, sticky-back stabilizer with a protective paper covering. Score the paper lightly with a needle or pin point and peel it away to reveal a slightly tacky surface that will hold trims in place for pucker-free stitching. Designed for machine embroidery on fabrics that would be crushed by a hoop—velvet, for example—you put this stabilizer in an embroidery hoop with the paper side up. Once the stabilizer is in the hoop, you score and remove the protective paper and lay the fabric on top, smoothing it in place on the adhesive side. The stabilizer, not the hoop, holds the fabric in place. It tears easily away from the stitching when you're done. Any tiny pieces of stabilizer left under the stitches won't add unwanted stiffness, but you can pull them out with tweezers, if you prefer.

EMBROIDERY WITH SILK RIBBON

As with silk ribbon embroidery by hand, this sewing machine work is most effective when one or more stitches are combined. Included here are the basic stitches and methods to get you started. You can master these techniques, then adapt and combine them to expand your stitch repertoire. No matter which stitch you're using, always start with the following setup.

Get Ready

Needle	Metalfil, Metallica, or embroidery
Needle thread	Transparent
Bobbin thread	Lingerie/Bobbin Thread or embroidery cotton
Notions	Lightweight weft-insertion fusible interfacing or tear-away stabilizer (optional); chalk pencil; machine embroidery hoop; 2- to 7-mm-wide silk ribbon; awl; long, blunt needle, trolley needle, or serger tweezers; large-eyed chenille needle*

Get Set

Presser foot	None
Stitch	Straight or zigzag
Stitch length	0
Stitch width	Narrow for zigzag only
Needle tension	Loosen by two numbers
Feed dogs	Disengaged or covered
Needle control	Down, if available

*Don't substitute a wooden hoop. You need to be able to leave the needle in the fabric while shifting the ring to a new position. Also, specified ribbon widths are those most commonly used for the stitch. Of course you are free to experiment with other ribbon widths.

Silk ribbon motifs can be positioned in a dense "garden" or scattered sparsely across the fabric. This camisole features several stitches. The upper edge is trimmed with bobbin couching, while the flowers consist of bullions, a chained rose, and French knots.

Sew

1. Back knit fabrics with a lightweight weft-insertion fusible interfacing in the design area. Back other fabrics with a tear-away stabilizer, if desired.

2. Draw your design on the fabric right side with the chalk pencil, or use a commercially available silk embroidery design and transfer it to the fabric. You can also adapt or combine many traditional embroidery designs for silk ribbon embroidery.

3. Load the fabric into the embroidery hoop and place it under the needle. Lower the presser bar.

4. Lower the needle into the fabric at the ribbon starting point and draw the bobbin thread to the surface. Tack by taking several small stitches very close together, moving the hoop back and forth by hand to slightly shift the position of the stitches to lock the threads. Clip the thread tails close to the work.

5. Position and stitch the ribbon in place to create the desired design. Refer to the instructions for specific stitches below through page 215 for further direction and finishing information.

Make It Easy

Build your skill and learn the basic steps for tacking, walk stitching, and looping by practicing stitches in the following order: chain, mock outline or cable, chained rose, loopy petal, French knot, bullion, and feather. Start with 2- or 4-mm-wide ribbon, then experiment with other widths.

Bullion Stitch

1. Cut a 12- to 16-inch (30- to 40.5-cm) piece of silk ribbon. (When making bullion stitches in clusters, you may want to make them from a single length of ribbon rather than starting and stopping for each one.) Tack the ribbon at the desired location on your fabric 4 inches (10 cm) from the end of the ribbon. To tack, take several stitches in place and end with the needle down. Wrap the ribbon around the needle at least six times, leaving a bit of slack in the wraps.

2. Slowly hand-turn the flywheel to raise the needle out of the little roll of ribbon and let the roll fall on its side, onto the fabric, in the desired direction (as dictated by the design that you're following). Take a few stitches in the fabric at the end of the ribbon roll that falls onto the fabric. You may catch the ribbon in the stitching, but this isn't necessary. See **Diagram 2.**

3. Stitch to get to the other end of the ribbon roll, then tack the ribbon to the fabric with a few stitches.

4. If you are making a single bullion stitch, you have two choices for finishing the stitching. One is to cut

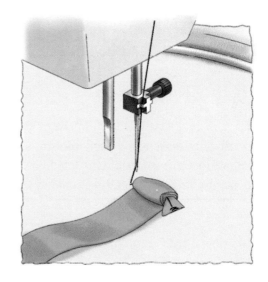

Diagram 2

the excess ribbon, leaving a tail. Use a large-eyed chenille needle to draw the ribbon ends through to the wrong side and tie off or weave in and out of the stitches on the underside to secure. The other finishing option is cutting the ribbon as close to the bullion stitch as possible and then covering the raw end with other stitches.

Chain Stitch

1. If desired, draw the placement for the chain-stitched line on the fabric with a chalk pencil. Cut a piece of silk ribbon twice the length of the line. Fold the ribbon in half lengthwise and lightly crease to mark the center. Tack the center of the ribbon to the beginning of the line by making several small stitches in the same place.

2. With the needle up, move the fabric so that the needle is positioned where the first chain stitch ends. Lower the needle.

3. Loosely cross the ribbon ends in front of the needle.

4. Hand-turn the flywheel to make the next stitch to cross over the ribbon. See **Diagram 3**. Repeat until you have created a line of the desired length.

5. Cross the ribbons for the last stitch and tack them in place. Use a large-eyed chenille needle to draw the ribbon ends through to the wrong side and tie off or weave in and out of the stitches on the underside to secure.

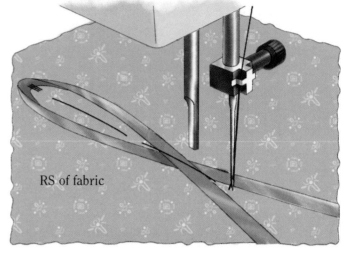

RS of fabric

Diagram 3

Chained Rose

1. To make a chained rose as shown in **Diagram 4,** use a chalk pencil to make three small dots in the desired location on the fabric right side to create a small triangle. Tack the center of a 12-inch (30-cm) piece of ribbon at one of the dots.

2. With the ribbon held out of the way, stitch across to one of the remaining dots. End with needle down.

3. Loosely cross the ribbon ends in front of the needle. Hand-turn the flywheel to make the next stitch cross over and secure the ribbon. See **Diagram 5** on the opposite page. Rotate the hoop and stitch to the remaining dot, then cross and stitch over the ribbon.

4. Continue making chain stitches in the same manner as described in Steps 1 through 3, circling

Diagram 4

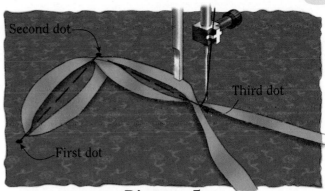

around the first three stitches to make a rose of the desired size. Take care that the beginning and end of each chain stitch does not line up with the one it lies next to in the growing circle.

5. Trim the excess ribbon, turn the ends under, and tack them in place. Or use a large-eyed chenille needle to draw the ends to the wrong side and tie off or weave in and out of the stitches on the underside to secure.

Diagram 5

Feather Stitch

1. Draw your design on the fabric right side with the chalk pencil, or use a commercially available silk embroidery design and transfer it to the fabric. Cut a piece of ribbon two to three times the length of the guideline. Place one raw end of the ribbon at the top of the guideline with the rest of the ribbon length extending behind the needle. Tack with several small stitches in the same place.

2. Fold the ribbon down to cover the raw end. Move the hoop away from you while walk stitching along one side of the ribbon to the starting point for the first feather. Stitch. Tack across the ribbon to secure it.

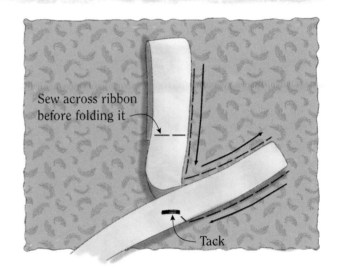

Sew across ribbon before folding it

Tack

Diagram 6

3. Fold the ribbon up, at an angle, away from the stitching guideline to form the first feather. Walk-stitch along the side of the ribbon and sew across the feather's "tip." You may catch a tiny pleat in the ribbon while you stitch a bit for added dimension and a more natural-looking stitch.

4. Fold the ribbon back on itself to hide the tacking and stitch along the other edge, back to the guideline. Tack the ribbon in place at the guideline. See **Diagram 6.**

5. Bring the ribbon down along the guideline and stitch alongside it to the next feather location. Tack across the ribbon. See **Diagram 7.** Make the next feather by folding, tacking, folding, and walk-stitching as described in Steps 3 and 4.

6. Repeat Steps 3 to 5 for additional feathers. Use a large-eyed chenille needle to draw the end to the wrong side and tie off or weave on the underside.

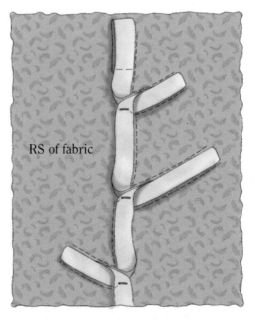

RS of fabric

Diagram 7

French Knot

1. Tack the end of a 9-inch (22.5-cm) length of ribbon at the desired location on the fabric by stitching up and down several times in the same place. End with the needle down.

2. Spin the hoop to loosely wrap the ribbon around the needle two or more times for the desired fullness. Let the ribbon relax into a loose tube around the needle. See **Diagram 8.**

3. Use a pointed tool, such as an awl, to hold the wrapped ribbon tube against the fabric while you take a stitch over one edge of the wraps, and then back into the center. Use a large-eyed chenille needle to draw the ribbon end through to the wrong side and tie off or weave in and out of the stitches on the underside to secure.

4. For a cluster of French knots, stitch to the next knot location and repeat Steps 2 and 3 to make the next knot. At the last knot, cut the ribbon end, turn it under, and tack it under the free edge of the last French knot, or secure as in Step 3.

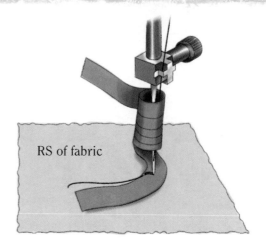

RS of fabric

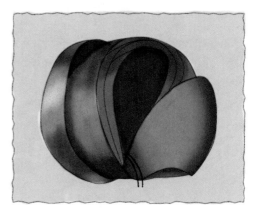

Diagram 8

Lazy Daisy

1. Determine where you will place the finished daisy, and, if desired, chalk-mark the center of the flower. This is where you start your work, by tacking one end of a 10- to 12-inch (25- to 30-cm)-long piece of ribbon to the center of the daisy. Ribbon loops, which represent petals, will extend out from this central point.

2. Moving the hoop toward you, sew several short stitches to reach the point where you want the first petal to end. The number of stitches will vary, depending on the length that you want each petal to be. Stop with the needle down.

3. Wrap the ribbon loosely behind the needle and tack

Diagram 9

it to the fabric right side, scrunching or pleating the ribbon in the stitches. Stop with the needle in front of the ribbon.

4. Stitch to the center of the daisy. Tack the ribbon in place. See **Diagram 9** on the opposite page.

5. Rotate the machine embroidery hoop and create the remaining petals in the same way. Clip the ribbon, tuck the raw end under, and tack it in place.

Loopy Petal Stitch

1. Tack an 8-to 10-inch (20- to 25-cm)-long piece of ribbon to the fabric right side at the flower center. End with the needle down.

2. Make a ¼- to ⅜-inch (6- to 10-mm)-long loop over a needle or awl.

3. Tack the ribbon layers together at the starting point (flower center). See **Diagram 10.**

4. Rotate the hoop and repeat Steps 1 through 3 to add as many petals as desired around the flower center. Trim off the excess ribbon. Tuck under and tack the ribbon ends at the flower center.

Diagram 10

Mock Outline or Cable Stitch

1. With a chalk pencil, draw a stitching guideline for the chain on the fabric right side. Cut a piece of 2-mm-wide ribbon twice the length of the line. Fold the ribbon in half lengthwise and lightly crease to mark the center. Tack the ribbon center to the beginning of the guideline.

2. Take three or four short stitches while moving the hoop away from you. Stop with the needle down.

3. Cross the ribbon ends in front of the needle and snug them up against the needle. Hold the ribbon ends in place with a finger on the left and a pointed tool on the right.

4. Stitch to the next stitch location. Repeat Steps 2 through 4 along the remainder of the stitching guideline. See **Diagram 11.** The stitching should look like a tight cable, covering the walking stitches.

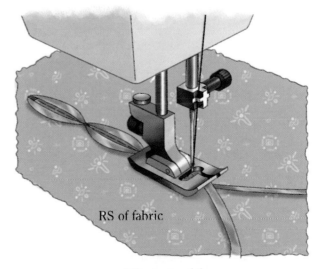

RS of fabric

Diagram 11

SUCCESSFUL STRATEGIES FOR RIBBON EMBROIDERY

Haste makes waste. Avoid wasting precious silk ribbon by practicing first with less expensive soft woven, knit rayon, or polyester ribbon.

Walk in the garden. For connected flowers or French knots, simply stitch to the next location, allowing the ribbon to drape along the stitching.

At"tack" it. When starting the ribbon, cut the end at an angle and keep it perpendicular to the foot while tacking across its width.

Awl's well. For stitches that look more like handwork, use an awl, trolley needle, or tweezers to "scrunch" or pleat the ribbon against the needle before you tack it in place.

Spin it. To wrap ribbon around the needle, it's easier to insert the needle in the fabric, hold the ribbon to one side, and spin the hoop around the needle. Count each complete revolution as one wrap.

Stay flat. Your work will look its best if you keep the ribbon flat and twist-free the entire time that you are stitching.

Wrong is right. Ribbon tails that are not clipped or hidden can be drawn to the wrong side of your stitched fabric. The easiest way to do this is to thread the ends, one at a time, through a large-eyed chenille needle. After you've pulled them through, weave the tails in and out of previous stitches to secure them.

Be handy. For interesting effects, combine machine work with hand work. You may want to add machine embroidered highlights, using regular embroidery thread and straight or zigzag free-motion stitching. Try a bartacked flower center, a straight-stitched stamen, and a French-knot pistil, for example, or add beads or groups of beads. You can do all of these suggestions on your sewing machine.

Take care. It would be a pity to damage the three-dimensional effect of your silk embroidery by pressing the ribbon flat. To press your completed work, place it face down on a pile pressing board or a scrap of velvet. Then steam it, rather than pressing it with the weight of the iron.

Stitch last. Add embroidery to completed garments by drawing the desired design on tear-away stabilizer. Pin or apply the stabilizer over the area to be embroidered. Remove the stabilizer carefully when the work is complete.

Make a new hue. To make a colorful statement, combine two ribbons of different colors for a variegated effect.

Knock wood. Most of your silk ribbon embroidery work needs to be mounted in a machine embroidery hoop. Don't try to get by with using a wooden hoop. You need the flexibility of being able to leave the sewing machine needle in the fabric while you remove the ring, move it to a new position, and snap it back in place.

Bar none. Lower the lever for the presser foot, even when you don't have a presser foot mounted on the machine for your stitching. Otherwise your stitches will knot up when you start, creating an unsightly "nest" of threads on the wrong side.

Pick posies. To form a group of posies, stitch a cluster of French knots. Singly, the French knot can represent the center of a flower.

Cross 'n stitch. To help you remember the correct way to make a chain stitch, just keep in mind that every time you cross the ribbon ends you need to secure them with small machine straight stitches.

Extend yourself. Don't draw a line for every extension along your line of feather stitching. Perfectly matched feathers aren't as charming as the varied look achieved when you make yours with random lengths and positions.

Smocking

If you've never considered smocking because you think of it as strictly handwork, think again. All of the methods shown here can be done on your sewing machine or serger.

Some of the most popular "smocking" methods draw up the fabric with elastic thread. This is actually "shirring," which is explained on page 203. The methods in this entry are closer imitations of true hand smocking. These techniques are easier to do, plus the resulting fabric is more stable.

GATHERED SMOCKING

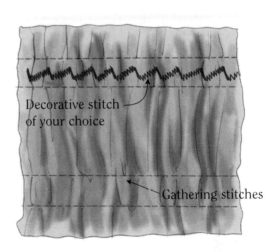

This technique is most reminiscent of traditional hand smocking. To create it, two rows of gathering are anchored with a centered row of decorative machine stitching. What a perfect opportunity to use the machine embroidery stitches built into your sewing machine or, if you own a computerized machine, to try your hand at programming your own stitch pattern.

Decorative stitch of your choice

Gathering stitches

Diagram 1

Get Ready	First Pass	Second Pass
Needle	Appropriate for fabric and thread	Embroidery
Thread	All-purpose to match fabric	Embroidery
Notions	Fabric scrap larger than the smocking area or heat-sensitive, iron-away stabilizer; quilting guide (optional)	

Get Set	First Pass	Second Pass
Presser foot	All-purpose with quilting guide, if desired	Embroidery
Stitch	Straight	Decorative*
Stitch length	6 spi (4.5 mm)	As desired
Stitch width	—	As desired

*Stitches commonly used for this type of work are zigzag, stretch zigzag, honeycomb, feather, and double-stretch overlock.

Sew

1. Select your decorative stitch and note its width. Using the First Pass settings, stitch pairs of horizontal rows of gathering stitches. Make the space between the upper and lower stitched row of each pair as wide as the decorative stitch. Space the stitched pairs of rows ¾ or 1 inch (2 or 2.5 cm) apart.

2. Draw up the bobbin threads to gather each paired row. If you have several sets of rows, gather each pair a little, then go back and continue gathering them more, a little at a time, to keep the gathers even and parallel. Adjust the gathers to the desired finished size and tie off the threads.

3. Cut a strip of fabric slightly larger than the smocked fabric and pin or baste it to the wrong side. If you do not want the added bulk, use a heat-sensitive, iron-away stabilizer instead of the fabric.

4. Decorative stitch as indicated for the Second Pass. Sew between the paired rows of gathering stitches. See **Diagram 1** on page 217. Steam the completed smocking to set the stitches. Remove the gathering threads.

Sharp Notion

Eliminate the decorative stitching and instead accentuate the smocking by weaving ribbon across the unstitched spaces. Use a tapestry needle to thread ⅛-inch (3-mm)-wide double-faced or silk ribbon under the stitches, zigzag fashion, across the spaces.

PINTUCK SMOCKING

Combine serger pintucks and sewing machine bartacks to create a highly textured surface. This is done by using decorative thread in the upper looper with the rolled edge stitch to make spaced rows of tiny tucks, then joining them with bartacks. While this is a nice treatment for small parts of a garment, why not make enough fabric for the front of a jacket or a simple vest?

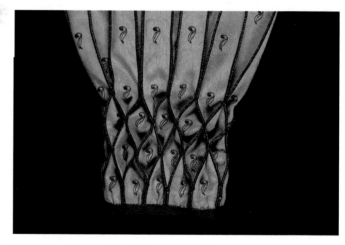

A decorative motif adds instant style to pintuck smocking. Do the stitching before bartacking the tucks together.

Get Ready

	Serger	Sewing Machine
Needle	Appropriate for fabric and thread	Universal
Needle thread	Decorative	Embroidery or all-purpose
Bobbin thread	—	Embroidery or all-purpose
UL thread	Decorative	—
LL thread	All-purpose	—
Notions	Water-soluble marking pen	

Get Set

	Serger	Sewing Machine
Presser foot	Standard	Open-toe embroidery
Stitch	Narrow rolled edge	Zigzag
Stitch length	Short	0
Stitch width	Very narrow	Medium
Feed dogs	Engaged	Disengaged or covered
Upper knife	Disengaged, if possible	—

Sew

1. Mark vertical lines for tucks on the fabric right side, spaced 1 inch (2.5 cm) apart.

2. Fold the fabric with wrong sides together along each marked line. Serge, being careful not to cut the folded edge.

3. On the fabric right side, make a mark every inch (2.5 cm) along each serged pintuck, making sure that the marks are exactly aligned from one pintucked row to the next.

4. If desired, machine embroider between the tucks, centering a motif between the pairs of marks.

5. At the sewing machine, on the fabric right side, bring the first two pintucks together at the top marks. Position them under the presser foot so the right swing of the needle clears the folded edges of the tucks. Machine bartack the tucks together at the marks. See **Diagram 2.**

6. Move down to the next row of marks and refold the fabric to bring the second and third pintucks together. Bartack at the marks.

7. Repeat Steps 5 and 6, working across and down the grid to form a honeycomb (alternating diamond) smocked effect.

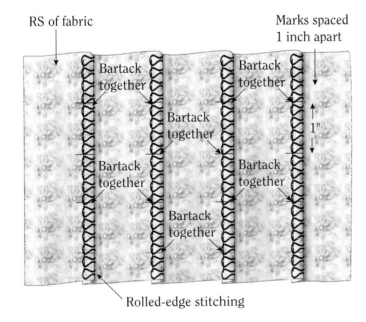

RS of fabric

Marks spaced 1 inch apart

Bartack together

Bartack together

Bartack together

Bartack together

Bartack together

Bartack together

1"

Rolled-edge stitching

Diagram 2

Sharp Notion

For pintuck smocking on the sewing machine, you can zigzag stitch narrow tucks or make pintucks using a double needle and pintuck foot. Try the blindstitch and be sure to start each row of twin-needle stitching at the same point in the stitch pattern. Join the zigzag stitches to create the alternating diamond pattern for "Pintuck Smocking" on the opposite page. Yet another idea is to try transparent thread in the needle so that the blindstitch is not obvious in the finished work.

TACKED SMOCKING

Tacked smocking, made at your sewing machine, is the perfect technique to add subtle texture. Because there are no gathers, it's particularly appropriate for heavier fabrics like velveteen and moiré satin. Bartack over folds and then pull the tacked tucks open on the right side. For added drama use a contrasting thread, like metallic embroidery.

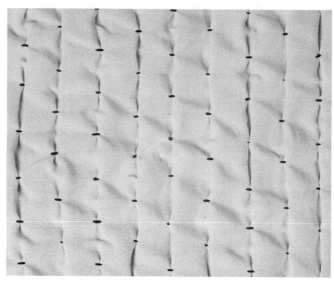

The effect of tacked smocking can be subtle or bold, depending on your design needs.

Get Ready

Needle	Appropriate for fabric and thread
Thread	All-purpose or decorative
Notions	Water-soluble marking pen

Get Set

Presser foot	Open-toe embroidery
Stitch	Zigzag or bartack
Stitch length	0
Stitch width	Medium (3.5 to 4 mm)
Needle position	Left, if possible

Sew

1. On the fabric wrong side, draw vertical lines 1 inch (2.5 cm) apart, following the straight of grain if possible. Make a mark every inch along the first line, beginning 1 inch (2.5 cm) from the edge of the fabric. On the second line, mark ½ inch (1.25 cm) down from the top edge of the fabric and then mark every inch (2.5 cm) along the remainder of the line. The marks on the second line are offset from those on the first line, each being halfway between two marks on the first line. Mark the remaining lines.

2. With right sides together, fold the fabric along the first line and position it at the machine so that the right swing of the needle just catches the edge of the fold. Bartack, with seven or eight stitches, at each mark on the first line. Change to a 0 stitch width and take several stitches in place to tie off. Return to the bartack width setting. Without cutting the thread, move to the next mark on the line and bartack. See **Diagram 3.** It isn't necessary to

clip the long threads between the bartacks unless the thread's shadow is visible on the right side of the completed work. Stitch each marked line in the same manner.

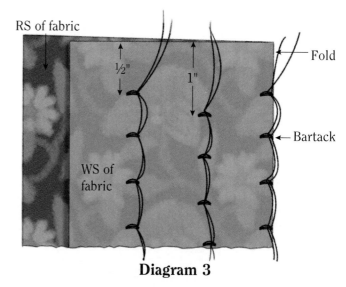

Diagram 3

3. The stitched side is the wrong side of the work. Open the completed work and tug gently at each bartack to expose the stitches on the right side.

Topstitching

Topstitching is one of the simplest yet most effective ways to add distinct details to even the simplest garment design—but only if it's done to perfection. Like many fashion details, the popularity of topstitching comes and goes, so take your cue from current ready-to-wear when planning topstitching. In this section you'll find helpful hints for serger topstitching applications.

DIMENSIONAL COVER STITCHING

Cover stitching, the latest arrival on the serging scene, offers some new possibilities for topstitching. It can copy the ready-to-wear appearance of twin-needle machine topstitching on ribbing (see the Sharp Notion on page 222), and also create a special "tucked" effect. Once you've mastered cover stitching basics, try adding tucklike texture with the twin-needle cover stitch. This technique works best on beefier fabrics like knits, synthetic suede, and heavier coating or suiting fabrics.

Get Ready

Needles	Appropriate for fabric and thread
Needle threads	All-purpose or decorative
Looper threads	Woolly nylon
Notion	Water-soluble marking pen, dressmaker's pencil, or chalk pencil

Get Set

Presser foot	Cover stitch
Stitch	Cover
Stitch length	Medium
Stitch width	Varies
Needle tension	Tighten slightly
Looper tensions	Tighten substantially
Differential feed	- (if available and if there's puckering)

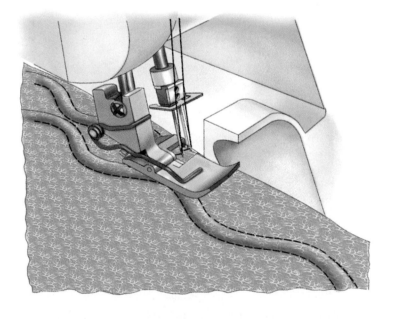

Diagram 1

Serge

1. Adjust all of the tensions (both on the needles and the loopers) so that the fabric puffs up between the two rows of needle stitching without causing thread breakage.

2. Mark the desired topstitching pattern on the garment right side with a water-soluble marking pen, dressmaker's pencil, or chalk pencil. Use this guideline for straight rows of topstitching, or follow more decorative patterns like intertwining cables, diamonds, or scallops if you'd like a more decorative effect. See **Diagram 1** on page 221.

3. Stitch on the right side of the fabric, following the pattern that you marked in Step 2.

Sharp Notion

Copy the look of ready-to-wear by using the double-needle cover stitch to topstitch ribbing in place after serging it to a garment edge. The appearance is much like twin-needle machine topstitching, which was once the only option for duplicating this look. (If you stitch with the garment face down, the more complex looper stitches appear on the right side of the garment. This is even prettier when you use a decorative thread in the looper.)

FLATLOCKED TOPSTITCHING

You can give a garment the look of serged flatlocked seaming with this type of topstitching. Flatlocked seams are best on ravel-free knit fabrics, but with this technique you can dress up plain seams on any garment. Woven fabrics require a special stabilizing treatment if you use a flatlocked seam, which makes this topstitching an appealing substitute. It also affords a more accurate fit along a set-in sleeve or around a band collar.

Get Ready

Needle thread	All-purpose serger
UL thread	Decorative*
LL thread	All-purpose serger

Get Set

Presser foot	Standard or blind hem
Stitch	Flatlock
Stitch length	Start with medium and adjust
Stitch width	Start with medium and adjust
Upper knife	Disengaged, if possible

Try pearl rayon or cotton, Burmilana acrylic, or heavy rayon such as Decor 6.

Serge

1. Assemble the garment, using plain seams wherever you want the flatlocked topstitching. Press the seam allowances open. Overlock the raw edges to prevent raveling, if you think that this is necessary for your fabric.

2. Fold the garment along the completed plain seamline with wrong sides together. Lightly press this stitching.

3. Adjust the pressed seam edge under the presser foot so that the stitches are half-on and half-off the edge of a test seam. See **Diagram 2.** Pull the fabric flat so that the flatlocked seam is flat. If you cannot pull it completely flat, stitch another seam sample, catching less of the seam edge in the stitching. Note how far the loops must hang over the edge in order to flatten the stitch, so that you can duplicate that spacing on the garment seamline. (Fabric thickness makes a difference.)

4. Serge over the garment seam edges where you want flatlocked topstitching and pull the seams open to flatten. Press lightly.

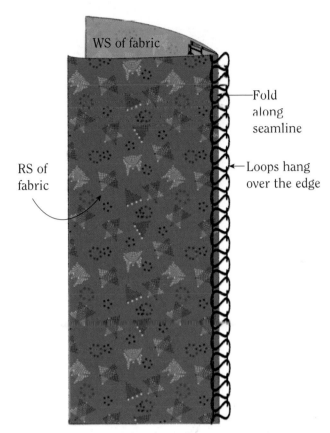

WS of fabric

Fold along seamline

Loops hang over the edge

RS of fabric

Diagram 2

Sharp Notion

Straight-Tape is a specially designed, clear, 1-inch (2.5 cm)-wide tape with ¼-inch (6-mm) dividing lines on which to stitch. Remove the backing paper, position as desired, and stitch on the solid lines. Fold against the stitching, then tear away carefully and save the unused pieces of tape by resticking them to the original backing paper. You can stitch five parallel rows of stitching ¼ inch (6 mm) apart if you use the outer edges and colored dividing lines, or ten parallel rows if you follow the ⅛-inch (3-mm) marks.

Sharp Notion

Single or multiple rows of chain stitching add wonderful textured topstitching detail. This stitch is available on five-thread sergers, some older four/two machines, and the new chain-and-cover stitch-only machine from Bernina. It requires only two threads and a single needle and must be stitched with the fabric right side down. Tape or draw stitching guidelines for multiple rows or use the edge of the presser foot to space them an equal distance. When using a heavier decorative thread, such as topstitching thread, pearl cotton or rayon, jeans thread, or heavy metallic thread, use a longer stitch than normal and loosen the looper tension a bit.

SUCCESSFUL STRATEGIES FOR TOPSTITCHING TROUBLES

Start fresh. Insert a new topstitching needle. If you're using metallic thread, use a special Metallica or Metalfil needle.

Clap it flat. On extra-thick fabrics, be sure to press enclosed edges as flat as possible. Use a tailor's clapper but be careful not to over-press.

Don't skip. Avoid skipped stitches at corners by making sure that the needle has completed the last stitch and is on the upswing, but not yet out of the fabric. Then pivot.

Use two. To keep your tension balanced when using two threads in the needle, wind two threads on the bobbin and thread them through the bobbin as one.

Just bobbin' along. When using a heavy thread for topstitching on a fabric that might be damaged by a heavier topstitching needle, wind the topstitching thread on the bobbin and stitch with the underside of the garment face up. To mark the location of the topstitching, machine baste from the right side using lightweight embroidery thread in a contrasting color in the bobbin.

Walk often. If possible, engage the even-feed mechanism or attach a walking foot to your machine to prevent the top fabric layer from scooting ahead of the bottom layer.

Slow down. Thicker threads and multiple layers require slow, even stitching for the best results.

Get stable. If your machine always eats the corner when you edgestitch and pivot, place a strip of tear-away stabilizer under the corner before you reach it. The corner won't sink into the needle hole with the stabilizer there to support it, and you'll take the corner with ease. When you're done, tear away the stabilizer.

Use tape. Narrow, ¼-inch (6-mm)-wide masking tape makes a great guide for even lines of stitching.

A shifty notion. You can prevent fabric from shifting by basting the fabric layers together. Or, try decreasing the pressure on the presser foot.

Beat the bugs. Special topstitching needles with longer eyes and wider scarves prevent thread fraying and skipped stitches, the two most common bugaboos.

Go long. Use a stitch length of 6 to 8 spi (4.5 to 3.5 mm).

Note the foot. A great array of presser feet can guide your stitching line—keeping it an even distance from the fabric edge, stitching line, or other reference point. Try an edgestitching, topstitching, adjustable blind hem, ¼-inch patchwork foot, or a quilting guide.

Set it free. "Release" the fabric every inch to prevent shifting fabric layers when you aren't using a walking foot or even-feed feature. Raise and lower the foot with the needle down.

Choose bulk. Needle and thread choice make a telling difference in the quality of your topstitching. Switch to a heavier or decorative thread to make your topstitching stand out. If you must use regular sewing thread but you want pronounced stitching, switch to a tri-motion straight stretch stitch.

Baste away. If you don't have an even-feed mechanism or walking foot for your machine, the top and bottom fabric layers may shift as you stitch. In this case, it's a good idea to baste the fabric layers together. Also try a stabilizer underneath the fabrics.

Expect twins. For perfectly aligned multiple rows, switch to a twin or triple needle. This will also save you time.

Tucks

Corded tucks, decorative tucks, twisted tucks, lettuce tucks, double-needle tucks, and serger tucks. These are just a few of the ways you can stitch interesting and unexpected style into a garment.

Even when your pattern doesn't call for tucks, you can add them to collars, cuffs, pockets—even an entire sleeve or the bottom edge of a skirt. Simply design and tuck the fabric, then cut the required pattern pieces from your fabric.

CORDED TUCKS

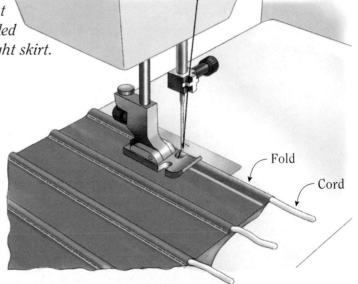

With precise measuring, marking, and stitching you can transform a lightweight fabric into "ribbed" yardage that rivals ready-to-wear. Start with a knit or woven fabric. Then, at your sewing machine, encase the cord inside single-needle tucks. Tuck a length of fabric to cut out pattern pieces for a complete jacket, or just add corded tucks to the sleeves or band at the bottom of a straight skirt.

Fold

Cord

Diagram 1

Get Ready

Needle	Appropriate for fabric and thread
Thread	All-purpose or decorative
Notions	⅛-inch (3 mm)-diameter cord, or other size as desired; tailor's chalk or water-soluble marking pen

Get Set

Presser foot	Zipper
Stitch	Straight
Stitch length	8 to 10 spi (3.5 to 2.5 mm)

Sew

1. Do a test to determine the tuck width (don't cut the cord for this test). Wrap a short, 1½-inch (4-cm)-wide strip of the garment fabric around the cord. Pin, placing straight pins parallel and as close as possible to the cord without catching it.

2. Using tailor's chalk or a water-soluble marking pen as appropriate for the fabric, open the raw edges of the strip and chalk-mark along both sides of the pins to establish the required size of the tuck. Remove the pins and measure the distance between the two chalk lines.

3. Mark parallel tuck placement lines on the right side of the fabric. The distance between each placement line should be no less than the tuck width determined in Step 2.

4. Fold the fabric wrong sides together around a length of cord at a marked line. Place pins with their points up along the marked line, catching both sides of the fabric (but not the cord).

5. Adjust the zipper foot to the left of the needle and stitch along the marked line, removing the pins as you go. See **Diagram 1** on page 225.

6. Make additional tucks in the same manner.

Sharp Notion

You can mark the tuck positions on fine fabric without a chalk pencil. Simply draw a thread at the tuck's fold. This will only work if you're making tucks along the straight grain.

DECORATIVE TUCKS

Add interest to narrow tucks with open decorative stitching made with the options on your sewing machine. Delicate floral and leaf patterns, for example, add lovely texture to the tucks on lingerie and delicate blouses. Sewing on a single layer of fabric before folding and straight stitching keeps the tucks soft and flexible. In addition, the underside of the decorative stitch won't be seen in the finished tuck.

Get Ready

Needle	Embroidery in size appropriate for the fabric
Thread	Embroidery
Notions	Tailor's chalk, water-soluble or tear-away stabilizer, quilting guide (optional)

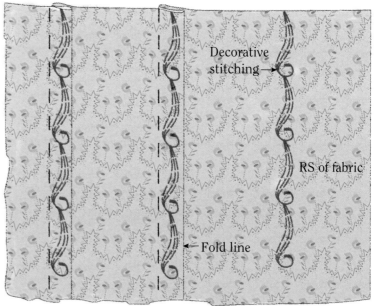

Diagram 2

Get Set

	First Pass	Second Pass
Presser foot	Embroidery	Zipper
Stitch	Decorative	Straight
Needle tension	Balanced or loosen*	Balanced or loosen*

Loosen, if necessary, to eliminate puckering.

Sew

1. Mark the tuck fold line. With the machine adjusted for the First Pass, stitch a row of the desired decorative stitch just to the left of the fold line that you already marked. Before you start stitching, place a layer of water-soluble or tear-away stabilizer underneath your fabric to prevent puckering when you do the decorative work. This stabilizer can be removed when the stitching for the tuck is completed to your satisfaction.

2. Fold the fabric to make the tuck. With the machine set up for the Second Pass, adjust the zipper foot so that it is positioned to the left of the needle. When sitting on the fabric, the decorative stitching should be visible. If the desired tuck width (from the stitching line to the folded edge) does not follow one of the engraved stitching guides on the needle plate, attach a quilting guide so that the edge of the tuck is against the metal bar on the guide while, at the same time, the straight stitching is to the left of the decorative stitching. Stitch along the left edge of the decorative stitching. See **Diagram 2** on the opposite page.

3. Make additional tucks in the same manner described in Steps 1 and 2.

Sharp Notion

You can do decorative stitching on completed tucks, too, especially when you want to use a stitch over the edge to draw it in a bit for the look of a scalloped or picot edge. Careful pressing of the completed tucks will ensure that the underside is not exposed.

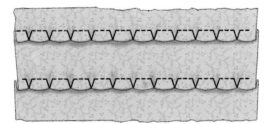

Picot tucks or blindstitch

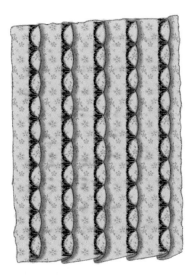

Closed or reverse scallop stitch

EXPOSED RELEASED TUCKS

Wait until you try this sewing machine technique! Avoid unsightly backstitching or knots at the interior edge of a released tuck. (This type of tuck ends in the interior of the garment, rather than going from one seam to another.) With this slick trick, everyone will wonder how you did it! It's a super technique on any fabric, but particularly on sheers, where knots can show through and backstitching is too bulky.

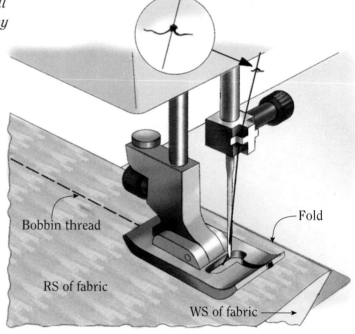

Diagram 3

Get Ready

Needle	Appropriate for fabric and thread
Thread	All-purpose or decorative
Notion	Needle threader (optional)

Get Set

Presser foot	All-purpose or straight stitch
Stitch	Straight
Stitch length	12 spi (2 mm)

Sew

1. With the wrong sides together, press the tuck along the fold and position the exposed end of the tuck (the end that's in the garment interior, not the end at the seam allowance) under the needle. (This may be backward to you if you're accustomed to stitching from the raw edge to the open end of the tuck and backstitching there.)

2. Lower the presser foot and hold on to the needle thread tail while you take one stitch to draw the bobbin thread to the fabric surface.

3. Lift the presser foot and draw up a length of bobbin thread, taking care to leave the fabric in place on the bed of the machine.

4. Remove the needle thread from the eye of the needle only and insert the bobbin thread through the needle eye from the back to the front. If this proves awkward or difficult, remove the needle to thread it. Thread from back to front, then replace the needle.

5. Tie the bobbin and needle threads together in an overhand knot above the eye of the needle, then carefully draw the bobbin thread up through all the thread guides and up to the spool. Draw up enough bobbin thread to stitch the entire length of the tuck. If necessary to keep the bobbin thread tidy, wrap it around the spool.

6. Lower the presser foot and stitch to the end of the tuck. Clip the threads. See **Diagram 3**. Repeat Steps 1 through 4 for additional exposed tucks.

Twisted Tucks

Twisted tucks have long been a popular embellishment. They take on new character when stitched with decorative thread on the serger, then secured in opposing directions in alternating rows with stitching done at your sewing machine. Imagine a vest front or the sleeves of a jacket sporting these textural tucks. Use metallic threads in the loopers to add holiday sparkle. Four-thread overlocked tucks offer some interesting decorative possibilities. Use thread in four different colors to thread the serger.

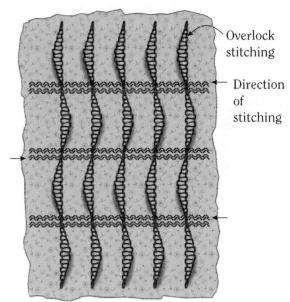

Overlock stitching

Direction of stitching

Diagram 4

Get Ready

	Serger	Sewing Machine
Needle	Appropriate for fabric and thread	Twin or triple
Needle thread	All-purpose serger	All-purpose or decorative
Bobbin thread	—	All-purpose or decorative
UL thread	Decorative	—
LL thread	Decorative	—
Notion	Water-soluble marking pen or tailor's chalk	

Get Set

	Serger	Sewing Machine
Stitch	Balanced three-thread	Straight, zigzag, or serpentine*
Stitch length	Short to medium†	6 spi (4 mm)
Stitch width	Narrow to wide	—
Upper knife	Disengaged, if possible	—

*You can substitute a serger cover stitch, if available, and do your tucks entirely on a serger.
†Adjust for the thread and desired coverage.

Serge and Sew

1. Mark the tuck fold lines on the right side of the fabric with a water-soluble marking pen or tailor's chalk, or pull a thread as explained in the Sharp Notion on page 226. You can also use the edge of the presser foot as a tuck spacing guide.

2. Fold a tuck along the fold line and serge over the fold. If you can't disengage your upper knife, take care that you don't cut through the fold in the tuck while you're stitching.

3. Mark evenly spaced topstitching lines perpendicular to the tucks.

4. Straight stitch with a twin or triple needle (or experiment with zigzag or serpentine stitching) along the first topstitching line. Turn the fabric 180 degrees and stitch on the next marked line. Sewing in the opposite direction will force the tuck to fold in the opposite direction, exposing the underside of the tuck. See **Diagram 4.**

Zippers

Think about using zippers for decorative, as well as functional, purposes. You can even use your serger to imitate a hand-picked zipper, finish the seam allowances at the same time that you're inserting an exposed zipper, or stitch in a zipper with decorative flatlocking.

To further expand your creativity, consider applying zippers in unexpected locations, or replace center front buttons and buttonholes, as shown in the illustration at right.

DECORATIVE FLATLOCKED ZIPPER

On some garments, you can turn an ordinary zipper treatment from mundane to sublime by exposing the teeth and some stitching. Think of the sheen of rayon or metallic thread along a heavy lace evening garment.

This look is easy to achieve with a serger by using decorative thread in the upper looper when you attach the zipper to the seam allowances. You'll need an extra-long zipper, and you'll have to insert it prior to sewing your seams.

Get Ready

Needle	Appropriate for fabric and thread
Needle thread	Decorative or all-purpose serger
UL thread	Decorative
LL thread	Decorative or all-purpose serger
Notions	Zipper at least 2 inches (5 cm) longer than the garment's opening

Get Set

Presser foot	Standard
Stitch	Two- or three-thread flatlock
Stitch length	As desired
Stitch width	As desired

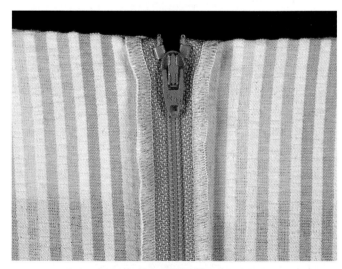

Insert this zipper in a garment that has a facing, waistband, or other pattern piece that makes a seam at the top of the zipper to create a top stop for the slider.

Serge

1. Trim off the seam allowances on both opening edges. Place the closed zipper face-up on the wrong side of the fabric. The zipper tape edge aligns with one seamline and extends past the top and bottom ends of the garment opening for the zipper.

2. Flatlock over the zipper tape and the raw edge of the fabric, trimming the seam allowance as you stitch. See **Diagram 1.** It isn't necessary for you to position your stitching on the guideline that's woven into the zipper tape. Instead, place your stitches according to the amount of tape that you want to show on the right side of your garment. Serge without trimming any of the seam allowance and zipper tape if you want wider exposure of the zipper tape on each side of the teeth. For less tape showing, trim away zipper tape and seam allowance while serging. After stitching, grasp the zipper tape in one hand and the garment in the other and fold them apart, tugging gently to pull the stitches and fabric flat.

3. Repeat Steps 1 and 2 on the remaining half of the zipper.

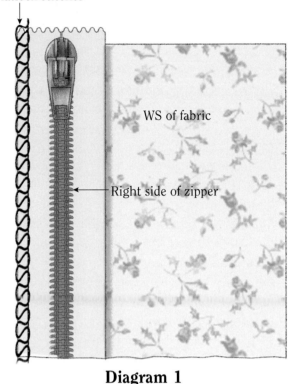

Diagram 1

4. Open the zipper before crossing the upper end with a seam. Cut off the excess after crossing it with a seam.

SUCCESSFUL STRATEGIES FOR INSERTING A ZIPPER

Top it. Always stitch the zipper from the bottom to the top for a smooth, wrinkle-free finish on the right side of the garment.

Baste with haste. Narrow double-faced adhesive basting tape will hold the zipper in position for sewing. No hand stitching!

Make footsteps. When inserting an invisible zipper, locating the optimal positions for your stitching lines is easy with a simple test. Center the needle and separately sew the first 3 inches (7.5 cm) of both sides of the zipper tape to a scrap of your fabric. Close the zipper to make sure that it slides smoothly and easily past the stitched areas. If it's too tight, slide the foot in the appropriate direction and test again. If the zipper shows after stitching and zipping, the stitching may be too far away from the teeth.

Pinch hit. If you can adjust your conventional zipper foot to the right or left (rather than moving the needle from side to side with a stationary foot), you can use it for an invisible zipper application. Baste the zipper to each seam allowance, then adjust the foot so you can stitch close to the teeth.

Lap it up. For a lapped zipper, use one that's at least 2 inches (5 cm) longer than the length of the garment opening. Position the zipper with the top of the tape extending beyond the top of the garment. When you topstitch, completely close the zipper to prevent an unsightly stitch "bump" at the top.

"Center" your stitches. Apply ½-inch (1.25-cm)-wide cellophane tape to the right side of the garment, centering it on the basted seamline for a centered zipper. Use the edges as stitching guides.

"HAND-PICKED" LAPPED ZIPPER

Often a signpost of quality in a couture garment, a hand-picked zipper is traditionally inserted with stitches that are carefully placed by hand.

The application process takes both skill and time, which is why garments with this detail are usually more expensive.

If you aren't inclined to spend your time hand stitching but you like the quality look, you can still re-create a version of a "hand-picked" zipper on your serger and sewing machine. The only "specialty" item you need for this work is a blind hem foot for your serger.

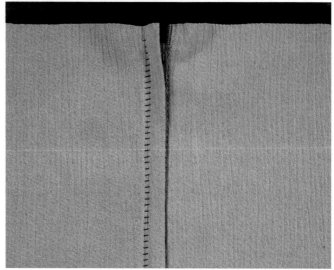

In this photograph, a contrasting color of thread was used for better visibility. For your garment, use matching thread.

Get Ready

	Sewing Machine	Serger
Needle	Appropriate for fabric and thread	Appropriate for fabric and thread
Thread	All-purpose	All-purpose serger
Notions	Zipper at least 2 inches (5 cm) longer than the garment's opening for the zipper	

Get Set

	Sewing Machine	Serger
Presser foot	Straight or zigzag, and zipper*	Blind hem
Stitch	Straight	Three- or four-thread overlock
Stitch length	8 and 12 spi (3.5 and 2 mm)*	4 mm
Stitch width	—	1.5 to 2 mm
Cutting width	—	1.5 to 2 mm

You adjust the stitch length and switch the presser foot several times while working at the sewing machine. See the step-by-step instructions for guidance.

Sew and Serge

1. Stitch the seam below the zipper opening, beginning at the bottom edge of the garment and ending at the bottom of the zipper opening. Backstitch, but don't cut the threads because you now finish the seam with a basting stitch. Sew the remainder of the seam (the zipper opening) at 6 spi (4.5 mm).

2. Press the seam allowances open. Place the garment right side up on your worktable, with the top of the zipper opening closest to you. Fold the garment away from the seam allowance on the right, along the seamline. Place the unzipped zipper face down on this seam allowance with the coil against the seamline. Pin, with the zipper's bottom stop at the end of the basted seam and the top extending approximately 1½ inches (4 cm) above the top edge of the fabric. Stitch close to the zipper coil at 12 spi (2 mm). See **Diagram 2.**

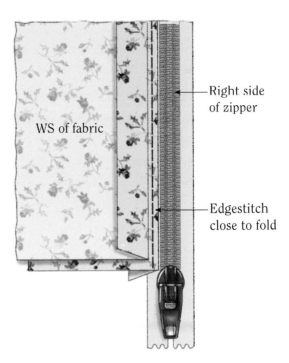

Right side of zipper

WS of fabric

Edgestitch close to fold

Diagram 3

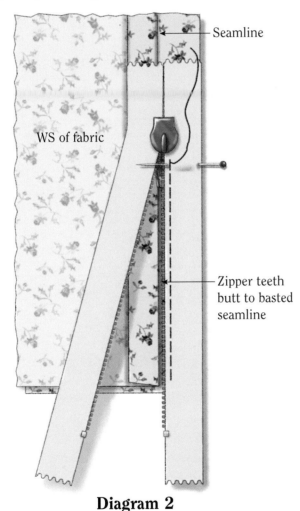

Seamline

WS of fabric

Zipper teeth butt to basted seamline

Diagram 2

3. Close the zipper. With the garment right side up and the top closest to you, press the garment, seam allowance, and seamline away from the zipper. Edgestitch close to the fabric fold from the stop at the bottom of the zipper to the end of the fabric at the top of the zipper. See **Diagram 3.** Backstitch at the beginning and end of the stitching.

4. Open the garment so that there is one layer of wrong side fabric and a seam allowance under the loose half of the zipper tape. Baste this remaining part of the zipper tape to the seam allowance and garment, stitching just inside the woven guideline in the zipper tape. See **Diagram 4.**

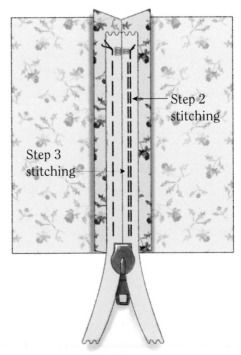

Step 2 stitching

Step 3 stitching

Diagram 4

5. With the garment right side up and the top of the zipper closest to you, fold the right side of the garment away from the seam allowance and the right side of the zipper tape. At the serger, position the fold of the fabric under the blind hem foot and adjust the guide on the foot so that the fabric fold is in line with the needle. Stitch with the fabric fold against the presser foot guide to ensure that each stitch catches the fold. See **Diagram 5.** You'll probably cut away some of the zipper tape and seam allowance as you stitch.

6. Press from the right side and remove all of the basting. You don't have to stitch across the bottom of the zipper.

7. On the inside of the garment, anchor the zipper tape tail to the left seam allowance with a few stitches.

8. Unzip the zipper before attaching a facing or waistband. Trim away the excess zipper tape above the seam allowance. Never cut off the excess zipper while the zipper is closed.

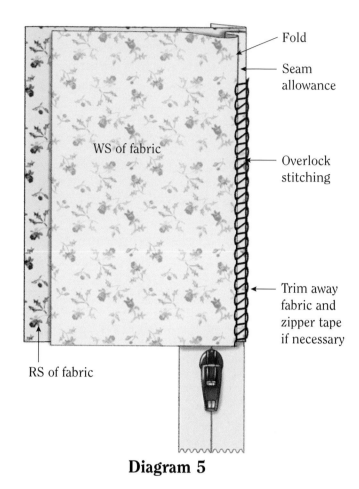

Diagram 5

SUCCESSFUL STRATEGIES FOR INSERTING AN INVISIBLE ZIPPER

Baste away. Before stitching the zipper to the fabric, machine baste just inside the ¾-inch (2-cm) seam allowance on both sides of the zipper opening. You can use the basting as a placement guide for the zipper coil.

Tack the tails. Stitch the portion of the zipper tape below the zipper's bottom stop to the seam allowances. This prevents stitches from breaking at the bottom of the zipper.

Switch feet. Don't own an invisible presser foot? Just substitute a five-groove pintuck foot. Insert the coil for the invisible zipper into a groove in the foot, and stitch with the coil in the foot for the required length.

Measure up. The position of your zipper stop has a significant impact on how the top of your garment lies. Place the top edge of the zipper stop ¾ inch (2 cm) below the upper raw edge of the garment if you will be adding a collar or facing. Place it 1 inch (2.5 cm) below the raw edge if you plan to attach a facing or waistband.

Press on. The invisible zipper coils automatically "roll" so that your stitching won't show after the zipper is installed. But it's much easier to stitch the zipper if you first press the tape flat. With the iron on the synthetic setting, press the zipper from the wrong side to "unroll" the coils away from the tape. Press until the tape is nice and flat, then stitch in place.

Recommended Reading

Allen, Alice and JoAnn Pugh-Gannon. *The Complete Sewer's Aid to Needles and Threads*. Wasco, IL: Sewing Information Resources, 1995.

Amig, Marya Kissinger, Barbara Fimbel, Stacey Klaman, Karen Kunkel, and Susan Weaver. *The Experts' Book of Sewing Tips and Techniques: From the Sewing Stars of America—Hundreds of Ways to Sew Better, Faster, and Easier*. Emmaus, PA: Rodale Press, 1995.

Baker, Naomi, Gail Brown, and Cindy Kacynski. *The Ultimate Serger Answer Guide*. Radnor, PA: Chilton Book Company, 1996.

Black, Lynette Ranney and Linda Wisner. *Creative Serging for the Home and Other Quick Decorating Ideas*. Portland, OR: Palmer-Pletsch, 1991.

Brown, Gail and Tammy Young. *Innovative Serging: Newest, Best, and Fastest Techniques for Overlock Sewing*. Radnor, PA: Chilton Book Company, 1989.

Curran, Doreen. *Free-Machine Embroidery*. Berkeley, CA: Lacis Publications, 1992.

Dodson, Jackie. *Know Your Bernina*. Radnor, PA: Chilton Book Company, 1988.

Dodson, Jackie and Jan Saunders. *Terrific Textures*. Radnor, PA: Chilton Book Company, 1996.

Fanning, Robbie. *Decorative Machine Stitchery*. New York, NY: Butterick Publishing, 1976.

Garbers, Debbie and Janet F. O'Brien. *Point Well Taken: The Guide to Success with Needles and Threads*. Marietta, GA: In Cahoots, 1996.

Harker, Gail. *Tassel Making*. Oak Harbor, WA: Gail Harker Design & Embroidery, 1996.

Nall, Mary Lou. *Cut Ups and Cut Outs with Bernina*. Pensacola, FL (for ordering information, e-mail mltbooks@juno.com).

———. *Foot Book–I with Bernina*. Pensacola, FL (for ordering information, e-mail mltbooks@juno.com).

———. *Heirloom Sewing with Bernina*. Pensacola, FL (for ordering information, e-mail mltbooks@juno.com).

———. *Just Needling with Bernina*. Pensacola, FL (for ordering information, e-mail mltbooks@juno.com).

Palmer, Pati and Gail Brown. *Sewing with Sergers: The Complete Handbook for Overlock Sewing*. Portland, OR: Palmer-Pletsch, 1985.

Palmer, Pati, Gail Brown, and Sue Green. *Creative Serging, The Complete Handbook for Decorative Overlock Sewing*. Portland, OR: Palmer-Pletsch, 1987.

Pepper, Philip. *Peppering: The Artistic Creations of Philip Pepper*. Huntsville, AL: Albright and Co., 1993.

Person, Ann. *Serge & Sew: Time-Saving Serger Tips*. Eugene, OR: Stretch & Sew, 1984.

Price, Ann Hesse. *The Serger Idea Book: A Collection of Inspiring Ideas from the Palmer/Pletsch Professionals*. Portland, OR: Palmer-Pletsch, 1989.

Pullen, Martha Campbell. *French Hand Sewing by Machine*. Huntsville, AL: Martha Pullen Company, 1995.

———. *Victorian Sewing and Crafts*. Huntsville, AL: Martha Pullen Company, 1985.

Saunders, Jan. *A Step-by-Step Guide to Your Sewing Machine*. Radnor, PA: Chilton Book Company, 1990.

———. *Sew, Serge, Press: Speed Tailoring in the Ultimate Home Sewing Center*. Radnor, PA: Chilton Book Company, 1989.

———. *Speed Sewing: 103 Sewing Machine Shortcuts*. New York, NY: Van Nostrand Reinhold, 1982.

Shepherd, Sandy. *Reader's Digest Complete Guide to Sewing: Revised and Updated Step-by-Step Techniques for Making Clothes and Home Furnishings*. Pleasantville, NY: The Reader's Digest Association, 1995.

Simmons, Judy. *Machine Needlelace and Other Embellishment Techniques*. Bothell, WA: That Patchwork Place, 1997.

Singer Sewing Reference Library: 101 Sewing Secrets. Minnetonka, MN.: Cy DeCosse, 1989.

Singer Sewing Reference Library: Decorative Machine Stitching. Minnetonka, MN: Cowles Creative Publishing, 1990.

Singer Sewing Reference Library: Sewing with an Overlock. Minnetonka, MN: Cy DeCosse, 1989.

Stanley, Isabel. New Crafts: *Machine Embroidery*. New York, NY: Anness Publishing, 1996.

Young, Tammy and Lori Bottom. *ABCs of Serging*. Radnor, PA: Chilton Book Company, 1992.

Zieman, Nancy. *Serger Feet on the Go*. Beaver Dam, WI: Nancy's Notions, 1991.

Index

Decorative stitching *(continued)*
  on serger, 36, 98
  tension for, 3, 24
  thread and, 134
  on tucks, 226, 227
Dental tools, 29, 36
Differential feed control, 29, 30, 87.
  See also Feed dogs
Drawn thread work, 127–28
Drawstrings, 109–10
Drinking straw, 17, 176

E

Ease, 30
Edgestitch, 59
Edgestitch foot, 59, 188
Elastic
  applying with cover stitch, 46
  applying with rolled-hem foot, 191
  in binding, 86–87
  casing for, 128, 129–30
  in lingerie, 131
  never-twist straps, 132
  presser feet for, 132, 191
  as seam gauge, 3
  stabilizing seams with, 131
  on stretch braid trim, 95
  stretch piping, 129, 133
  successful strategies for, 130
  in swimwear, 128
Elastic foot (elasticator), 37, 39, 92
Embroidery. *See also* Free-motion embroidery;
  Ribbon embroidery
  around buttonholes, 103
  on curves and corners, 136–37
  with fagoting, 147
  French knots, 65, 66
  Richelieu bars, 74–75
  on seamlines and edges, 135
  stitches for, 138–40
  successful strategies for, 134
  thread for, 134
Embroidery foot, 13, 18, 89, 134, 189. *See also*
  Open-toe embroidery foot
Embroidery hoop, fabric slippage in, 148
Entredeux. *See also*
  Heirloom sewing
  as heirloom sewing feature, 162, 164
  imitation, 143
  insertion, 141–42
  joining to flat lace, 142
Eyelets, 81, 144

F

Facings, fuse-basting, 69
Fagoting
  curved, 145
  flatlock, 146
  straight, 147
Fastube Foot, 14
Feather stitch
  on appliqué, 59
  for couching, 118
  free-motion, 149
  in ribbon embroidery, 213
Feed dogs, 3. *See also* Differential feed control
Filmoplast Stic, 209
Flagging, 3
Flat hemmer, 119, 190–91
Flatlock stitch
  applying elastic with, 131
  beading with, 78–79
  couching with, 117–18
  described, 47–48
  for fagoting, 146
  as heirloom sewing feature, 155
  hemming with, 48, 157–58
  lace insertion with, 163
  for making braid, 140
  shirring with, 203–4
  stitching seams with, 222
  topstitching with, 222–23
  for "tuck" creases, 121
  uses for, 48–50
  for zippers, 220–31
Foot pressure dial, 29, 126
Free-motion embroidery. *See also* Cutwork;
  Embroidery
  on appliqué, 62–63
  bobbin couching with, 118
  in drawn thread work, 127–28
  Richelieu, 74–75
Free-motion stitching. *See also* Battenberg lace;
  Needle lace
  beading with, 79–81
  in charted needlework, 104–5
  eyelets, 81, 144
  general directions for, 148–49
  making braid with, 92
  motif shirring, 206–7
  stitch-wrapping cord with, 112–13
French knot
  bartacked, 64, 65, 66
  in ribbon embroidery, 210, 214
French seams, mock, 191

Christmas with Jinny Beyer

Decorate Your Home for the Holidays with Beautiful Quilts, Wreaths, Arrangements, Ornaments, and More

by Jinny Beyer

Renowned quilt designer Jinny Beyer shares her ideas and techniques for making over 50 holiday projects, suitable for any skill level. Complete instructions and full-color illustrations accompany every project.

Hardcover   ISBN 0-87596-716-7

The Experts' Book of Sewing Tips & Techniques

From the Sewing Stars of America—Hundreds of Ways to Sew Better, Faster, and Easier

edited by Marya Kissinger Amig, Barbara Fimbel, Stacey L. Klaman, Karen Kunkel, and Susan Weaver

Learn the trade secrets of the top sewing experts in this easy-to-use guide. Hints and tips, from appliqué to zippers, are covered in alphabetical order.

Hardcover   ISBN 0-87596-682-9

Sewing Secrets from the Fashion Industry

Proven Methods to Help You Sew Like the Pros

edited by Susan Huxley

Learn the same tips and techniques that the industry professionals use in their sample rooms and production factories. Over 800 full-color photographs accompany the step-by-step directions.

Hardcover   ISBN -0-87596-719-1

Sew It Tonight, Give It Tomorrow

50 Fast, Fun, and Fabulous Gifts to Make in an Evening

edited by Stacey L. Klaman

Make one-of-a-kind gifts in no time at all. The projects, from golf club covers and a tea cozy to crib bumpers and holiday ornaments, are appropriate for sewers of all levels.

Hardcover   ISBN 0-87596-645-4

No Time to Sew

Fast & Fabulous Tips & Techniques for Sewing a Figure-Flattering Wardrobe

by Sandra Betzina

Sandra Betzina, star of the television series "Sew Perfect," helps you to sew in record time, offering stylish patterns, step-by-step instructions, time-saving tips, and wardrobe advice. A complete set of multi-sized patterns is included with the book.

Hardcover   ISBN 0-87596-744-2

High-Fashion Sewing Secrets from the World's Best Designers

A Step-by-Step Guide to Sewing Stylish Seams, Buttonholes, Pockets, Collars, Hems, and More

by Claire Shaeffer

Nationally known sewing expert Claire Shaeffer reveals the sewing secrets of fashion industry legends from Ralph Lauren to Yves Saint Laurent. You'll also discover that high-fashion sewing does not have to be difficult!

Hardcover   ISBN 0-87596-717-5